THE SOCIAL WELFARE INSTITUTION

THE
SOCIAL WELFARE
INSTITUTION
An Introduction

RONALD C. FEDERICO
University of Maryland

D. C. HEATH AND COMPANY
Lexington, Massachusetts Toronto London

Photos by Elsa Dorfman.

International Standard Book Number: 0–669–73866–2

Library of Congress Catalog Card Number: 72–4565

This book is dedicated to Eleanor Vosburgh in fond and grateful memory.

CONTENTS

LIST OF EXHIBITS

ACKNOWLEDGMENTS

A book is an undertaking of many people—those who have taught the author, those who have questioned him, and those who have helped him. A life is full of such people, and it is impossible to cite them all in one brief acknowledgment. Nevertheless, the following deserve special recognition: my parents; Phil and Sandra Hammond; Henry Meyer and Edwin Thomas; Lou MeKush; and Howard S. Becker, Ray Mack, and Arnold Feldman.

My colleagues at the University of Maryland have been of vital importance, especially Bob Hirzel, Ray Henkel, Bob Ellis, Donna Lichvar, Phyllis Svitak, Bonnie Mandell Shuer, Fern Komenarsky Berkman, and Charles Perticari. Win Thomet, Ruth Schwartz, Les Levin, Mary Ellen Elwell, Tom Walz, the Southern Regional Education Board, and the Council on Social Work Education were all valuable stimulants and resources. The book is greatly enriched by the sensitivity and talent of Bob Wright, who gave basic ideas for the photographs included in this book. A special gratitude is owed to Wanda Bair, who contributed a great deal of work, interest, and enthusiasm in making this book a reality.

INTRODUCTION

The effectiveness of the American social welfare system has been undergoing increasingly pointed examination in the past few years. The questioning of the system has resulted from changes in American society as well from the suspicion that the welfare structure has not always been successful in implementing its societal mandate. The changes occurring in society and their effects on the welfare system have created a period of flux in the welfare professions. We are in the midst of a shift from the traditions of the past to new values and behavior patterns that will be more effective in the society of the future.

Any transitional period creates anxiety and uncertainty. Possessing advanced degrees or professional certification does not necessarily avoid the common reluctance to step out of the past, or the honest perplexity in looking to the future. Social welfare practitioners have felt the anxieties, and many have reacted quite normally in trying to deny the need for change. For others, the reactionary phase is now over. The traditional order was indeed ripe for reexamination. Uncertainty is being faced and will be an issue in social welfare for many years, since the building of a new social order always takes time and experimentation.

The personal and structural dislocations that the present transitional period has created have brought with them many exciting and promising possibilities. A major result is the reevaluation of social welfare objectives, methods, and task allocations, which in turn has led to the rapid growth of several levels of social welfare education. At the undergraduate level, courses are often closely tied to a social science base. Undergraduate social welfare education has received its major organizational impetus from the Council on Social Work Education (CSWE). The complex relationship of social welfare to social work will be examined in more detail in Chapter 1. CSWE's attempts to codify appropriate content at the undergraduate level led to the identification of four major objectives for undergraduate social welfare education.[1]

1. Preparation for informed citizenship—enabling the college graduate to understand the social welfare issues of our time and to be active citizens regarding them (at the polls, in the community, etc.).
2. Preparation to enter social welfare work—enabling the undergraduate social welfare major to fit into appropriate work contexts with basic but minimal on-the-job training.

3. Preparation to enter graduate programs in social welfare areas.
4. Preparation for employment or graduate training in a variety of fields related to social welfare.

Some believe these tasks cannot all be met in any given undergraduate program. I believe they can, although I feel the heart of the program lies in the second objective, with the others following from its attainment. The attempt to meet these CSWE objectives seems most logically to begin with the study of social welfare as a social institution, in which the broad, fundamental knowledge of the liberal arts can be joined with specialized knowledge relating to professional means and goals.[2]

This book is written as an introduction to the issues and knowledge upon which social welfare and social work curricula are built. It illuminates the scope of social welfare as a concept, the structures which have grown out of the concept, and the theory and practice techniques enabling the structures to function. The attainment of the CSWE objectives requires this breadth and this essentially interdisciplinary approach. An attempt is made to provide a reasonably objective picture of the subject, while openly recognizing the current transitional period. The reader should have an elementary background in sociology, psychology, and political science so that major theories can be introduced and analyzed with minimal foundation material.

A theoretical focus is maintained in the analysis of historical background, values, structures, concepts, methods, and contexts. There is no attempt to develop a sophisticated level of practice skills or an in-depth knowledge of all practice contexts. The emphasis is more on helping the reader to understand the present social welfare structure and societal needs, the values forming the core of our social welfare system, traditional practice techniques, relevant social science concepts from which new techniques will ultimately come, and current attempts to reformulate techniques. The book is not a "how-to" manual. Becoming a social welfare professional depends in part on the mastery of basic social science and social welfare concepts. Sometimes theory seems very far removed from practice; actually it simply helps us to organize what we know so that we can use our knowledge more effectively as practitioners.

A final characteristic of the book needs explanation. It is very much an introductory text, in that it covers an extensive subject matter in a relatively concise manner. One book cannot hope to explore all the issues involved in so many diverse areas, and an introduction to these issues should not get enmeshed in all of their ramifications. By seeing the major issues, the interested reader can pursue them as he wishes, using the basic material and the related bibliographies, presented at the end of each chapter, as reference points. Adopting this approach will hopefully allow the book's momentum to be maintained, since it is questionable whether further exploration by a reader is encouraged by an overly complex and static introductory text. At the same time, the broad focus of the book should enhance its value at several points in social welfare and social work curricula, since various facets of each area can be reintroduced in some detail at different points in the student's development.

Specific, real-life examples, in the form of Exhibits, are scattered throughout the text, and reflect both this author's interests and actual experiences. It is hoped that the reader will be encouraged in some small way by this book to adopt one of the social welfare professions as a life-long vocation or avocation.

Suggestions for Instructors

This book is not intended to stand alone in a course. It is assumed that other books will be used to supplement parts of this one. Which parts you choose to supplement depends on the course and your own teaching approach. A "Social Welfare as a Social Institution" course might use books such as Romanyshyn,[3] Rein,[4] or Wilensky and Lebeaux,[5] all of which emphasize certain parts of the overall view presented here. A "Interventive Methods" course might use Combs,[6] Avila,[7] Frank,[8] Loewenberg,[9] Collins,[10] or any of the numerous well-known books that deal with specialized methods. A "Social Policy" course could include Rein,[11] Perlman and Gurin,[12] Piven and Cloward,[13] Kershaw,[14] Zurcher and Bonjean,[15] or Steiner.[16] This book could form a stable referent for a student as he progresses through an undergraduate social welfare or social work program. He can grow from it into the areas you wish to emphasize in your teaching, but he can return to it periodically to see the structure of the whole, and to review the basic foundation material in each area covered.

No single "theory" of social welfare is propounded: this is more a guidebook than a scholarly study. The student is provided with the foundation knowledge necessary to follow the instructor. A conscious effort was made to create a text that is unique in its scope and coverage.

This book deals with the contemporary United States. The history of social welfare is only briefly and selectively covered, and there is no attempt to generate cross-cultural perspectives. Both of these areas may be further emphasized through supplemental readings.

REFERENCES

1. The basic guide to objectives is the Council on Social Work Education's *Undergraduate Programs in Social Welfare: A Guide to Objectives, Content, Field Experience, and Organization* (New York: Council on Social Work Education, 1967), especially pp. 5–6.
2. A concise, interesting statement of the general perspective being adopted here is Verl Lewis, "The Relevance of Social Welfare to the Liberal Arts," in Margaret Long and Edward L. Protz, eds., *Issues in Planning for Under-*

graduate Social Welfare Education (Atlanta: Southern Regional Education Board, 1969), pp. 1–8.

3. John Romanyshyn, *Social Welfare: Charity to Justice* (New York: Random House, 1971).
4. Martin Rein, *Social Policy: Issues of Choice and Change* (New York: Random House, 1970).
5. Harold Wilensky and Charles Lebeaux, *Industrial Society and Social Welfare* (New York: Free Press, 1958).
6. Arthur Combs et al., *Helping Relationships: Basic Concepts for the Helping Professions* (Boston: Allyn and Bacon, 1971).
7. Donald Avila et al., eds., *The Helping Relationship Sourcebook* (Boston: Allyn and Bacon, 1971).
8. Jerome Frank, *Persuasion and Healing* (Baltimore: Johns Hopkins Press, 1961).
9. Frank Loewenberg and Ralph Dolgoff, *Teaching of Practice Skills* (New York: Council on Social Work Education, 1971).
10. Alice Collins, *The Lonely and Afraid* (New York: Odyssey, 1969).
11. Rein, op. cit.
12. Robert Perlman and Arnold Gurin, *Community Organization and Community Planning* (New York: John Wiley, 1972).
13. Francis Piven and Richard Cloward, *Regulating the Poor* (New York: Pantheon, 1971).
14. Joseph Kershaw, *Government Against Poverty* (Chicago: Markham, 1970).
15. Louis Zurcher, Jr., and Charles Bonjean, *Planned Social Intervention* (Scranton: Chandler, 1970).
16. Gilbert Steiner, *The State of Welfare* (Washington, D.C.: Brookings Institution, 1971).

I

AN OVERVIEW OF SOCIAL WELFARE

BASIC CONCEPTS

1

Social welfare is a concept that is operationalized through the interaction of a number of separate but related professions. For example, vocational rehabilitation is a profession that helps individuals to overcome handicaps and develop appropriate job skills, while social work helps individuals and groups develop skill in the procurement and use of emotional, social, and financial resources. Each profession is a means to attain one or more social welfare goals, and as such forms part of a societal social welfare structure. However, each social welfare profession has its own distinctive concerns and techniques that distinguish it from others. Undergraduate social welfare education, then, must begin by identifying and clarifying several important points: (1) the meaning of social welfare as a concept; (2) the ways in which social welfare professions operationalize this concept through the provision of concrete resources and services; and (3) the range of social welfare professions and their interrelationships. Because all of the social welfare professions spring from the same conceptual base, they share major concepts, practice techniques, and organizational characteristics. These common elements comprise the core content of undergraduate social welfare education, and subsequent specialized professional education is built on this base.

The number of distinct professions and sub-professions that comprise the social welfare institution are too numerous for each to be discussed in detail. Instead, social work will be used to exemplify the ways in which social welfare professions translate the concept of social welfare into concrete resources and services. Of the many professions that might have been selected for illustrative purposes, social work suggests itself because of the integrative position it occupies among the many specialized social welfare professions. Also, the fact that social work as a profession has commonly been confused with social welfare as a concept provides the opportunity to clarify the distinction between this concept and its operationalization in various specialized but interrelated professional contexts.[1]

Social welfare is difficult to define precisely, partly because of its relationship to various professions and partly because of its unusually wide scope. It can be thought of as an institution,[2] meaning a set of norms clustered around a societal function and operationalized by a social structure of positions and roles.[3] As a social institution, social welfare has three important characteristics: (1) it is an organized structure of activities; (2) it develops from the effort to meet societal needs; and (3) it grows out of the normative (value) system which characterizes a society. It is apparent that social welfare as a social institution exists as one part of a large, complex societal structure and that it must operate within a given set of values. At the start of our understanding of social

3

welfare, we can see why social welfare professionals need a sound grasp of social science theory, and the political sophistication necessary to work within a societal system to attain one's professional goals.

There have been many attempts to formally define social welfare. It may be helpful to review some of the definitions used by others before developing a working definition to be used in this book. Philip Klein refers to social welfare as "the administration of certain services to individuals and families who find it difficult or impossible to maintain themselves and their dependents in material solvency and in health by their own efforts."[4] Crampton and Keiser "define social welfare operationally as a system that embodies a multifaceted approach to social and economic problems, reflecting social values and using the expertise of interrelated disciplines for the collective good."[5] Friedlander defines

---

EXHIBIT 1–1
The Scope and Focus of Social Welfare

The magnitude and complexity of the American social welfare system can make it a difficult one to comprehend. Below is an attempt to illustrate the kinds of social welfare services that would exist in various types of systems using the framework presented in the text. Concrete examples of existing services are provided for illustrative purposes.

An Institutionalized Social Welfare System

Social welfare services are built into the normal functioning of the social system. They are available as a matter of course to the participants in the social system. The American social welfare system has some institutionalized segments, such as public education, but most social welfare services are available only upon evidence of need and qualification for the service.

1. *Curative Institutionalized Services.* Institutionalized services to help when a problem arises. Free hospital care would be an example of such a service, since it would provide needed care for all in the event of illness. Few curative institutionalized services actually exist in contemporary North America. The legal system is one of the closest approximations of such an existing service, since it is available to all in times of need. This includes the police as a social service resource available to all to handle an extremely wide range of personal and social problems.

2. *Preventative Institutionalized Services.* Institutionalized services to prevent the future occurrences of personal and social problems. Free medical care would be an example of such a service, since it would enable everyone to enjoy the benefits of preventative medicine. Preventative institutionalized services are not common in our society, but free public education is one example of such an existing service. It is intended to guarantee an education to a certain level, helping to prepare the individual for a satisfying and productive life in the social system of which he is a part.

3. *Rehabilitative Institutionalized Services.* Institutionalized social welfare services to help those with an existing problem overcome the problem and avoid similar problems in the future. An example would be free marital counseling, whereby those experiencing marital

social welfare as "the organized system of social services and institutions, designed to aid individuals and groups to attain satisfying standards of life and health, and personal and social relationships which permit them to develop their full capacities and to promote their well-being in harmony with the needs of their families and the community."[6] Wilensky and Lebeaux define welfare by distinguishing traits of the contemporary social welfare structure. These are: (1) formal organization; (2) social sponsorship and accountability; (3) absence of a profit motive as a dominant program purpose; (4) an integrated view of human needs; and (5) direct focus on human consumption needs.[7] Finally, Smith and Zeitz say simply that "the social services institutionalize, as public policy, the philanthropic impulse."[8]

Although there are clearly many ways to define social welfare, all of

---

problems could be helped to solve these problems and develop the skills to avoid similar problems in later years. One of the very few rehabilitative institutionalized services available in our society is the United States Employment Service. It assists the unemployed to find work, as well as providing job training to try to avoid unemployment in the future.

A Residual Social Welfare System

Social welfare services are provided only to those in crisis who also qualify for the service. Therefore, residual social welfare services are only selectively available. The majority of the United States social welfare system is of the residual type.

1. *Curative Residual Services.* Services to help those who qualify when a problem arises. Medical care is an excellent example, since medical services are available only to those sick persons who can afford it (either by paying cash, by having health insurance, or by being on public assistance).

2. *Preventative Residual Services.* Services to help prevent the future occurrence of personal and social problems. Prevention and residual are almost by definition mutually exclusive. Nevertheless, some preventative services do exist for selected groups in American society. Social security is an example, in that eligible individuals contribute to a fund that will provide income when they are no longer able to work, thereby helping to prevent poverty in old age.

3. *Rehabilitative Residual Services.* Services to help selected persons with an existing problem overcome the problem and avoid similar problems in the future. Here again, there is a certain inconsistency between rehabilitation and residual, but programs that are both do exist. The WIN (Work Incentive) Program for public assistance mothers is an example. Unemployed mothers are given job training so that they can hopefully become self-supporting, thereby improving their self-image and their family's standard of living.

The above analytical framework is not completely comprehensive or mutually exclusive. For example, the line between prevention and rehabilitation is not always clearcut, and residual services shade into institutionalized services in some cases. Nevertheless, it is helpful when trying to disentangle some of the complex characteristics of the social welfare system in the United States, since it is such a mixture of all of the parts of the framework.

the above definitions focus on the organization of services to solve personal and social problems, with the major goal of improving the functioning of persons in all their social contexts. Working from these common elements, but emphasizing the importance of the social structure, social welfare, as defined in this book, is a means of *improving social functioning and minimizing suffering through a system of financial and social*

EXHIBIT 1–2
The Social Welfare System in Action: Skid-Row Alcoholics

Professional Contexts in which Social Welfare Service to Skid-Row Alcoholics Is Offered:	Official Goal Is Rehabilitation of the Alcoholic. Means Used in Goal Attainment:
City jail	Place to sober up and dry out; context in which alcoholic is punished for public drunkenness (norm violation).
Alcoholism school	Education on the evils of alcoholism.
County jail	Same as city jail, except more severe (longer sentences) for repeaters (chronic norm violators).
State mental hospital	Drying out and psychological therapy (emphasis on alcoholism as an illness).
Jail branch clinic	Same as state mental hospital.
Out-patient therapy center	Psychological therapy.
Welfare home for homeless men	Drying out; informal therapy; food and shelter provided.
Clinics and hospitals	Detoxification; treatment for physical problems caused by alcoholism or skid-row life.
Christian missionaries	Spiritual renewal; food and shelter provided; employment.

Analysis of Implications

Structural. Welfare services provided in structures especially for the specific problem (missions, alcoholism schools) and in multi-purpose structures (hospitals, jails, welfare homes).

Professional. A variety of professions is involved in the provision of services (medical, corrections, social work, religious, etc.).

Values. Two value bases are made clear by Wiseman: (1) "Punitive-Correctional Strategies" focusing on control and containment when alcoholism is seen as "sheer self-indulgence"; (2) "Strategies of Therapy" when alcoholism is seen as the result of psychological and physiological problems, or moral and spiritual problems.

---

services at all levels in the social structure. This system may be structured to service only those who have already experienced need or problems (a residual social welfare system), or to provide services to all as a normal part of the social environment (an institutionalized system).[9] The focus of the social welfare system may be on solving existing problems (curative), preventing the future occurrence of problems (preventative), or

Routes by which Skid-Row Alcoholics Enter Treatment Contexts

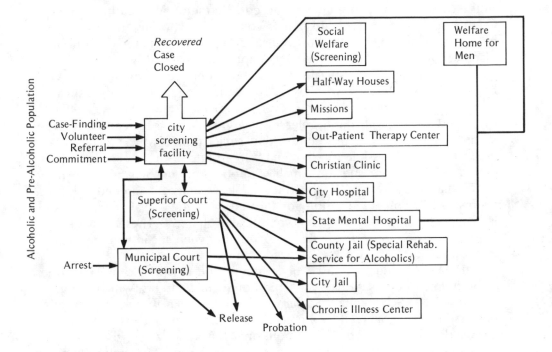

Analysis of Implications

Structural. Specialized services are interrelated into a total system which the recipient traverses (the "loop"). This system includes the nonwelfare contexts which feed into the specialized services (the family, friends, etc.).

Professional. Note the addition of the legal professions to the system.

Values. The multitude of possible moves within the system implies that the actual experience within it will depend on the value orientation of the person making the original referral (arrest leads to jail, while welfare contact leads to social work or psychiatric services). Note also how the legal system makes service (treatment) decisions on the basis of its referrals (either to jail or a hospital).

Table and figure from Jacqueline P. Wiseman, *Stations of the Lost: The Treatment of Skid Row Alcoholics,* © 1970, pp. 51 and 55. By permission of Prentice-Hall, Inc., Englewood Cliffs, N. J.

rehabilitating those with problems to prevent future problems (rehabili-tative). Obviously the scope and focus of the system represent two con-tinua, with any given system representing a given place along them.

Using any definition of social welfare, it becomes clear that social welfare as an institution cannot be detached from the social value struc-ture out of which it grows. One can think in terms of "improving social functioning" and "minimizing suffering" only with reference to accepted standards of living existing in a given society at a given time. Questions of scope and focus can only be considered using societal conceptions of the causes of social dysfunction, acceptable methods of curing or pre-venting such dysfunction, and beliefs concerning who has the responsi-bility for minimizing dysfunction and suffering. These value issues will be discussed at more length in the next chapter.

Looking at the way social work has been defined by others, we may begin with Ruth Smalley, who says: "The underlying purpose of all social work effort is to release human power in individuals for personal fulfill-ment and social good, and to release social power for the creation of the kinds of society, social institutions, and social policy which make self-realization most possible for all men."[10] In an attempt to make this gen-eral definition more specific, Smalley quotes Karl de Schweinitz, who states that social work is "the body of knowledge, skill, and ethics, professionally employed in the administration of the social services and in the development of programs for social welfare."[11] These two state-ments clearly establish the basic distinction between social welfare as an institution and social work as a profession.

Elizabeth Ferguson cites a definition of social work, formulated by a committee of the National Association of Social Workers, which is con-sistent with de Schweinitz: "Social work practice, like the practice of all professions, is recognized by a constellation of value, purpose, sanction, knowledge, and method."[12] Skidmore and Thackeray assert that "social work may be defined as an art, a science, a profession which helps people to solve personal, group (especially family), and community problems and to attain satisfying personal, group, and community relationships through use of certain methods including casework, group work, com-munity organization, and the enabling processes of research and adminis-tration. Social work not only helps people to solve problems, but also assists them to prevent problems and enrich daily living."[13]

Summarizing these attempts to define social work, it becomes clear that it is a socially legitimated profession (with all the characteristics of professions). It uses a body of methods (tied to specific knowledge bases) to solve individual, group, and community problems, and utilizes the resources of the social welfare system (institutionalized values, services, and structures). Seen in this way, social work is obviously only one of many socially defined professions that use their own methods to solve problems within the broad framework of the social welfare system, such as medicine, corrections, physical therapy, teaching, psychiatry, etc. The distinctions between these professions are partially arbitrary, since they all share certain bodies of knowledge and methods (knowledge of physical functioning and its effect on social relationships, for example); they may all interact in the same problem area (criminal behavior resulting in injury and apprehension, for example); and they all draw heavily on the social welfare system (the society's mandate for welfare and governmental support of the institutional structure, for example). Nevertheless, each profession specializes in certain problem areas or in the use of certain methods. Social work's specialty can perhaps best be seen in its non-specialty. It concerns itself with social relationships, an enormously broad area which cuts across the specific concerns of many other professions in the social welfare system.

Exhibit 1–2 analyzes an extensive excerpt from a recent sociological study by Jacqueline Wiseman, *Stations of the Lost*.[14] Her study is a superb contemporary analysis of one small part of the social welfare network, and in it the distinction between social welfare and social work is clarified. In talking of a "service loop" for skid-row alcoholics, she presents a network of specific social welfare services offered in a variety of professional contexts, all intentionally or unintentionally related, and all founded in a societal and professional value system. In Exhibit 1–2, the institutional nature of social welfare becomes apparent.[15]

REFERENCES

1. A good discussion of some of the confusion in the use of social welfare as a concept may be found in Philip Klein, *From Philanthropy to Social Welfare* (San Francisco: Jossey-Bass, 1968), p. 7.
2. The student not familiar with the sociological definition of this term should refer to a basic text. See, in particular, Melvin L. De Fleur et al., *Sociology: Man in Society* (Glenview: Scott, Foresman, 1971), p. 95.
3. Ibid., pp. 40–41.
4. Klein, op. cit., p. 7.
5. Helen Crampton and Kenneth Keiser, *Social Welfare: Institution and Process* (New York: Random House, 1970).
6. Walter A. Friedlander, *Introduction to Social Welfare* (Englewood Cliffs, N.J.: Prentice-Hall, 1961), p. 4.
7. Harold Wilensky and Charles Lebeaux, *Industrial Society and Social Welfare* (New York: Russell Sage Foundation, 1958), pp. 140–147.
8. Russell Smith and Dorothy Zeitz, *American Social Welfare Institutions* (New York: John Wiley, 1970), p. 3.
9. Wilensky and Lebeaux, op. cit., pp. 138–140.
10. Ruth E. Smalley, *Theory for Social Work Practice* (New York: Columbia University Press, 1967), p. 1.
11. Ibid., p. 4.
12. Elizabeth Ferguson, *Social Work: An Introduction* (Philadelphia: Lippincott, 1969), p. 7.

13. Rex Skidmore and Milton Thackeray, *Introduction to Social Work* (New York: Appleton-Century-Crofts, 1964), p. 8.
14. Jacqueline P. Wiseman, *Stations of the Lost: The Treatment of Skid Row Alcoholics* (Englewood Cliffs, N.J.: Prentice-Hall, 1970).
15. Ibid., pp. 46–62.

SELECTED READINGS

Dolbeare, Kenneth, and Patricia Dolbeare. *American Ideologies*. Chicago: Markham, 1971.

Howard, Donald. *Social Welfare: Values, Means, and Ends*. New York: Random House, 1969.

Klein, Philip. *From Philanthropy to Social Welfare*. San Francisco: Jossey-Bass, 1968.

Rein, Martin. *Social Policy: Issues of Choice and Change*. New York: Random House, 1970.

Romanyshyn, John. *Social Welfare: Charity to Justice*. New York: Random House, 1971.

Towle, Charlotte. *Common Human Needs*. New York: Family Service Association of America, 1952.

Wilensky, Harold, and Charles Lebeaux. *Industrial Society and Social Welfare*. New York: Free Press, 1958.

A BRIEF HISTORY

2

The development of social welfare in England and the United States is a historical study of enormous scope and detail. The purpose of this chapter is to establish a historical perspective within which the present welfare institution can be more fully understood. In spite of their vividness, many details are unimportant for such a purpose. Therefore, this chapter will concentrate on the major events and developmental threads crucial to the social welfare institution as it currently exists in the United States. The fascinating details of the personal and societal conflicts and crises that accompanied the events so briefly described here may be found in the many excellent historical accounts of social welfare's growth and development. Change has rarely been accepted without resistance, and the struggles of our day are but the contemporary expression of many earlier struggles along the road to a more adequate concept of social welfare.

Before beginning with the early attempts to formalize and unify social welfare services in the 1500s, a brief overview of the basic importance of the social bond is important. Group life derives its essential justification from its social welfare utility. Early man probably joined into groups because of the greater functional utility of the group in accomplishing various tasks. At first, these tasks no doubt centered around life-sustaining activities such as physical protection, food gathering, and sexual intercourse. The need to care for the resulting children was a likely stimulus for the development of early forms of the family and the tribe. The family, then, became a stable welfare unit in which many common human needs were performed for a clearly identified group of family and tribal members. As such, the concept of responsibility for others was established, and the future history of social welfare can be seen as the progressive expansion of the group for which responsibility is felt. The family continues to be an important social welfare unit, in spite of the development of other major social welfare units in our society.

The Industrial Revolution and the English Response

The Judeo-Christian beliefs expressed in the Old and New Testaments, which commanded that the needy be served, were perhaps the earliest formalization beyond the family of a concern for the poor, the sick, and the aged.[1] In medieval England, the poor were accepted as unfortunates whom the fortunates were normally obligated to help, the help being provided through churches, monasteries, guilds, and other benevolent groups.[2] In the Tudor period, the parish (the local governmental unit most analogous to contemporary counties) organized the provision of charity by parceling out responsibility for the poor to both religious and secular organizations. Gradually a series of societal changes created an increasing strain on existing systems, and eventually led to their modification. Three of these changes were the breakdown of the medieval feudal system, the centralization of political power in national governments, and the displacement of church power by secular governments. These changes reduced church funds available to meet the needs of persons displaced from feudal estates, while at the same time consolidating the power of local and ultimately national governmental units in caring for the poor.[3]

Many of these changes were caused by the early stirrings of the Industrial Revolution. As England became the world's greatest wool-producing country, the wool trade became more productive than farming, with much land being removed from cultivation and given over to grazing. This displaced many workers from the land, and was a force breaking the economic feasibility of the feudal manorial system. This in turn decreased the need for men previously in the service of nobles. These dislocations occurred at the same time that monasteries were broken up and their resources confiscated, thereby greatly weakening one of the earliest welfare resources in a period of increasing need. By 1518 the swelling ranks of the unemployed was a serious enough problem to generate efforts to block migrants and the unemployed from wandering around the countryside in search of work or aid. Later in the sixteenth century, the English commission responsible for studying unemployment noted that the societal conditions of grazing enclosures and erratic commerce were the main causes of unemployment, removing the blame from personal shiftlessness.[4]

Regardless of the reasons for unemployment, the large number of vagrant and often starving people became troublesome. To protect themselves against these paupers, the more affluent passed legislation to control the moral and social order,[5] with the Elizabethan Poor Law of 1601 ("43 Elizabeth") being an important early piece of such legislation.[6] Three categories of the poor were identified: the helpless, the involuntarily unemployed, and the vagrant. The helpless, or needy by impotency of defect, were the aged, decrepit, orphaned, lunatic, blind, lame, or diseased. They had their needs met by the parish, being given necessary food, clothing, and housing. The involuntarily unemployed, including those made poor by misfortune such as fire, robbery, or being "overcharged with children," were set to work or sent to a house of correction.[7]

Instead of having their need for adequate food, clothing, and housing met through charity, these poor people were expected to "pay," either through forced work or the relinquishing of their freedom. This lack of charity reflected the belief that these poor people's need was at least partly their own fault. The vagrant, including drifters, strangers, squatters, and beggars, were ostracized. Each parish felt responsible only for its own members. Since the social dislocations of the time created forced vagrancy for many people, the fact that the Poor Law encouraged parishes to ostracize nonmembers tended to create a group of the poor who belonged nowhere. This has led some later observers to blame the Poor Law for having caused many of the poor to remain vagrant.[8] The Settlement Act of 1662 further legitimated the concept of a residence requirement, a carryover of which was one of the qualifications for public assistance in the United States until the Supreme Court decision of 1969 (*Shapiro v. Thompson*) that declared it unconstitutional.[9]

The Elizabethan Poor Law of 1601 had several other significant components. It recognized the desirability of national coverage and administration of public welfare, a feature of most contemporary programs. It never accomplished total national coverage, however, and the parish continued to be the local unit through which the legislation was administered. Each parish had an Overseer of the Poor appointed every Easter by the Justice of the Peace. Social welfare funds were obtained through voluntary contributions and a public land tax. The Poor Law tried to strengthen the family unit, which was felt to be the foundation of the community. It made parents and grandparents responsible for their children (unless married) up to the age of twenty-four for boys and twenty-one for girls. If relatives could not care for their children, they were apprenticed. Finally, able-bodied individuals were set to work in special public factories, establishing the principle still used today that the more people working, the less the tax burden on the affluent. If the able-bodied refused to work, they were sent to a house of correction. Ultimately the competition between private and public factories led to the demise of the latter, but the work ethic for the poor has remained in many other guises.

To summarize, the parish welfare structure consisted of almshouses for the helpless (called indoor relief), help in the home for the aged and handicapped helpless (called outdoor relief), workhouses or houses of correction for the able-bodied, and indenture for children. Relief was basically tax-supported, but was supplemented by private charity. A distinction was made between the legitimately needy and the shiftless.[10]

As the number of needy increased, attitudes changed, and by the 1700s harsher laws and the narrowing of poor relief occurred. The attitude in workhouses became more punitive and less benevolent. Virtue was tied to thrift, industry, sobriety, and wealth, and poverty and dependency were stigmatized. Amendments to the 1601 law went so far as to evict anyone from the parish who might "become" dependent. In 1776, Adam Smith published *The Wealth of Nations*, in which he advocated the amassing of wealth. People should operate to the best of their ability with minimal societal restraints—laissez-faire capitalism. Though he did not call for the end of the poor laws, he felt that giving freely to people would only result in dependency and misery.[11] Others followed in pointing out the evils of supporting those in need, with Thomas Malthus in

1798 arguing that population growth would soon outrun food production. Further impetus for the making of relief more punitive was the rise of Protestantism in Europe and England. It stressed the importance of individual effort, and did not stress charity and the help-your-neighbor attitude of the Judeo-Christian tradition. Gradually the punitive aspects of the poor laws came to be stressed over the rehabilitative components.[12]

Social conditions worsened between 1740 and 1850 as the Industrial Revolution gained momentum. The shift from agriculture to technology continued; the population greatly expanded and the numbers needing to be clothed and fed shot up rapidly. The uncontrolled growth of towns and factories created many new social problems. In response to increasing need, the Speenhamland Act was passed in 1796. It broadened relief by making aid available when one's wages fell below a subsistence level. This subsistence level was based on family size and food costs, and was called the "bread scale." However, after the postwar depression of 1815 it became apparent that broader political changes were essential.[13]

Poverty was widespread and was aided by the Speenhamland Act, since employers reduced wages knowing that workers would get at least the bread scale through welfare. Taxes to support the Poor Law had tripled by 1832, and the law was called "a bounty of indolence and vice" and "a universal system of pauperism."[14] In the New Poor Law of 1834, the able-bodied poor were to receive no relief except for employment in workhouses. Outdoor relief was sometimes granted in an attempt to maintain the family at home, but relief payments were usually meager because they were supposed to supplement income rather than replace it. Widows and the aged constituted the two groups receiving the majority of aid. Despite the lower payments provided, the New Poor Law was praised for its more orderly, firm guidelines which were open to less misuse, and for speeding up special reforms in the medical, housing, and sanitation areas.[15] Nevertheless, its restrictive and punitive features were evident.

To summarize the development of social welfare in England from 1601 to 1834, we have seen that the poor laws sought to stem disorder during rapid economic and social changes that made many members of society dysfunctional. The needy were distinguished from the criminal, and originally, involuntary unemployment was accepted as a necessary outcome of industrialization. Only in the 1700s, when wealth became a virtue, was poverty considered a sin and vice. The Industrial Revolution brought insecurity to many while others achieved wealth; but those who had prospered because of the economic changes would not take a charitable attitude toward those who had not. The poor were a burden with whom few wanted to contend.

The colonies developed a system of relief appropriate to their needs, but also inherited many attitudes developed in England from 1601 to 1834, including the concept of community-based welfare, stigmatizing relief recipients, distinguishing between worthy and unworthy relief recipients, establishing homes for the sick and aged removed from community life, and so on.

The Colonial Social Welfare System in America

Considering the conditions of life in the colonies, it wasn't at all surprising to find many people in the 1600s and 1700s in need of public assistance and charity. Some of the original settlers were paupers, criminals, and indentured servants of whom England was trying to dispose, while others were seeking religious freedom, adventure, fortunes, or a new life. The colonists often landed in America in poor financial condition, and turned to subsistence farming as a livelihood or settled in communities which became cities, such as Boston, Philadelphia, and Charleston.

Since the value system and conditions of life in the new country were compatible with the negative attitudes toward dependency that had been developing in England, the English Poor Law of 1601 and the Law of Settlement and Removal of 1662 were adopted. The public did acknowledge its responsibility to protect and care for the needy, but this did not mean that the needy were accepted or understood.[16] Throughout its history the United States has reaffirmed this responsibility to care for the needy, but along with it the fear that public care of the needy fosters dependence.[17] Carried over with the Poor Law were the practices of residence requirements, parental responsibility, classification of the needy, and indoor and outdoor relief. Residence requirements in the colonies included the practices of "worming out"—the turning away of persons who might become dependent—and "passing on," whereby a person was transported to his legal residence if he became dependent.[18] Assistance was provided in four ways: private citizens could be paid to house the destitute (similar to foster-care today); the destitute could be auctioned to the lowest bidder; the needy could be placed in almshouses; or they could obtain outdoor relief (the heart of our present assistance system). The able-bodied were required to work, a practice finding increasing popularity in our contemporary assistance systems.

Though originally the concept of self-help was strong, two major events helped to modify these early beliefs. Between 1760 and 1820, the French and Indian Wars left many families fatherless and drove frontier people to seek safety along the coast. Unemployment increased and wages fell as a result, while bad crop years, low yields, and other natural catastrophies made costs skyrocket. These conditions created need under circumstances which called into question the New England Puritan values of self-sufficiency, the goodness of work, piety, and the strength of the family.

A series of bloody revolutions at the end of the eighteenth century, of which the American and French were the most famous, created societies more equalitarian than ever before. The greater power of the common man over the social institutions which governed his life generated the rise of Romanticism. Romantic ideals countered ascetic Puritan beliefs with a faith in the goodness, uniqueness, and value of each individual, thereby supporting attempts to increase individual autonomy and provide basic social welfare services to all. The depression after the Napoleonic Wars (1815–1821), the growing population, and the arrival of over six million immigrants between 1820 and 1860 were all factors which supported the adoption of some of the practical implications of Romanticism.

These effects were first felt in prison reforms, starting with the opening of the Walnut Street Prison in Philadelphia in 1790. Greatly improved conditions in almshouses followed, and auctioning of the needy was gradually replaced by their placement in almshouses. The almshouses became important as poor men's hospitals, a development fostered by the large number of immigrants who often arrived destitute, ill, with language barriers, and encountering difficulty finding work. These immigrants were highly motivated and usually needed temporary care until they could regain their health and become somewhat acclimated to their new society. In response to such needs, medical care in almshouses was usually excellent, with some of the greatest physicians in the country working in them. Manhattan's Bellevue Hospital, Philadelphia's General Hospital, and Baltimore City Hospital were all originally almshouses.

Though many thought the residents of almshouses were capable of work, studies showed this to be false. In Philadelphia's Blockley Almshouse in 1848, only 12 percent of the men and women were able-bodied. Nevertheless, there was growing criticism that they were too costly, too crowded, had unhealthy conditions, and were ineffective in reaching the needy whose pride would not let them be confined in an almshouse. These criticisms stimulated a period of vigorous social reform from 1830 to 1860. Thoreau, Emerson, and other intellectuals recognized the need for social reform, and stimulated attempts to establish experimental social communities to find better ways of life. Brook Farm and the Oneida Community were two examples of their day, while the communes of our day continue the search for more satisfying community contexts. Education, woman's suffrage, temperance, trade unionism and slavery were other important issues of the time that reflected society's struggles with early industrialization and the values of freedom and democracy.

In the Jacksonian era, 1830–1846, movements to correct the social ills of industry, eliminate religious intolerance, and provide better treatment of the insane increased.[19] There continued to be conflicting views on welfare, however. Some felt that hard-working individuals shouldn't have to pay taxes to support the idle, while others felt that those people who had once contributed to society should be aided in troubled times. Some felt volunteer charities should be the only source of aid, while others felt volunteer charities were too limited and unstable to bear the sole responsibility for aiding those in need. While these issues were being debated, the evidence of need included anti-rent wars staged in New York;

constant looting and burning in opposition to the hard times in Baltimore; and Boston's need to cope with a massive influx of Irish immigrants.

New Patterns of Helping: The Legacy of the 1800s

From 1860 to 1900, the population of the United States rose from 31.5 million to 76 million, with 13.7 million being immigrants. The Industrial Revolution was having a profound effect on the United States during this period, and the nation was rapidly becoming a large, urban society increasingly cognizant of its many problems. During the 1800s, social welfare progress occurred in three major spheres: public social welfare services; private social welfare services; and services for special groups.

Starting in 1857, outdoor relief (relief provided in one's own home) replaced many almshouses, indicating its increased social acceptance. This resulted from studies that showed it to be less costly than relief provided in almshouses, as well as an increasingly prevalent belief that those temporarily in need should not be subjected to the degrading conditions of almshouse life. Outdoor relief payments were small, since many continued to believe that low payment levels would encourage recipients to seek work, in spite of evidence indicating that the majority of the needy could not work.[20] Relief payments in cities were usually in cash, but in rural areas relief was usually given "in kind" (giving the actual products, such as food and clothing, instead of money to buy these items).[21]

The Civil War and its aftermath led to other changes in the public welfare system. In this period of intellectual and social upheaval, equality of all men and the struggle between competing political and economic systems became issues of high priority with profound moral consequences. Congressional response to these issues included the passage of the Morrill Act and the establishment of the Freedman's Bureau in 1865. The former gave states land grants to build colleges and other institutions. The latter was created to help the needy, especially ex-slaves, by providing financial assistance and free education in the South.[22] It was supported by the first federal tax legislation to care for the poor, a clear governmental declaration of its responsibility for citizens who were the pawns of the political and economic dislocations of the Civil War.

The public welfare realm was increasingly supplemented by organized private charity. In spite of progress in the public sphere, relief was strained to the limit by such events as the depressions of 1815–1821 and 1837–1843, as well as the panics of 1847 and 1857. Soup kitchens, collections through newspapers, and old clothing and bread funds were used to supplement public relief channels, but it became clear that more organized procedures would be more effective. An early attempt at such organization appeared in 1817. The New York Society for the Prevention of Pauperism stressed prevention and rehabilitation within a rather moralistic framework for dealing with problems. The New York Association for Improving the Condition of the Poor (AICP), founded in 1843 and subsequently copied in several other cities, was modeled after the New York Society for Prevention of Pauperism, and superseded it. This association developed a classification system for the needy: those who were needy by "unavoidable causes," by "own improvidence and vices," or by laziness. Like the society on which it was modeled, the AICP felt intemperance was a main cause of poverty. However, it realized that social reform was as important as moral reform, so in addition to moral preaching,

---

EXHIBIT 2–1
Progress?

The following editorial and pictorial comment appeared on p. 37 of the June 22, 1971 issue of the New York Daily News. *It does seem to support the old adage that history has a way of repeating itself.*

And So, to Work

A new state law requiring able-bodied reliefers to get to work goes into effect July 1.

There are an estimated 60,000 employables on the local welfare rolls. They are being directed to pick up their semi-monthly relief checks after July 1 at state employment offices.

From there, it should be a short hop in most cases to paying jobs, or to public work that needs to be done in hospitals, parks, schools, etc. Failure, without good reason, to appear at the state employment office to which a reliefer has been assigned is to result in removal from the welfare rolls.

We hope the new system may get a fair tryout here, as a small measure of relief (no pun intended) for taxpayers.

In which connection, we note that Social Services Commissioner Jule M. Sugarman already is voicing doubts of the plan's feasibility and thinking out loud about reasons why he fears it won't work.

So why shouldn't Mr. Sugarman betake himself forthwith to some job in which he will be happier? If his heart no longer is in his present job, doesn't he owe it to the public to make way for a successor who will give it his best efforts?

Reprinted by permission of *The New York News.*

attempts were made to improve sanitation and housing, and to lessen alcoholism, promiscuity, and child neglect.

The associations were in turn superseded by the development of the Charity Organization Society (COS). Begun in England in 1869, COS opened its first United States affiliate in Buffalo in 1877. By 1892, America had ninety-two COSs. Care in investigating claims, meeting individual needs, and providing minimal relief payments were stressed. Help was to be provided only to the "truly needy."[23] Case records were taken, and agents increasingly found education helpful in preparing such records. The workers kept accounts of all persons receiving aid, made regular visits, and paid agents to check up on welfare recipients. The COSs followed the teachings of Josephine Shaw Lowell in her *Public Relief and Private Charity*. She believed that all relief should be voluntary, and made unpleasant enough so that few would stoop to ask for aid. Mrs. Lowell felt almshouses and workhouses should be rehabilitative, with those working there finding moral regeneration.

Lowell's relief system was based on some insidious values. Her underlying belief was that most needy people were capable of work, a belief no truer then than it had been earlier or is today. She also continued to distinguish between deserving and undeserving poor, and used a means test to determine eligibility for aid. Such values and practices continue to undermine contemporary efforts to formulate an adequate social welfare system, and as such were unfortunate parts of Lowell's work. However, she did make some beneficial changes to the practices then existing. The individual was considered for relief according to his personal set of circumstances, although if a person was found worthy of aid, relatives, the church, and others were asked for charity first. A scarcity of other resources eventually led the COS organizations to have their own relief funds, and since few people volunteered to visit relief recipients, both the investigation of claims and the visiting of relief recipients became the job of a paid agent.

The COS played an important role in the development of welfare in the United States in other ways also. It countered the harshness of Social Darwinism by focusing on individual circumstances that might create need. It influenced and enlisted the support of scholars from university campuses, and set standards of case evaluation by which all charity and relief organizations could be measured. COS also offered auxiliary services: an employment bureau; a savings and thrift class; a loan office; a workroom; legal aid; a day nursery for working mothers; and visiting nurses. Not until 1863, with the establishment in Massachusetts of the State Board of Charities, were the beliefs against welfare and the restrictive welfare standards of the COS partially reversed.[24] By 1897, sixteen states had such boards, which in addition to improving institutional conditions and supporting outdoor relief, created special services for children, the handicapped, and the mentally disturbed.

In response to continued assertions by some groups that outdoor relief did not properly discourage the temptation to take relief instead of trying to improve one's condition, other solutions to the relief problem were sought. The settlement house movement caught on as a possible alternative, and in 1887, Neighborhood House in New York; Hull House, under Jane Addams, in Chicago; the South End in Boston; and Northwestern University Settlement in Chicago, were opened. They operated to meet special community needs and often specialized in helping immigrants get a foothold in America. They formed ties with universities and the community in which they existed, and proved more understanding of the causes of poverty than the COS. In addition, Hull House was able to offer auxiliary services, such as a free kindergarten, a day nursery, a playground, clubs, lectures, a library, a boarding house, passage of laws governing sweatshops, and meeting rooms.

Settlement houses personified a community approach to problem solving, a perspective important for two major reasons:

1. It focused on concrete needs of people rather than looking for psychological or moral flaws in individuals. This reduced many of the then-existing value barriers in the provision of services, it rendered services in very practical forms, and it helped counteract the dominance of Freudian psychology that began in the 1920s.
2. It encouraged individual participation in solving one's own problems, and demonstrated that people can organize themselves to become very effective agents of change. This reduced the feelings of helplessness in facing social problems, and provided a basis for the development of consumer advocacy groups.

We are just emerging from a long period in which a psychological approach was thought to be the most effective one to adopt in the solution of problems. The limitations of such an approach in terms of problem abstraction, loss of client power, reduced quantity of services, and inequitable distribution of services have led many contemporary social welfare practitioners back to a more community focused approach. Indigenous movements to reduce inequality and improve the quality of life in today's society are logical successors to the principles established in the settlement house movement. Today we speak of consumer advocacy, participation of the poor, community organization, and the like. While the terminology may be contemporary, the ideas were sown in the earlier community settlement house movement.

Progress in the provision of services for special groups moved ahead in several areas during the 1800s. As American society industrialized, distinctions between the laborer and the industrial manager were becoming more apparent. It became increasingly evident that the old "moral code of an individualistic, agrarian society" was being applied "to the practices of a corporate and industrial society."[25] Social Darwinism was the philosophy of the times, and it discouraged governmental intervention

in the realm of business. The formation of groups such as the National
Labor Union in 1866, the Knights of Labor in 1878, and the American
Federation of Labor in 1886, was the result of workers' attempts to organize to protect themselves against such beliefs and their results. Such
organizational attempts were vigorously and often violently opposed
by managerial and entrepreneurial groups. The contemporary efforts of
Cesar Chavez to organize migrant farm workers in spite of economic and
social reprisals by the food industry gives some flavor of what early organizational efforts were like.

The needs of the physically and mentally ill were issues at mid-cen-
tury. The American Medical Association (AMA) was founded in 1847, giving powerful support to early attempts to improve standards of medical
care and practice. Movement of mentally ill prisoners from houses of correction to mental hospitals in 1844 improved their chances for receiving
humane treatment. However, President Pierce vetoed legislation in 1854
that would have provided federal money to build homes for the mentally
ill, in spite of Dorothea Dix's eloquent appeals. From our contemporary
perspective, the AMA may be seen as maintaining professional privilege
as much as supporting standards of medical practice, and the wisdom of
Dorothea Dix's attempts to remove the mentally ill from the community
into isolated institutions may be questioned. However, at the time, the
formation of the AMA was seen as a positive act, and the refutation of
Dorothea Dix's goals slowed reform considerably.

Children and prisoners were two final groups for which services
were improved during this period. Legislation passed in 1878 prohibited
the removal of children from their homes solely because of poverty, while
legislation in 1887 and 1890 improved the procedures used when children
had to be placed in foster homes or institutions. Reform schools to rehabilitate youthful delinquents were developed, and juvenile courts were
established in 1899. Related to these changes were more general prison
reforms resulting in the separation of male and female prisoners, and attempts to eliminate political influences in jails and prisons. In 1891, the
National Conference of Charities and Correction (now the National Conference on Social Welfare)[26] recommended maximum and minimum sen-
tences, a reformatory system, encouraging prisoners to learn a trade,
letting the disabled practice their trade within the institutions, rewarding
good behavior, keeping total records of each prisoner, giving classroom
instruction, and allowing prisoners to attend regular religious services. As
can be seen, more humane care was slowly being attempted for additional
groups in society. Events like the atrocities documented in the Arkansas
prison system and the spectacular Attica disaster serve as periodic re-
minders of the as yet inadequate nature of attempts to deal more humanely with all human beings regardless of the problems or the offenses.

As the 1900s began, many people increasingly recognized economic
and social conditions as causes of poverty, and conceded that the majority
of those on relief were ill-fit to work. If one appeared to be able in body,

then the mind was considered disabled, or vice versa. Outdoor relief was still widely contested, and its administration was frequently poor. Therefore, private relief was preferred until public relief could be better organized. The period up until 1900 had been the time when the stigma of poverty was most keenly felt, a result of Social Darwinism and the COS blaming dependency on personal failure. But the developing social and biological sciences were helping men realize that social, economic, and other environmntal factors played large roles in men's lives. In spite of the progress toward an adequate social welfare system, substantial challenges remained as America moved into the twentieth century.[27]

Social Welfare in the Twentieth Century in the United States

Between 1900 and 1925 the population of the United States reached the 100 million mark, with 50 percent of the people living in the cities. The United States had become an important industrial nation and world power, attaining unheard of prosperity and wealth; the GNP reached $104.4 billion just before the stock market crash of 1929. The publication of Robert Hunter's *Poverty* in 1904 showed that the growing society was developing a new regard for the poor. Hunter's statistics on the prevalence of unemployed men, low wages, and poor working conditions showed the poor to be victims of unfortunate circumstances. After John A. Ryan published *A Living Wage* in 1906, the value of more than a minimum standard of living became more accepted. He and other economists calculated what a family needed to live comfortably, and the discrepancy between the then-current wage scale and the estimated living wage was enormous.

Immigrants, though they didn't comprise the entire group of unemployed, formed a vast majority. The communication problem, slum conditions caused by overcrowding, and the fear of a great number of men flooding the labor force caused much adverse feeling toward the new arrivals. The pressure became so great that in 1921 legislation was passed that set strict quotas on further immigration.[28] In 1924 the Immigration Act was passed by Congress.[29] Unfortunately, this did not raise wages, and did not stem the migration of impoverished farm families to the cities in search of work.

In the period from 1900 to World War I, a group of concerned citizens called Progressives sought to expose the evils of low wages, long hours, bossism, health hazards, and all other problems facing the poor in the cities. Social workers also tried to help, and at the 1912 Conference on Charities and Correction, the Committee on Standards of Living and Labor recommended a liberal list of much needed reforms. Among them were the eight-hour workday for women, children, and some men; a six-day workweek; and an end to work hours at night.[30] In 1912, Woodrow Wilson took office on the platform of New Freedom, and before the outbreak of World War I he pushed strongly for reform. He established the

Federal Reserve Act, the Federal Trade Commission, the Sixteenth Amendment, the federal income tax, the eight-hour workday for railroad workers,
laws against interstate transportation of goods made by child labor, and
the Clayton Antitrust Act of 1914.

   Children were of prime concern in the early 1900s. Theodore Roosevelt held the first White House Conference on Children in 1909. It dealt
with the care of dependent children, and one of its outcomes was the
formation of the Children's Bureau in the Department of Labor in 1912.[31]
The bureau, in the capable hands of Julia Lathrop and Grace Abbott, carefully regulated the laws and reforms concerning child abuse practices in
this country.[32] President Wilson held the second White House Conference
on Children in 1919, which resulted in the Maternity and Infancy Act of
1921 (Sheppard–Turner Act);[33] in 1930, President Hoover held the third
conference, which produced the Children's Charter. The Charter emphasized the child's need for love, security and understanding, as well as
protection, recreation, proper schooling, and preparation for adulthood.
The fourth conference was held in 1940 by President Roosevelt. The topic
was children in a democracy, and concern was for economic and social
security for each child.[34] In 1918, the Children's Bureau did a study of the
existing juvenile courts and found only a few acceptable. Reforms included hearings held in the judge's private chambers under informal conditions (i.e., no warrants or indictments); the provision of probation
services; and special detention centers and psychiatric services.[35] Unfortunately, the unintended effect of these well-intentioned reforms was to
deprive juveniles of their basic legal rights, and many have since been
reversed by the courts. Special health services for children were also
sought, and by 1934, thirty-seven states had developed programs for
diagnostic services, medical treatment, and convalescent care for crippled
children.[36]

   By the 1920s reformers had established the futility of trying to indict
people for personal failure. There was a greater awareness of the effects
of such factors as poor sanitation facilities, low wages, poor safety pre-
cautions in industry, and various other occupational hazards. Unemployment, illness or incapacity, death of the breadwinner, and old age were
also accepted as legitimate causes of need. These value changes provided
a foundation for further legislation. Between 1900 and 1920, forty-three
states passed workmen's compensation laws,[37] although many of these
laws were ineffective and there was no uniformity in coverage or administrative structure from state to state.[38]

   Assistance programs were gradually developed to aid various special
groups in addition to those already mentioned. By 1920 forty states had
passed acts to aid needy mothers, and soon after, similar aid was made
available to the aged. Lobbies were formed to improve facilities for the
destitute aged, and by the Depression this was one of the most powerful
groups pushing for social security.[39] Unfortunately, other needy groups

were not as successful in organizing to protect against low levels of aid and geographically variable coverage.

The early 1900s saw the continued growth of voluntary organizations financed by dues, donations, and subscriptions. Some of the best known groups were the Boy Scouts, Girl Scouts, National Tuberculosis Association, American Cancer Society, Camp Fire Girls, Goodwill Industries, National Association for the Advancement of Colored People (NAACP), and National Child Labor Committee.[40] During World War I, the Red Cross performed important functions under the directorship of Harry Hopkins. It provided a communications link between servicemen and their families and provided assistance to needy dependents of servicemen. It also advanced money to families that had not received their allowance from the Soldier's and Sailor's Insurance Law of 1919, which was supposed to protect the enlisted man's family from hardship due to his military service.[41] Charitable trust funds were also growing during the early 1900s. Some of the best known were the Rockefeller and Carnegie Foundations, the Rockefeller Institute for Medical Research (1901), General Education Board (1902), Carnegie Foundation for the Advancement of Teaching (1905), and the Russell Sage Foundation (1907).[42]

The Depression answered once and for all the question of whether relief should be primarily public or private. The crisis was so widespread that private agencies could not hope to alleviate the unemployment and resulting need.[43] It was this impetus that finally made the federal government assume the major responsibility for economic stability. Keynes and other influential economists of the time called for full employment, but private business could not control business cycles. Factors such as lack of economic opportunity and resources were seen as responsible for poverty and unemployment, particularly in the cases of youth, the aged, women, minority groups, and farmers.[44] The Great Depression after World War I was the major reason for poverty coming to be seen as a societal rather than an individual problem.[45]

The New Deal and Its New Perspective

The Great Depression (1929–1933) forced a change in the administration and financing of outdoor relief. It stimulated increased public works and work relief programs, an expanded categorical approach to relief, and eventually a new program of social insurance and social assistance.[46] To help with unemployment relief, some state governments established emergency relief administrations,[47] while the Wagner–Rainey bill of 1932 authorized the Reconstruction Finance Corporation to make loans to states for public works and unemployment relief.[48] In 1933, President Roosevelt established the Federal Emergency Relief Act (FERA), appropriating $500 million for grants-in-aid to states for work relief and unemployment relief. When FERA was abolished in 1936, it had allocated over

$3 billion to assisting the states.[49] In November of 1935 President Roosevelt created the Civil Works Agency, administered by FERA, "to give work to able-bodied poor."[50] The Public Works Administration was also formed, with goals to increase the demand for heavy or durable goods and to stimulate purchasing power. In spite of their good intent, the flurry of experimental and often hotly contested legislation ultimately proved incapable of dealing with the need for a new approach to social welfare in the United States.

Legislation following the Great Depression constituted what was termed the New Deal, and it accelerated the increase in the amount of public control imposed on the nation's economy. "The New Deal, however, was more concerned with the social repercussions of industrialization, rather than with more narrowly economic problems."[51] A long-range economic security plan by President Roosevelt, the Social Security Act, passed Congress in 1935. Two social insurance programs were established on the national level to meet need created by old age and unemployment: Old Age and Survivor's Disability Insurance (OASDI, or social security), a federal system of old-age benefits for retired workers; and a federal-state system of unemployment insurance. The program also provided for federal grants to states to help them provide financial assistance to the aged, the blind, and dependent children. Some health services and vocational rehabilitation were also included. "The creation of a foundation of social insurance was laid, and areas previously considered the exclusive province of the private sector were brought under the scrutiny of a democratic government."[52]

The Social Security Act laid the foundation of the present public welfare system in the United States. The social security program itself affirmed the social desirability of social insurance versus grant programs, and was intended to provide for need during old age when earning capacity was minimal. Payment levels were never intended to be sufficient to meet living costs in and of themselves, but were to be supplemented by personal savings. Although social security payments have steadily risen, they remain low enough to require some supplementation. Unemployment insurance was intended to be a temporary income maintenance program during periods of temporary unemployment, and it continues to be a program of limited duration. By far the most controversial programs in the Social Security Act were those providing the nucleus of the present public assistance programs. These were direct grant programs for the blind, dependent children, and aged persons not covered by social security, whose funding involved a complicated federal-state matching formula (see Appendix A). These programs were controversial because recipients received direct cash grants rather than the money they had previously paid into a fund, as was the case with a social insurance. Because the public assistance programs were so controversial, they were restricted to helpless groups with obvious need: the destitute aged, the blind, and dependent children.

Over the years, the programs established in 1935 have been gradually expanded in scope and the benefit levels have risen, although benefit levels continue to be minimal. However, the basic structure of the Social Security Act has not been changed, and as the number of recipients and the number of program components have grown, so has the unwieldiness of the structure. This has been especially true in public assistance where federal-state sharing is involved. The current administrative costs of the public assistance network are very high, as are the costs of the benefits themselves. Yet it is obvious that in spite of high costs, need is being inadequately met both financially and socially. The Social Security Act established the social acceptability of a national attack on need, but contemporary needs are probably too different from those in 1935 to be adequately served by legislation formulated and enacted almost forty years ago.

There are several areas in which the Social Security Act is presently inadequate:

1. It was limited in scope, reflecting the political and social realities of 1935. By its very passage, it paved the way for a more comprehensive view of needed social welfare legislation. New legislation will no doubt continue some parts of the 1935 act (such as social security and unemployment insurance), but it will probably change the whole basis for handling other social welfare needs (health care, financial assistance, social services, and so on).
2. Contemporary society is vastly different from what it was in 1935. Rural-to-urban migration, civil rights progress, automation, and changes in educational opportunity have each had a significant impact on the nature of social life and the definition of social problems. New legislation must take account of these changes.
3. Funding and political realities have changed. The crisis in local and state fiscal affairs has shifted the burden of funding needs to the federal government. Patterns of cooperation and funding established in 1935 will have to be reexamined and altered.
4. National priorities have changed. Minority groups are more vocal and more powerful. Domestic and foreign priorities are being reexamined. Affluence and its effects are being reevaluated. All of these priority adjustments must be reflected in national social welfare policy.

In summary, the Social Security Act of 1935 marked recognition of governmental responsibility for needs in a new and creative manner. The act continues to support the basic framework of the social welfare system in the United States, but will probably be supplemented or replaced by more contemporary legislation in the near future.

The period directly following the passage of the Social Security Act focused mostly on World War II and its effects. "The road to social change from F. D. Roosevelt's third inauguration in 1940 until the election

of President John F. Kennedy in 1960 was circuitous at best and impass-
able at times."[53] The volunteer and public agencies were concerned with
providing for the needs of men and women in the military, and their
dependents, leaving postwar plans for the economy somewhat undirected.
The Servicemen Readjustment Act (G.I. Bill) of 1944, which provided for
medical benefits and a maintenance allowance for education, was the
major legislation of the forties in which government intervention for social
welfare was continued at a minimal level. Foreign policy concerns and
ideological questions continued as dominant ones in the fifties. "Many
social insurance measures and programs involving social spending were
defeated in a rising tide of reaction against social legislation and a virulent
anticommunist hysteria that convulsed the nation at midcentury."[54] Although revisions in the social security programs were made during both
the Truman and Eisenhower administrations, radical innovations were
rejected.

In 1953, Congress reorganized the welfare structure with the hope
of gaining administrative efficiency and more coordinated planning. Modi-
fications of the Social Security Act in 1954 and 1956 brought into the
system many members of the labor force left out of the original act.
Unemployment insurance coverage was broadened, while the amount
of assistance and the duration of coverage were increased. The Social
Security amendments of 1962 made significant funds available for the
training of public assistance workers, and social services were added
to financial aid in public assistance programs. The concept of public welfare as a rehabilitative program was stressed, maintaining the view of
welfare as temporary until people could once again independently participate in a competitive society.

The Development of the Contemporary Social Welfare Scene

A new dimension of welfare began to come into focus in the fifties. In
1954, the Supreme Court found school segregation unconstitutional on
grounds that "separate but equal" is inherently unequal, and ordered
desegregation of the public school system "with all deliberate speed."
President Eisenhower ordered federal troops to Arkansas to enforce integration of Little Rock Central High School in defiance of Governor Orval
Faubus in 1957. The same year, Eisenhower signed the Civil Rights Act
authorizing the Justice Department to bring to federal courts cases involving discrimination in voting. The Civil Rights Act of 1960 made legal
action against state and local officials possible. The seeds of the black
movement were sown through legal and legislative battles provoked by
courageous nonviolent blacks and students in sit-ins and other demon-
strations under the leadership of men like Martin Luther King and his
associates.

At the onset of the decade of the 1960s, President Kennedy gave
social problems the perspective of his New Frontier policies, in the hands

of concerned intellectuals. Social Security revisions were liberal; the Re-development Act was passed in 1961; and in 1962 the Manpower Develop-ment and Training Act was enacted. Food stamps were initiated as a new method of helping to meet the nutritional needs of welfare recipients. Kennedy's assassination burdened the American conscience, and enabled President Johnson to pass numerous pieces of social legislation. "The Great Society was envisioned as a perfectable society in which social justice can be created by the development of institutions to meet the needs of the citizens."[55] Under the Johnson administration the following legislation was passed: in 1963, the Mental Retardation and Community Mental Health Centers Construction Act; in 1964, the Economic Oppor-tunity Act (the plan to mobilize the "war on poverty"), and a civil rights act; in 1965, Medicare, Appalachia Regional Development Act, Depart-ment of Housing and Urban Development legislation, and another civil

---

EXHIBIT 2–2
Public Assistance in the United States: Some Illustrative Data

The Growth of Aid to Families with Dependent Children, 1965–1970

The figures below indicate the growth of public welfare in recent years. Although the data are only for one program, and the one experiencing the most rapid growth, they do suggest the magnitude of the public welfare system in the United States at the present time.

	Recipients			
Fiscal Year	*Monthly Average*	*% Increase From Previous Year*	*Average Monthly Payments*	*Expenditures for Assistance Payments*
1965	4,237,000	—	$31.25	$1,588,663,000
1966	4,395,000	3.7	32.90	1,734,301,000
1967	4,714,000	7.3	36.10	2,043,339,000
1968	5,349,000	13.5	39.50	2,536,437,000
1969	6,154,000	15.0	42.55	3,141,660,000
1970	7,429,000	20.7	45.70	4,074,043,000

Source: Trends in AFDC 1965–1970 (NCSS Report H-4), U.S. Department of Health, Education, and Welfare, Social and Rehabilitation Service, National Center for Social Statistics, p. 17.

---

rights act; in 1966, a housing act; and in 1967, legislation further revising the Social Security Act.

The Economic Opportunity Act, which established the Office of Eco-nomic Opportunity (OEO) with its Vista, Job Corps, and Head Start pro-grams to name a few, was one of the most significant acts of the times. For the first time the "participation of the poor" in the power structure of the war on poverty was attempted in the form of community-action agencies. This new direction for welfare threatened local political structures and entrenched welfare organizations whose structures were poorly adapted to include client participation. The American dilemma of private versus common good arose again under the guise of federal and state funding conflicts, and in the shocking exploitation of OEO contracts by private contractors. Many communities had little experience in organizing to obtain potential grants, and often deteriorated into many squabbling groups competing for resources to end their own deprivation. The lack of success of many programs reflected inadequate funding, inadequate planning, inadequate knowledge of needs, and inadequate client partici-pation in planning. The ultimate failure of most of the programs estab-lished by the Economic Opportunity Act underlined the need for more adequately conceptualized and implemented legislative solutions to the nation's welfare needs, the entrenched complexity of most social prob-lems, and the obstacles created by the welfare bureaucracy itself.

The first massive violence in the civil rights movement broke out in 1965 in Watts, Los Angeles. The black riots were continued the following summers, and served to make Americans aware of how much poverty and inequality had still not been eradicated. In April 1968, Martin Luther King was killed in Memphis, Tennessee, and dissipation of the direct action through peaceful public protest phase of the civil rights movement was signaled by the ineffectiveness of the Poor People's Campaign that same year. Thereafter, more militant and more politically sophisticated approaches were adopted as exemplified by the National Welfare Rights Organization (NWRO).

Students also had a period of militancy spurred by the escalation of the Vietnam War in 1966, the assassination of Robert Kennedy in the spring of 1968, and the invasion of Cambodia in 1970. "The SDS (Students for a Democratic Society), the leading group in campus unrest, in 1968 had only 250 chapters with 35,000 members, but could mobilize up to 300,000 supporters."[56] Not only the poor were organizing to demand a measure of influence in the nation's social policy.

The emerging new politics, social legislation, and living styles of the sixties and seventies seem to be seeking a way to bring American ideals closer to reality. The New Left is a revolt against the bureaucracy of gov-ernment, the depersonalization of universities, the inhumanities of war, the social and economic deprivation of minority groups and the poor, and the discrepancy in some areas between what America stands for and what it practices. The New Left has drawn its support mostly from college students, middle-class youth, and discontented blacks, and has empha-sized community and social change.

Governmental responses to the problems posed by the Vietnam War, civil rights, and welfare reform have been slow and often ineffective. At present, "there is no clear definition of purpose, nor central direc-tion in welfare effort as a whole. . . . Acceleration of programs toward the abolition of poverty seems unlikely."[57] The war has been divisive and costly, yet meaningful peace negotiations stood at stalemate while seemingly meaningless destruction continued. President Nixon's resistance to school busing as an effective civil rights tool stimulated anti-busing legislation in 1972 that has seriously weakened school busing in concept and practice, a discouraging reversal of hard-won gains. Attempts to deal with the need for an overhaul of the nation's basic social welfare system have shown similar inconsistencies in 1972. Legislation already passed requires a public assistance applicant to make himself available for work as a condition for the receipt of aid, in spite of high unemployment rates, low wages, and the unsuitability of most assistance recipients for gainful employment.[58] The prospect of a nationally administered system of cash grants to replace the present public assistance system seems promising, and would lead to greater simplicity and equity. However, serious problems are tied to such grants, such as grant levels, the reduction of present assistance levels for some recipients, forced work requirements, inadequate day-care facilities, and the loss of food stamps. The future role of many types of social welfare professionals is also a potential problem area in pending social welfare legislation.

Expansion on the only meaningful frontier, that of individual men and their relationships with each other, is essential. President Nixon's strengthening of the police and corrections structures of the nation at the expense of other social welfare structures cannot hope to attain such expansion. Millions continue to live in poverty. Inequality continues to be a way of life for many blacks, Chicanos, Indians, and women. Social priorities continue to be questioned. The social welfare student and practitioner of today is living through a period of crucial importance to the future of social welfare in the United States. As is always the case, knowledge of the past will help all of us to make more intelligent decisions about the future.

REFERENCES

1. Philip Klein, *From Philanthropy to Social Welfare* (San Francisco: Jossey-Bass, 1968), p. 10.
2. S. H. Steinberg, ed., *A New Dictionary of British History* (New York: St. Martin's Press, 1963), p. 280.
3. Blanche D. Coll, *Perspectives in Public Welfare* (Washington, D.C.: Government Printing Office, 1969), p. 2; Wallace Notestein, *The English People on the Eve of Colonization* (New York: Harper & Row, 1954), p. 245.
4. Samuel Mencher, *Poor Law to Poverty Program* (Pittsburgh: University of Pittsburgh Press, 1967), p. 11.
5. Klein, op. cit., p. 11.
6. Actually the Statute of Laborers of 1349 is sometimes regarded as the first poor law in England. For a good summary discussion of the breakup of feudal organization, and the replacing of church authority by secular power, see Paul A. Kurzman, "Poor Relief in Medieval England: The Forgotten

Chapter in the History of Social Welfare," *Child Welfare* 49 (November 1970): 495–501.

7. E. M. Leonard, *The Early History of the English Poor Relief* (New York: Barnes & Noble, 1965), p. 16.
8. Mencher, op. cit., p. 12.
9. Russell Smith and Dorothy Zeitz, *American Social Welfare Institutions* (New York: John Wiley, 1970), p. 14.
10. Leonard, op. cit., p. 137.
11. Coll, op. cit., p. 9.
12. Mencher, op. cit., p. 27.
13. Steinberg, op. cit., pp. 174–175.
14. Coll, op. cit., p. 10.
15. Ibid., p. 14.
16. Ibid., p. 18.
17. Mencher, op. cit., p. 144.
18. Coll, op. cit., p. 20.
19. Nathan E. Cohen, *Social Work in the American Tradition* (New York: Dryden Press, 1958), p. 49.
20. Coll, op. cit., p. 30.
21. Ibid., pp. 36–37.
22. Smith and Zeitz, op. cit., p. 43.
23. Ibid.
24. Frank Bruno, *Trends in Social Work* (New York: Columbia University Press, 1957), p. 108.
25. Cohen, loc. cit.
26. Ibid., p. 7.
27. Coll, op. cit., p. 60.
28. Ibid., p. 63.
29. Walter Friedlander, *Introduction to Social Welfare* (Englewood Cliffs, N.J.: Prentice-Hall, 1961), p. 107.
30. Coll, op. cit., p. 63.
31. Friedlander, op. cit., p. 113.
32. Coll, op. cit., p. 72.
33. Friedlander, op. cit., p. 114.
34. Ibid., p. 116.
35. Arthur P. Miles, *An Introduction to Social Welfare* (Boston: D. C. Heath and Company, 1949), p. 200.
36. Ibid., p. 200.
37. Coll, op. cit., p. 74.
38. Miles, op. cit., p. 175.
39. Coll, op. cit., p. 81.
40. Richard H. Bremner, *American Philanthropy* (Chicago: University of Chicago Press, 1960), p. 117.
41. Bruno, op. cit., p. 232.
42. Bremner, loc. cit.
43. Coll, loc. cit.
44. Mencher, op. cit., p. 363.
45. Ibid.
46. Duncan M. MacIntyre, *Public Assistance—Too Much or Too Little?* (Ithaca:

New York State School of Industrial and Labor Relations, Cornell University, 1964), p. 14.

47. Mencher, loc. cit.
48. Miles, op. cit., p. 219.
49. MacIntyre, op. cit., p. 15.
50. Miles, op. cit., p. 224.
51. Daniel Bell, ed., *The Radical Right* (New York: Anchor, 1964), p. 213.
52. Smith and Zeitz, op. cit., p. 101.
53. Ibid., p. 107.
54. Ibid., p. 108.
55. Ibid., p. 200.
56. Ibid., p. 151.
57. Clair Wilcox, *Toward Social Welfare* (Homewood: Richard D. Irwin, 1969), pp. 360, 377.
58. John Romanyshyn, *Social Welfare: Charity to Justice* (New York: Random House, 1971), pp. 173–175, 219–222, 231–232.

SELECTED READINGS

The history of social welfare is an area that is exceedingly well-covered in published materials. These works give a good overview. The student wishing more detail should use the excellent bibliography provided in Smith and Zeitz.

Coll, Blanche. *Perspectives in Public Welfare: A History*. Washington, D.C.: Government Printing Office, 1969.

Kershaw, Joseph. *Government Against Poverty*. Chicago: Markham, 1970.

Lubove, Roy. *The Professional Altruist*. New York: Atheneum, 1969.

Schottland, Charles. "The Changing Roles of Government and Family," in Paul Weinberger, ed., *Perspectives on Social Welfare*. New York: Macmillan, 1969, pp. 132–147.

Steiner, Gilbert. *The State of Welfare*. Washington, D.C.: Brookings Institution, 1971.

Smith, Russell, and Dorothy Zeitz. *American Social Welfare Institutions*. New York: John Wiley, 1970.

STRUCTURE AND EVALUATION

The social welfare system in a large, complex, urban, industrial society like the United States in the 1970s cannot be summarized in any simple way. It is an enormously complex, overlapping, interrelated system with some rather visible major programs and many smaller ones more difficult to enumerate. Yet the student of the social welfare structure must be able to get some perspective that is relatively comprehensive and still not too full of easily forgotten details. It is more important for our purposes here to obtain a sense of the whole rather than accenting the vast web of details.

Appendix A presents some of the major social welfare programs, with the exception of the educational, corrections, legislative, and judicial systems. Obviously education is an essential social welfare service; it is a major base upon which patterns of individual and social functioning are built. However, it is also a huge system with many marginally relevant parts, and so it has been omitted here (except for certain small segments, such as school feeding programs, which are directly tied to other services and discussed in Appendix A). The judicial and legislative systems are similarly important and marginal. Such legislation as the civil rights acts, when tied to the legislated structures that made the legislation workable, is highly significant. Yet so much of both the legislative and judicial systems is peripheral to the purposes of this book that neither system is discussed in detail. Finally, the corrections system is itself so vast and specialized that the specialized corrections literature would be a better source for reviewing existing programs.

Appendix A illustrates some of the concrete services which comprise the social welfare system. It is organized into five parts, each representing a major category of services: (1) public income transfer programs; (2) private income transfer programs; (3) public social service programs; (4) private social service programs; and (5) programs for special groups. These parts are not mutually exclusive, and in many cases it is intended that they work together. Each of these parts will be analyzed for its policy significance in this chapter. Selected major programs in each category are presented in Appendix A.

1. *Public Income Transfer Programs.* Any public program is characterized by governmental policy-making and public funding. In a public income transfer program, public funds collected from certain population groups are spent on behalf of other groups. Such income transfers may be made in four ways: (1) through cash grants, as when tax money is paid to public assistance recipients; (2) through in-kind payments, as when public monies are used to purchase food, housing, training programs, etc., which are then made available to client groups; (3) through tax allowances, in

which money due the public treasury is purposefully not collected so that client groups may keep more of their resources (various income tax exemptions are examples of tax allowances); and (4) through social insurances, in which individuals contribute to a fund on which they will ultimately draw. Since any insurance spreads the risk, some never live to draw their contributions, while others draw more than they contribute. In this way, a social insurance may be seen as an income transfer program. Any income transfer focuses on the importance of financial resources for the maintenance of an adequate life pattern. A public income transfer program is recognition of the society's commitment to utilize public policy and public resources to help those in need.

2. *Public Social Service Programs.* A social service is a noneconomic service which contributes to the improvement of social functioning. Public social services involve the use of governmental policy-making and public funds to establish and maintain such services. There are many kinds of public social services which are used in conjunction with public income transfer programs, such as marital counseling, birth-control information, personal counseling, psychological testing, and others, when provided for public assistance recipients. However, public social service programs need not be tied to income transfer programs, just as income transfer programs do not necessarily have integral social service programs. Any social service program is recognition of the fact that many problems exist which are not created solely by a lack of financial resources.

When considering public programs, it is important to realize that there are several governmental levels at which public policy is made and public funds collected and distributed. The federal government has the most wide-ranging responsibility for policy-making and financial management. Many of the most significant public welfare programs originate and operate at this level, including social security, various poverty programs, and medical research programs. State governments have the next greatest impact on public policy and funding, including public assistance, education, law enforcement, and consumer protection. Local governments have smaller spheres of influence, but have important effects on some types of public welfare, including recreation facilities, law enforcement, and public transportation. The diversity and complexity of public social welfare are major causes of problems in the formulation and operation of public programs. Such factors also make it difficult for change to occur in public programs.

3. *Private Income Transfer Programs.* Private income transfer programs share many characteristics with similar public programs. They involve a reallocation of resources through cash grants, through in-kind payments, and through various types of insurance. However, a private social welfare program draws upon voluntary funding, and policy is established in privately supported social welfare organizations. This distinction between

public and private income transfer programs can be exemplified by tax allowances. A tax allowance must be a public policy, since taxes are determined by appropriate governmental bodies. However, part of public policy can be (and in fact is) to allow contributions to recognized private welfare organizations to be deducted as exemptions from taxable income. Here we can see the cooperation of public and private social welfare programs, as well as the greater resource potential of public programs over their private counterparts.

4. *Private Social Service Programs.* Private social service programs are privately supported noneconomic services, very similar in nature and intent to public social service programs. The more limited resource base for the support of such programs is again an important consideration. However, it should be noted that private programs can be considerably more flexible than public programs. Without the need for public ratification of private social welfare policy, private organizations are better able to change their policy more rapidly, to focus on specialized problem groups and problem areas, and to supplement public programs. These are important advantages, and they help private programs to remain important parts of the total social welfare system in the United States. Increasingly, however, many private agencies are obtaining public funds through contracts with public agencies, and it appears that private giving to social welfare is stabilizing or even declining. These factors may ultimately reduce the potential advantage of private agencies vis-à-vis public agencies.

5. *Programs for Special Groups.* A variety of public and private programs exist for the benefit of special groups. These may be income transfer and/or social service programs, and result from public and private concern with special groups due to various social and historical circumstances. Some examples include groups affected by war (servicemen and their families, refugees, prisoners of war, etc.); groups affected by natural disasters; groups of persons suffering from chronic, particularly disabling or disfiguring illness; and groups unusually disadvantaged in the social structure. The special circumstances giving rise to such programs frequently give them characteristics quite different from other programs. In some cases, such special programs duplicate already existing programs.

Many income transfer programs may be viewed as income maintenance programs. Income transfer programs usually affect the income levels of recipients, increasing them in most cases. To the extent that this is true, they are income maintenance programs. In the extreme case of the financially indigent, income maintenance is crucial to survival. However, we have seen that some income transfer programs, such as social insurances and tax allowances, may benefit those who are not financially indigent. Income transfer programs that involve direct cash grants, such as public assistance or the currently debated family assistance program, have a direct, immediate effect on income maintenance. Other programs that involve deferred or reduced contributions by participants, such as social insurances and tax allowances, have a more indirect effect on current income.

In-kind income transfer programs, such as food stamps and public housing, also have indirect effects. They make it unnecessary to spend current income for the resources provided on an in-kind basis, thereby conserving income. Social services can also serve as indirect income maintenance programs to the degree that they provide free services that

---

EXHIBIT 3–1
Differences between Governmental and Voluntary Agencies

Arthur Dunham, in The New Community Organization, *has a very helpful summary of sources of the major differences between public (governmental) and private (voluntary) agencies on pp. 121–122. This summary is reproduced here as a way of helping the reader to understand the different sanctions, functions, problems, and potential of each.*

Sanctions

Governmental	Voluntary

1. Established by law:
  a. Legal authority for its activities;
  b. Must carry out provisions of the law;
  c. Cannot go beyond the law.
	1. Usually established by interested group of persons. Articles of incorporation, constitution, by-laws, or charter from national agency is usually its instrument of government.

2. Law tends to define powers and duties fairly precisely; relatively inflexible.	2. Objectives and functions may be expressed in fairly general terms; program may be potentially quite flexible.
3. Law is difficult to amend; requires legislative action.	3. Constitution and by-laws usually easy to amend. Articles of incorporation usually stated in general terms. National charter amendable only on national level.

Structure

4. Part of the larger structure of local, state, or federal government.	4. Usually more or less autonomous association, sometimes a subsidiary unit of a national agency. The agency's governing board usually determines most of the policies.
5. More tendency toward large size and bureaucratic organization.	5. Size varies, though usually not as large as major governmental agency in same size community.

would otherwise have to be purchased. Free personal counseling by a family service agency may be used in lieu of costly counseling by a psychiatrist, for example. However, social services are usually more concerned with their effects on individual and community functioning than on income maintenance. The latter only becomes important if it would interfere with the use of needed social services.

Even if in-kind income transfer programs are effective as income maintenance devices, they raise the important issue of recipient autonomy. One of the important structural characteristics of an income maintenance program is the degree to which the income can be spent as the recipient

---

Structure (cont.)

Governmental	Voluntary
6. Personnel usually employed under civil service.	6. Employment standards usually determined by agency; may be determined or influenced by national agency or united fund.
7. Subject to outside administrative controls—chief executive (governor, mayor, etc.), personnel, budgeting auditing, legislative committees, courts.	7. Outside administrative controls usually limited mainly to united fund, national agency, laws regarding licensing, etc.
8. Agency is a part of a political "administration." It is related to governmental and political power structure and may be subject to partisan political pressures.	8. Agency is related to the "community power structure"—primarily the economic power structure.

Support

9. Income derived primarily from tax funds, appropriated by a legislative body.	9. Income (in the past) usually derived primarily from voluntary contributions, either to the united fund or the national agency.
10. Funds obtained through governmental budgeting and appropriation process.	10. Funds obtained usually through united fund budgeting process or through arrangements with national agency.
11. Accounting and auditing procedures subject to law and governmental regulations.	11. Accounting and auditing procedures usually subject to procedures of united fund or national agency.

wishes. Food stamps do improve nutritional levels of users, but they also deprive users of the choice of purchasing nonfood items with their resources. For this reason, in-kind programs may be avoided by persons who need income support, but who find lack of choice demeaning or wasteful of scarce resources. Since in-kind programs also usually require a complex administrative structure for resource distribution and supervision, unrestricted cash income maintenance programs would seem to have several structural advantages.

In-kind income maintenance raises the question of the purpose of income transfer programs. Social service programs generally focus on the development of social skills that facilitate individual and community functioning. Income transfer programs, however, in fulfilling their primary income maintenance function, commonly focus primarily on the provision of concrete resources. Concrete resources are essential to social functioning, and often problems of personal and social functioning are generated by a lack of such resources. On the other hand, the provision of concrete resources is no assurance that related social or personal problems will be helped. In-kind programs are justified on the basis that they tie needed concrete resources to the solution of a specific problem, thereby increasing their effectiveness and economy. For example, food stamps can only be used to purchase food, thereby increasing nutritional levels of users. However, such a paternalistic approach to problem-solving is a poor mechanism for the development of social skills. Is the goal to simply support income, or through income support to help an individual or community develop the strengths and skills to function autonomously and effectively? Income transfer programs may achieve income maintenance in such a way that they are consistent with social service goals of improved individual and community functioning. This would seem to be the most logical and organized manner of structuring social welfare services.

A final structural consideration is whether an income transfer or social service program focuses on the individual or the group. Programs to aid individuals sometimes isolate recipients, meeting the needs of each but never helping them to share their resources to overcome their common problems. Welfare mothers may have minimal economic needs met through public assistance, but it took the National Welfare Rights Organization to meet their needs for recognition, hope, and activity. Focusing on groups encourages individuals to plan together and combine their resources to achieve their goals. For example, urban renewal involves income transfers, income maintenance, and social services of various kinds. It may focus primarily on the provision of housing for individuals or the creation of a community. When the latter approach is adopted, participants can help plan how the resources and social services that are to be expended can help them collectively and individually to attain a more satisfying and effective life. Obviously some needs must be met individually, but the issues involved in the structuring of income transfer, income maintenance, and social service programs come together when considering individual and group approaches to the solution of social welfare problems.

Given the tremendous diversity of social welfare programs, it is helpful to have a framework to use in analyzing any given program. This encourages a comparative perspective in which each program's essential characteristics and social impact can be made explicit. Unfortunately, it is much easier to develop such a framework for public than for private programs. The procedures that public policy must follow give public programs a visibility and consistency not found in private programs, which result from an assortment of policy procedures. The framework to be discussed below is usable in examining any program, but its application will normally be easier for public programs. Eight criteria may be used to analyze a program.[1]

1. *Objectives.* The purposes of the program as formally stated. A program may be successful in attaining these objectives, it may be partially successful, it may attain other objectives not planned for, or it may simply be unsuccessful. Therefore, the objectives guide one's evaluation of a program, but should not preclude seeing unanticipated objectives which may be accomplished by the program.

2. *Legislative authorization.* This will normally be applicable only to public programs. Considering legislative authorization helps to relate programs to others created at the same time, as well as establishing historical perspective for such programs. This perspective also helps one to see that when programs fail, it is often because the legislation did not build in adequate implementation procedures.

3. *Source of funding.* Funding is crucial to program implementation. Attention to the source of funding is a quick way to estimate a program's chances of success.

4. *Administrative structure.* The administrative structure is also crucial to implementation. It may include cooperation between various parts of the welfare system, and is another way in which historical perspective is obtained.

5. *Eligibility requirements.* This bears directly on the institutional versus residual nature of a program. Societal values relating to social welfare tend to surface in the specification of who is eligible to participate in a program, and often create such stringent requirements that the utility of a program is seriously lessened.

6. *Coverage.* Eligibility requirements establish the boundaries of the potential client population, while coverage refers to the number actually participating in the program. It is a good measure of the program's effectiveness in reaching the target population.

7. *Adequacy*. Adequacy is a measure of the program's effectiveness in meeting the need of the target population. It is common for programs to be based on meeting some percentage of the estimated total need which exists. Such planning seeks to encourage self-help and to spread scarce resources as far as possible.

8. *Equity*. Whereas coverage is a measure of the actual population being served by a program, equity examines the built-in inequities of a program. It is commonly the case that eligibility requirements systematically discriminate against certain potential target groups.

The utility of the above eight criteria are demonstrated in the selected summary of programs in Appendix A. On the basis of these criteria, the social welfare student should begin to evaluate social welfare programs. One should develop the skill to know when a program is ineffective, what characteristics tend to destroy the potential utility of a program, what gaps exist in present programs, and which groups are systematically disadvantaged in the present social welfare system. The work of social welfare is laden with value issues, and skill in program evaluation helps a professional identify and fight for his particular value system.

REFERENCES

1. Winnifred Bell, "Obstacles to Shifting from the Descriptive to the Analytic Approach in Teaching Social Services," *Journal of Education for Social Work* 5 (Spring 1969): 5–13.

SELECTED READINGS

Specific details of services can be dull, overwhelming, and easily outdated. However, a few sources with such details are provided for those interested in getting such a flavor. There are also some sources for factors involved in the development of services.

Congressional Quarterly. *Guide to Current American Government*. Washington: Congressional Quarterly, Inc., 1735 K Street, N.W., Washington, D.C. 20006. Published twice a year.

Edgar, Richard. *Urban Power and Social Welfare*. Beverly Hills: Sage Publishers, 1970.

Morris, Peter, and Martin Rein. *Dilemmas of Social Reform*. New York: Atherton, 1967.

Steiner, Gilbert. *Social Insecurity: The Politics of Welfare*. Chicago: Rand McNally, 1966.

U.S., Office of Economic Opportunity. *Catalog of Federal Assistance Programs.* Washington: Government Printing Office, 1967.

U.S., President's Commission on Income Maintenance Programs. *Background Papers.* Washington: Government Printing Office, 1969.

Wilcox, Clair. *Toward Social Welfare.* Homewood, Ill.: Richard D. Irwin, 1969.

BUREAUCRATIZATION AND PROFESSIONALISM

4

The welfare system has responded to the rapid industrialization and urbanization of society by developing a complex system of specialized services, as outlined in Chapter 3 and detailed in Appendix A. As the welfare system has grown in complexity and scope, and as services have become more specialized, welfare practitioners have had to become proportionately more sophisticated. Consequently, the medical doctor is no longer primarily a general practitioner, the school teacher no longer teaches in a combined one-room school, and the social worker is no longer merely a friendly visitor. The welfare practitioner has become professional at all levels, a paid person working in an organizational setting with specialized training and a codified set of professional values.

This has created a structure which is characterized by greater precision and competence than was likely when the welfare practitioner was less highly trained and when he worked in a less formalized setting. It has also led to several problems, some of which will be the focus of this chapter. After looking at the theory of bureaucracies and professions, some of the problems arising from the bureaucratic organization of social welfare professions will be investigated. Since the social welfare institution comprises many distinct professions functioning in a bureaucratically organized society, the interaction of the bureaucratic form of organization and social welfare professions is an area of considerable importance for the student of social welfare.

To the extent that social welfare services have been successful in obtaining a societal mandate and establishing themselves in the social structure, they have had to cope with the problems of success. When over one million persons receive public assistance in New York City,[1] the need for such services is evident. However, enormous organizational problems have been encountered in meeting such widespread need. These problems are not unique to social welfare services, of course, since many services in society have had to cope with increasingly large numbers of users. The Industrial Revolution began the process of task specialization in work contexts, ultimately providing the foundation for mass production and massive organizational growth and centralization.[2] The bureaucracy is a form of organization well-suited to such work contexts, accounting for its contemporary pervasiveness.

The bureaucracy is a way to formally organize multivariate functions into "a system of control based on rational rules. . . ."[3] When organizational goals and means can be specified, when tasks can be broken into their component parts and rationally organized, and when tasks can be organized into hierarchical spheres (bureaus) of control, a bureaucracy can be an extremely effective form of social organization. For example, the calculation and payment of social security benefits is relatively straightforward, and is generally conceded to be effectively accomplished by the Social Security Administration bureaucracy. Clearly the bureaucratic form of organization is the major one in contemporary American society, and its pervasiveness encourages its use in all organizational contexts. Its appropriateness in social welfare contexts, however, depends on the nature of social welfare tasks to be performed and their suitability for the organizational characteristics of bureaucracies.

The formal characteristics of bureaucracies may be summarized as: (1) a high degree of specialization; (2) hierarchical authority structure with specified areas of command and responsibility; (3) impersonal relations between members; (4) recruitment of members on the basis of ability; and (5) differentiation of personal and official resources.[4] In the ideal bureaucracy, rational rules govern behavior, and individuals are expected to interact as organizational role occupants rather than as individual people. Given the above characteristics, a bureaucracy has several potential advantages: efficiency in the performance of set tasks in set ways by trained bureaucrats; predictable behavior; impersonal behavior which stresses competence more than subjective preference; and the possibility of rapid goal attainment given the trained personnel and routinized activity.

On the other hand, the bureaucracy has several practical disadvantages. It can become quite inefficient when its highly formalized structure must be changed. It can be inhuman in responding to the human needs of those within it, which can seriously affect the motivation of workers and in turn impair both the quantity and quality of productivity. Workers can become so highly specialized that they may be unable to adapt to new working conditions and tasks (trained incapacity), as well as losing sight of the goals by focusing so intensively on the means (technicism). Finally, in an attempt to gain personal satisfaction and power from the basically impersonal, rational structure, various types of informal organization may arise.[5] Such organization may either complement the formal organization and increase productivity,[6] or it may conflict with the formal organization and disrupt or restrict productivity.[7]

Turning now to the application of bureaucratic characteristics to social welfare needs, a first point is that bureaucracies require that goals and means are able to be specified in such a way that appropriate tasks can be defined and ordered. This is possible in many welfare fields, such as those related to medicine. In others, such as social work or corrections, general goals and treatment approaches can be specified, but it is very difficult to identify exactly what task helps attain what organizational purposes. This is compounded by manpower utilization problems whereby specific levels of training are only vaguely related to actual tasks to be performed.[8] When these conditions prevail, it is questionable how appropriate the bureaucratic form of organization is, since specialization, impersonal relations, focusing on ability, and hierarchical organization become problematical or arbitrary. These questions arise, of course, quite aside from the built-in potential problems (disadvantages) of any bureaucracy.

A second problem area centers around professionalization. There are some who question the wisdom of all social welfare professions attempting to become highly professionalized.[9] Professionalization has advantages in terms of status, professional self-regulation, and professional rewards, but some fear an elitist detachment from social problems[10] and, of particular concern here, certain incompatibilities with the bureaucratic form of organization.[11]

Hall identifies the following five characteristics of professions: (1) the use of the professional organization as a major reference; (2) a belief in service to the public; (3) belief in self-regulation; (4) a sense of calling to the field; and (5) professional autonomy.[12] Using the profession as a major reference can be seen in the various professional social welfare organizations, such as the National Association of Social Workers. They usually have local chapters, which offer their members a full range of services and activities including meetings, group life insurance, professional publications, certification, and group travel arrangements. It is through such mechanisms that the professional's identity is reinforced and maintained. A belief in self-regulation and professional autonomy is based on the fact that professions have specialized knowledge bases and socialization procedures. For example, physical therapists have a specialized physiological knowledge base supplemented by technical skills, both learned through a well-documented socialization process;[13] public school teachers specialize in their content area as well as specific teaching skills. Professionals maintain that the nonprofessional is not equipped to evaluate their competence since he has not mastered the specialized knowledge base. It follows that professionals must be trusted to evaluate each other, and impose necessary sanctions when appropriate. It becomes difficult for the consumer to sanction the professional, although this may be needed in cases where the professional structures are too weak to be effective regulating bodies (social work, for example), or where instances of gross incompetence may be overlooked to protect the professional image from potentially intrusive legal action (medicine is a case in point).

A belief in service to the public and a calling to the field are important in creating a professional value system. Such values are often codified by the professional organization, and set the standard for professional behavior. In the social service professions, such values usually emphasize the value of human life, the significance of judgment and self-awareness to help others in a professional way, and the equal accessibility of service to all who need it. For example, medicine has its Hippocratic Oath, and social work values emphasize client self-determination, confidentiality, and impartiality.

Comparing the structural features of bureaucracy to the profession, some potential problem areas can be identified. A profession that seeks to have self-regulation and professional autonomy may encounter some difficulty with a bureaucratic structure that establishes a hierarchy of authority and impersonal relations between members. Self-regulation assumes a sharing of knowledge and information between members, which a hierarchical structure and impersonality can impede. Professional autonomy can at times conflict with an elaborately codified set of rules governing behavior and relationships. On the other hand, both the professional and bureaucratic structures demand ability as a prerequisite for membership. Self-regulation and professional autonomy both derive from the professional's claim to expertise in his field, and successful self-regulation permits autonomy at a high level of competence, unifying bureaucratic and professional goals.

Use of the profession as a major reference, belief in service to the public, and a sense of calling all bring the professional into possible value

---

EXHIBIT 4–1
Social Work Professional Values

Analysis

The following is the Code of Ethics of the National Association of Social Workers (NASW), the social work professional association. Until 1969, only social workers holding the Master of Social Work degree were eligible for membership. In 1969, a membership category was created for graduates of B.A. social work programs approved by the Council on Social Work Education, reflecting the increasing differential use of manpower in the social welfare professions. This NASW Code of Ethics is a good example of the codification of professional values, although naturally in practice there may be considerable deviation from such values. This Code of Ethics was provided by the National Office of NASW in Washington, D.C.

Social work is based on humanitarian ideals. Professional social workers are dedicated to service for the welfare of mankind; to the disciplined use of a recognized body of knowledge about human beings and their interactions; and to the marshaling of community resources to promote the well-being of all without discrimination.

Social work practice is a public trust that requires of its practitioners integrity, compassion, belief in the dignity and worth of human beings, respect for individual differences, a commitment to service, and a dedication to truth. It requires mastery of a body of knowledge and skill gained through professional education and experience. It requires also recognition of the limitations of present knowledge and skill and of the services we are now equipped to give. The end sought is the performance of a service with integrity and competence.

Each member of the profession carries responsibility to maintain and improve social work service; constantly to examine, use, and increase the knowledge upon which practice and social policy are based; and to develop further the philosophy and skills of the profession.

This Code of Ethics embodies certain standards of behavior for the social worker in his professional relationships with those he serves, with his colleagues, with his employing agency, with other professions, and with the community. In abiding by the code, the social worker views his obligations in as wide a context as the situation requires, takes all of the principles into consideration, and chooses a course of action consistent with the code's spirit and intent.

As a member of the National Association of Social Workers I commit myself to conduct

conflicts with a bureaucracy. A commitment to helping others on the basis of their need, which reinforces one's identification with the profession, sometimes conflicts with bureaucratic rules that specify who is to receive service and under what conditions. Stanton's study of the Pangloss Mental Health Association provides an excellent example in her description of a Christmas party for mental hospital inmates which meets bureaucratic needs and rules much more than client needs or desires.[14] The confrontation of bureaucratic rules and professional values is also seen in several major social welfare system problems: gaps in service, dividing the client, and competition for resources. Since it is typically necessary to establish a bureaucratic structure with certain goals and means in mind, the resulting structure may very efficiently perform its tasks even though these tasks may only partially meet client needs. A fine, albeit tragic, example of the

---

my professional relationships in accord with the code and subscribe to the following statements:

- I regard as my primary obligation the welfare of the individual or group served which includes action for improving social conditions.

- I give precedence to my professional responsibility over my personal interests.

- I hold myself responsible for the quality and extent of the service I perform.

- I respect the privacy of the people I serve.

- I use in a responsible manner information gained in professional relationships.

- I treat with respect the findings, views, and actions of colleagues, and use appropriate channels to express judgment on these matters.

- I practice social work within the recognized knowledge and competence of the profession.

- I recognize my professional responsibility to add my ideas and findings to the body of social work knowledge and practice.

- I accept responsibility to help protect the community against unethical practice by any individuals or organizations engaged in social welfare activities.

- I stand ready to give appropriate professional service in public emergencies.

- I distinguish clearly, in public, between my statements and actions as an individual and as a representative of an organization.

- I support the principle that professional practice requires professional education.

- I accept responsibility for working toward the creation and maintenance of conditions within agencies which enable social workers to conduct themselves in keeping with this code.

- I contribute my knowledge, skills and support to programs of human welfare.

- I will not discriminate because of race, color, religion, age, sex or national ancestry, and in my job capacity will work to prevent and eliminate such discrimination in rendering service, in work assignments and in employment practices.

gaps in service and division of the client that can result from bureaucratic solutions to professional problems is found in the case of Freddy (see Exhibit 4–2).

The scramble for resources that social welfare agencies face compounds the problems of providing professional services. The structure's survival must precede the provision of any services, yet attempts to insure organizational stability may conflict with professional values.[15] When, for example, a Traveler's Aid office is forced to close for varying periods of

---

EXHIBIT 4–2
Battered Freddy

The following is a discussion of Adam Kline's "Battered Freddy's New Chance at Childhood," an article that appeared in a 1970 issue of the Baltimore Sun Magazine.

At 17, one year after his parents were arrested for child abuse and he had had the benefit of warm professional care, Freddy was 4 ft. 6 in. and weighed 75 pounds. One of Freddy's doctors said, "I think he can grow to about five feet now, maybe a little more. . . . But it's pretty certain he'll always be stunted."

Before his aunt swore out a warrant for the arrest of Freddy's parents on child abuse charges, "Freddy's name slipped in and out of the files of three city agencies, a private organization for retarded children, and the police, all to no avail."

1. A policewoman visited the home and, noting Freddy was small for his age, referred him to a special school at Rosewood State Hospital. "However, there were no vacancies at the time," and contact was ended.
2. Since Freddy was first brought to public school at age 12, he was not allowed to register as a regular student, and was referred to the Department of Education's Psychological Service Division for testing and evaluation. Contact was ended when ". . . the Psychological Services Division was completely unsuccessful in getting the parents to bring Freddy in for an evaluation. . . ."
3. The Psychological Service Division referred Freddy to a public health nurse who noted ". . . that although he was 12 years old, he seemed no more than 5." She made several attempts to get the parents to bring Freddy to the Health Department's diagnostic and evaluation center, which they never did. "After more than a year of frustrated attempts to have the boy taken to a doctor, and after an appointment at Johns Hopkins Hospital was broken by the parents, the nurse gave up."
4. The case was referred to the Baltimore Association for Retarded Children. After futile attempts at contact, "The Association notified the Health Department . . . that no progress could be made."
5. Referral was next made to the Department of Social Services. The worker there was allowed to take Freddy to the Department of Education for comprehensive psychological and intelligence testing. They recommended he be placed in a city school for trainable retarded children, but his parents refused to grant their permission. After another broken contact initiated by the parents, the Department of Education closed their file on Freddy. The Health Department did the same since it ". . . had not been able to obtain evidence of physical maltreatment. . . ." This was followed by similar action by the Department of Social Services.

weeks or months due to inadequate funding, continuity in the attainment of professional values is seriously jeopardized.

Having raised some of the rather serious issues of appropriateness of the bureaucratic form of organization for the nature of the tasks and the characteristics of a profession, the alternatives need to be explored. The fact that so much of the social system in which the welfare network exists is bureaucratically organized, and given the massive scale at which the social welfare system operates, strong pressures are exerted by both social welfare

---

6. The warrant for the arrest of the parents was sworn out by Freddy's aunt.

Regarding this case, the agencies said:

Health Department. ". . . There was never any evidence of physical maltreatment that we could get a handle on. . . . If we sense a case of child neglect, we can only turn it over to Social Services; technically it would do no good to notify the school system of truancy, because he was never registered in a school to begin with. If there is any department that could have taken it to Juvenile Court then, it's Social Services, not us."

Social Services. "A charge of contributing to the delinquency of a minor would be irrelevant. They kept him out of school, sure, but what school would have taken him anyway by the time it was brought to our attention? And not only that, he was almost 16, the age when school attendance becomes optional. If the parents weren't going to cooperate at that point, we felt there was nothing we could do. Look, it seems there was so much happening to the child, but we had no evidence of that; to tell the truth, we had no real evidence of anything other than that the boy was retarded and that they weren't doing anything to help him. The only way we could have found out more is by breaking down their front door, and this isn't a police state, we don't do things like that. The papers said the neighbors seemed to know what was going on, but, damn it, they never told us a thing."

Analysis

This case is an excellent example of each agency having followed the rules, but none having solved the problem. Note that each agency is right—each one did what it was structured to do. However, in terms of fulfilling professional values, each was quite ineffective, and looking at this case from a professional value perspective, it is disheartening at best. This case is also a good example of many parts of the social welfare system being brought to bear on a problem, with several social service professions becoming involved. Note the ultimate reliance on the family to mobilize the social service network in a meaningful way, and the final ability of the system to act being based on the societal mandate given to certain professional systems (in this case the police) to forcibly intervene in the family. As the social service worker says, this is a serious decision requiring a great deal of evidence because of its police-state implications, and it illustrates the delicate societal value decisions often encountered in social welfare work.

From Adam Kline, "Battered Freddy's New Chance at Childhood," *Baltimore Sun Magazine*, October 11, 1970, pp. 20ff. Used with permission.

professions and organizations to embrace bureaucratization. Yet even when the scale of services and demands of interorganizational communication seem to require a highly developed bureaucratic structure, more humane and effective adaptations of the bureaucracy need to be explored,[16] along with methods of making professional characteristics operable in a formal organization.[17] Alternative organizational forms are increasingly being tried, and provide some practical adaptations to the dilemmas of providing adequate services effectively, efficiently, and humanely.

In discussing the applicability of the bureaucratic form of organization to social welfare tasks and goals, two problem areas have been identified: (1) the need for clearly specified goals and means; and (2) the relationship between bureaucratic and professional characteristics. A third problem area should also be noted, however. Since bureaucracies have specialized tasks organized into a rational, hierarchical structure, it is difficult for users of the services provided to have input into that structure. Decisions affecting what those services will be and how they will be provided are usually not directly accessible to users. Bureaucracies that operate within a market system are presumed to permit user feedback, through their decisions to use or not use the service offered. Chapter 7 will examine the validity of this assumption, but it is irrelevant in the many social welfare service areas that are not provided in a market system. If a recipient of public assistance is unhappy with the amount of his benefits or the procedures governing the distribution of them, his alternative is usually no assistance rather than assistance from another source.

The problem of user participation in bureaucratic decision-making takes on added significance in social welfare because of the importance of values in social welfare services. Social welfare bureaucracies are not simply providing consumer conveniences, and variations in services are not merely a matter of taste or luxury. The average American automobile offers numerous insignificant options, but few meaningful mechanical choices. Such lack of meaningful choice may be frustrating, but it does not prevent the consumer from having his basic need met, which is transportation. In contrast, whether or not a hospital provides safe, adequate services is a matter of life or death to an accident victim who has little choice or control. Social welfare bureaucracies, then, often serve to manipulate the value system within which users must function.

The concept of user feedback and participation can founder on the rock of competence. Complex bureaucracies like General Motors or a large hospital can rarely be fully understood by users. Users are usually interested in what affects them directly rather than all of the many problems and tasks that go into the total organization. However, competence in the performance of tasks is a separate issue from deciding what tasks are appropriate. The user of a bureaucratic service has the expertise and the right to determine the values by which he wishes to live and which the bureaucracy may affect. When meaningful value choices do not exist among bureaucracies, then the dominant bureaucracy has the responsibility of allowing users to help determine the services to be provided. Skilled bureaucrats may be best able to select and organize tasks to meet organizational goals, but in most welfare contexts the goals should be selected in consultation with users. This is rarely the case. The problem is obviously exacerbated when there is disagreement among user groups or between users and bureaucrats as to what the goals ought to be.

Organized user groups, such as the National Welfare Rights Organization, can be an effective way for consumers to force bureaucracies to take their needs and wishes into account. They, themselves, also may provide concrete services of various kinds. Another type of organization is exemplified by cooperatives, which allow consumers to provide for their own perceived needs through the use of procedures more personalized and attuned to the group's values. A third organizational type, exemplified by groups such as Alcoholics Anonymous or Parents Without Partners, concerns itself with providing information and emotional support for its members. These groups may develop into active lobbying groups as well as developing concrete services for members. A fourth alternative is the decentralized, multipurpose structure that brings a variety of coordinated services to users on a scale that is more attractive to them. These are only four examples of the basically nonbureaucratic solutions to the types of problems commonly encountered in social welfare. By involving consumers in the services that so heavily affect their lives, they may feel less trapped in a faceless, uncaring bureaucracy.

In spite of the problems that have been noted, the bureaucracy gives some semblance of order and objectivity to the massive, fragmented social welfare system, and gives it some strength relative to competing societal structures. Yet at the same time it can block the humane attainment of social welfare goals and in so doing erode professional motivation and performance. This leads to what can be called the professional's dilemma.

There are some fundamental decisions the professional must make in trying to reach a personal solution to this structural conflict. The first is deciding how much of one's responsibility is to the agency for which one works and how much is to the clients one serves. If the balance of one's commitment is to the agency, then there will be a tendency to follow established agency rules rather than challenging those rules when they interfere with attempts to provide service to clients. A related decision involves the extent of one's identification with an agency's goals compared to identifying with professional goals. When agency goals are dominant, there will usually be more willingness to follow agency procedures rather than a more flexible approach to problems growing out of professional values and skills. A third decision involves the willingness to inconvenience oneself if necessary to help others. A desire to keep one's professional commitment within clearly delimited boundaries tends to make the order, predictability, and limited range of activities of the bureaucracy more appealing. A final decision relates to the commitment to follow social norms versus a belief in the appropriateness of norm violation

EXHIBIT 4-3
Welfare as a Bureaucracy: The Department of Health, Education, and Welfare

The complexity of the social welfare system is a major impetus for its bureaucratic organization. The organization chart of the Department of Health, Education, and Welfare is a good example of the diversity of functions encompassed in such a massive welfare structure and the high level of organization necessary to coordinate these functions.

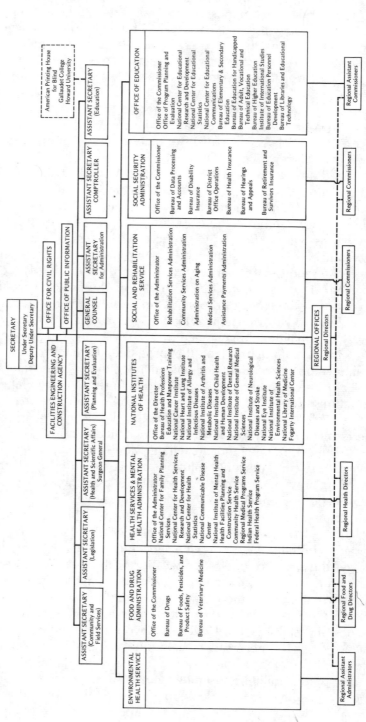

Source: *United States Government Organization Manual 1970–71,* Office of the Federal Register, National Archives and Records Service, General Services Administration, p. 614.

when necessary. Adherence to the established social norms tends to make it more likely that the bureaucracy's inherently conservative qualities will be accepted.

Clearly these four decisions are related, and have related consequences. The professional who generally accepts the limits defined by the bureaucracy will tend to resist any information or pressures that suggest his work is ineffective. To the extent that such pressures exist, the worker may be tempted to minimize his professional identification; or, if the pressures are great enough, he may resolve the problem by retreating into apathy or simply leaving the field. Decisions made favoring professional values and commitment are likely to generate substantial frustration with bureaucratic limitations. These frustrations can lead to frequent job changes in the search for a more acceptable structure, cynical exploitation of the bureaucratic structure to attain one's professional goals, or direct confrontation with the bureaucratic structure. Such confrontation can take many forms—personal actions, such as complaints or suggestions for more appropriate bureaucratic regulations; group actions, such as strikes, petitions, or informal organizations to counteract the bureaucratic structure; or group organization, as in the mobilization of consumer power to intervene in the agency structure, political action, or drawing on the strength of other professional groups.

The ways in which the professional's dilemma can be solved are many and varied. Some are consistent with professional values, while others are closer to bureaucratic rules. Some are conservative, and others are more radical. Some involve quiet, personal thoughts; others include involvement in turbulent political and organizational activities. Which are selected comes down to a very personal decision based on one's financial and personal needs. There are no best solutions; there are only those that each individual can devise and accept for himself. Finding acceptable solutions is difficult and their impact will only be known when actually on the job. However, early recognition of the interaction between societal, bureaucratic, and professional values will foster a mature approach to the fundamental value and organizational issues that underlie the contemporary social welfare institution in American society.

REFERENCES

1. In February 1971, there were 1,181,310 recipients of public assistance in New York City, according to Department of Health, Education and Welfare figures. *Public Assistance Statistics, February 1971* (NCSS Report A-2, 2/71), p. 4.
2. For an excellent discussion, see Alfred Chandler, Jr., *Strategy and Structure: Chapters in the History of the Industrial Enterprise* (Garden City: Anchor, 1966).
3. Nicos Mouzelis, *Organization and Bureaucracy: An Analysis of Modern Theories* (Chicago: Aldine, 1968), p. 39.

4. Ibid.
5. Ibid., p. 99. He defines informal organization as "the structure and culture of the group, which is spontaneously formed by the interactions of individuals working together."
6. Ibid., pp. 102–103.
7. See Donald Roy, "Quota Restriction and Goldbricking in a Machine Shop," *American Journal of Sociology* 57 (1952): 427–442.
8. See Robert Teare and Harold McPheeters, *Manpower Utilization in Social Welfare* (Atlanta: Southern Regional Education Board, 1970), pp. 4–8.
9. Martin Rein, *Social Policy: Issues of Choice and Change* (New York: Random House, 1970), pp. 281–301.
10. Ibid., pp. 47–99.
11. Richard N. Hall, "Professionalization and Bureaucratization," *American Sociological Review* 33 (February 1968): 92–104.
12. Ibid., p. 93. See also Harold Wilensky and Charles Lebeaux, *Industrial Society and Social Welfare* (New York: Free Press, 1958), pp. 284–285.
13. A classic example of occupational socialization is Howard S. Becker et al., *Boys in White* (Chicago: University of Chicago Press, 1961).
14. See Esther Stanton, *Clients Come Last* (Beverly Hills: Sage Publishers, 1970), pp. 145–158.
15. Ibid., Chapters 1, 4, 7, and 9.
16. Eugene Litwak has explored possible relationships between bureaucracies and primary groups. See his "Reference Group Theory, Bureaucratic Career, and Neighborhood Primary Group Cohesion," *Sociometry* 23 (1960): 72–84; and, with J. Figueria, "Technological Innovation and Theoretical Functions of Primary Groups and Bureaucratic Structures," *American Journal of Sociology* 73 (1968): 468–481. Carol Meyer, in *Social Work Practice* (New York: Free Press, 1960), suggests individualization and decentralization as possible adaptations (pp. 105–185).
17. Hall, op. cit.; and Ronald Akers and Richard Quinney, "Differential Organization of Health Professions: A Comparative Analysis," *American Sociological Review* 33 (1968): 104–121.

SELECTED READINGS

The problems of bureaucratization and professionalism in social welfare are major ones, and of great importance for the future of social welfare. The following sources examine various facets of these issues.

Bucher, Rue, and Anselm Strauss. "Professions in Process," in Mayer Zald, ed., *Social Welfare Institutions.* New York: John Wiley, 1965, pp. 539–553.
Etzioni, Amitai. *Modern Organizations.* Englewood Cliffs, N.J.: Prentice-Hall, 1964.
McLeod, Donna L., and Henry J. Meyer. "A Study of the Values of Social Workers," in Edwin J. Thomas, ed., *Behavioral Science for Social Workers.* New York: Free Press, 1967, pp. 401–416.
Stanton, Esther. *Clients Come Last.* Beverly Hills: Sage Publishers, 1970.
Vinter, Robert D. "Analysis of Treatment Organizations," in Paul Weinberger, ed., *Perspectives on Social Welfare.* New York: Macmillan, 1969, pp. 428–443.
Wiseman, Jacqueline. *Stations of the Lost: The Treatment of Skid Row Alcoholics.* Englewood Cliffs, N.J.: Prentice-Hall, 1970.

II

SOCIAL SCIENCE AND SOCIAL WELFARE: A BASE FOR PRACTICE

PSYCHOLOGICAL BASES

5

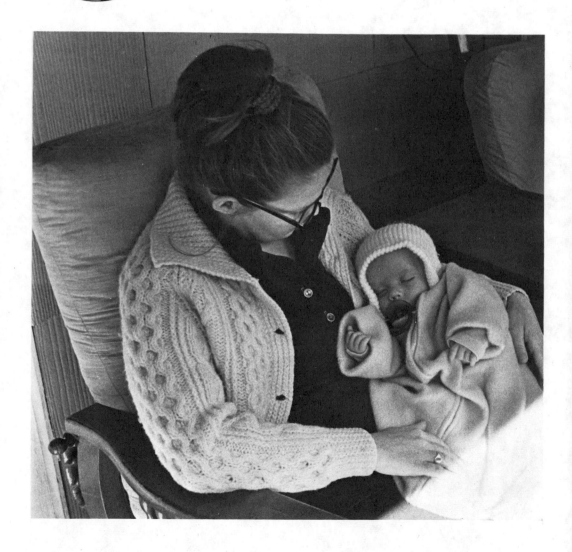

One of the most persistent problems in the social services has been the search for adequate conceptual frameworks within which to develop practice principles. This search has been made considerably more difficult by the unfortunate division between theory and practice, an outgrowth of societal specialization and professionalization resulting in academic disciplines separate from practice contexts. For example, while the origins of sociology can be found in attempts to understand social phenomena in order to solve social problems, especially those accompanying the Industrial Revolution, a division gradually emerged between sociology as a theoretical discipline and social work as its social action component. In spite of Merton's eloquent statement of the relationships between theory and empirical research,[1] in which practice contexts can be seen as empirical in nature, many theoreticians continue to see social welfare as irrelevant to their main task. At the same time, social welfare practitioners often resist the codification of their practice into more general theories.

In the preceding chapters, the organizational characteristics of the social welfare institution have been investigated. The remaining chapters are oriented toward interventive methods, the actual practice skills which social welfare practitioners use in carrying out their tasks. The analysis of interventive methods begins with a review of major social science knowledge in this chapter and the two following ones. The social welfare system is built around the knowledge existing in society. Such knowledge consists of theory and data derived from academic approaches to social behavior, as well as "practice wisdom," the accumulated experience of social welfare practitioners. Practice wisdom is an important source of knowledge, but is subject to individual biases, unique situations, and limited verification. Codified theory and its supporting empirical data tend to be much more objective and consistent, but can be remote from specific behavioral contexts in which social welfare practitioners must operate. Therefore, throughout these next three chapters the focus will be on the utility of specific social science principles for social welfare practice.

These are three of the most crucial chapters in this book. It seems fruitless to try to train social welfare workers who do not understand the theoretical bases for their work. In a rapidly changing world, and in a rapidly changing social welfare system, all options must be kept open in order to change and grow into the future. The great value of theory is precisely this overarching flexibility, since it allows the practitioner to derive new practice principles from a general body of interrelated propositions, and allows him to fit specific behaviors observed in his work into a theoretical framework that can help explain them. Since social science principles provide the major foundation and justification for the contemporary social welfare institution, an adequate understanding of it must be based on a mastery of relevant social science knowledge.

Psychoanalytic Perspectives

A psychological perspective on behavior focuses on the internal mental development and functioning of the individual. This entails a three-pronged approach: (1) the individual organism begins with a biological inheritance, which has developmental potential and internal organization; (2) the organism is affected by its social environment; and (3) the organism perceives, organizes, and responds to its internal and external environment.

Clearly, a psychological perspective can be turned either inward or outward. Looking inward, one can focus on such internal processes as cognition, perception, and reflex responses. An outward view would include personality and the environment, behavior and its social reinforcers, environmental effects on learning and perceptual organization, and so on. Since the social welfare system attempts to improve individual functioning and increase personal gratification, both psychological perspectives have great utility. However, the outward view has been the one which has had greatest use in developing generic practice principles, and is the one to be discussed at some length in this chapter. So far, the inward view has been of greatest utility to psychologists, and has generated theory still to be translated into practice principles.*

One of the persistent problems faced by social welfare practitioners has been that of understanding the social-organic totality that is the human being. The social sciences are founded on the belief that human behavior is more or less patterned and regular, but the attempts to explain how this happens have been many and varied.[2] In trying to understand why Freud's work had such a dramatic impact on the course of social welfare thinking and practice, one out of the many possible explanations is most important: Freud presented a comprehensive theory of personality development and functioning within a relatively scientific (for the time) framework. "As a result of the specificity and generality of psychoanalytic theory, it seems fair to say that at the present time no theory of human behavior comes closer to accomplishing the full purpose of a behavioral theory; no other theory accounts for all the data of human behavior, its development, and its pathological deviations in terms of a basic set of postulates and derivations."[3]

Personality has been defined as "the sum of an individual's inter-related drives, temperament, and social roles; the unique concatenation

---

*Internal psychological processes obviously affect behavior. However, the point being made here is that practice relies most heavily on external behavior. Theory which is useful in understanding internal processes must still be translated into its external behavioral effects, whereas theory focusing directly on external behavior avoids this two-step progression.

of characteristics which the individual manifests in his behavior."[4] Freud postulated that the human personality develops "through the stages of psycho-sexual development as the primary source of libidinal gratification shifts from the mouth to the anus to the genitals."[5] These stages are the oral, anal, phallic, latency, and adolescent. The major functioning personality units become differentiated as a result of stage development. These units, which Freud called "mental structures," are the id, ego, and superego. They may operate at one or more of three levels: the unconscious, the preconscious, and the conscious.[6] Since the Freudian personality is one with limited psychic resources (libidinal energy), the ego and superego grow by using energy originally utilized by the id.

Freud, then, saw the personality developing as a result of two processes: the confrontation of the physical organism (id) with the social world, which results in the formation of the ego and superego; and passing through five stages in the course of the transformation of the physical organism into a fully socialized personality. The importance of the stages is that:

Each stage can be thought of as confronting the child with a new problem, exposing him for the first time to a particular interpersonal relationship. . . . As a consequence of each stage, a certain amount of the individual's cathexes are fixated at that stage, and thus certain attitudes, fears, fantasies, defenses, and expectations are more or less permanently built into the personality. Major psychopathology results when excessive amounts of libido are fixated at an early developmental stage and the accompanying pattern of adjustment developed at that stage is maladapted to the demands of adult life.[7]

Consequently, we can see that the Freudian theory of personality development is a stage and conflict theory. The features of the personality develop through a series of stage transitions and grow out of the competition by each of the mental structures for its share of the existing libidinal energy.

Freudian theory generated a number of "neo-Freudians" who modified Freud's work in a variety of ways. For example, Otto Rank emphasized separation trauma as a motivating personality force;[8] C. G. Jung developed his analytical psychology;[9] and Carl Rogers produced his client-centered, nondirective therapy based on a view of man as basically rational and self-equilibrating.[10] Although each of these men have influenced social welfare practice, along with other descendants of Freud's theory not mentioned, perhaps one of the most influential neo-Freudians is Erik Erikson. His significance rests in his representativeness as an ego psychologist, and his further development of the concept of stages of development. Erikson's work is in part an attempt to elaborate the stages beyond adolescence, the last used by Freud.

Erikson begins with "an epigenetic principle of maturation,"[11] which postulates that each individual has a physical timetable governing his maturation. This timetable determines when libidinal energy will be shifted from one part of the body to another.

This means that stages of development do not grow out of each other. For example, the stage when anal-type functioning is dominant does not result from the child-environment interaction necessary to successful passage through the oral stage. . . . The primary condition (for the oral to anal transition) is his maturational code, which determines when the locus of instinctual investment will be shifted from the oral to the anal zone. . . . But continuity between stages is also implied by the epigenetic principle insofar as each organ must already be a potential part of the ground plan in order for it to grow out of it and mature at the proper time.[12]

Erikson, then, is giving a different kind of emphasis to the biological component of personality than did Freud. Whereas the latter saw the personality being shaped by a confrontation of internal biological and external social forces, Erikson says biological forces set a timetable to which social forces must adapt if the personality is to be a healthy one. Once a given biological stage is passed, the individual must move on, whether he has achieved a successful social adaptation to the earlier stage or not.

The combination of a genetic time clock and the fact that biological changes occur throughout the life span made it natural for Erikson to extend Freud's stages beyond adolescence. Erikson's eight stages in the life cycle are:[13]

1. Oral stage—Crisis of trust in the person on whom one is most dependent for one's sustenance.

EXHIBIT 5–1
The Freudian Personality at a Glance

Although an artificial construct for illustrative purposes, an effective way to see the scope of the Freudian theory of personality is in the following diagram taken from class notes of a lecture by Dr. Westman at the University of Michigan School of Social Work on October 23, 1962.*

The diagram (opposite) schematically represents the three mental structures and the functions that each plays in the personality. The total psychic (libidinal) energy within the system is fixed and it is a closed system; therefore, if the boundaries between any structures are to be changed, it will necessarily mean a redistribution of energy (which is why it is called a "hydraulic theory"). These structures develop in the process of moving through stages. Since the hydraulic nature of the system means one structure's gain is another's loss, defense mechanisms exist for each structure's use in trying to protect itself; hence the conflict nature of the system.

*For an elaboration of any of the concepts used, refer to Charles Brenner, An Elementary Textbook of Psychoanalysis (Garden City: Doubleday, 1957).

---

2. Anal stage—Crisis of whether one will develop feelings of autonomy or shame and doubt about oneself, one's actions, and one's ability to be autonomous.
3. Phallic stage—Crisis of acquiring a sense of moral responsibility resulting from the initiative and consequent guilt in the resolution of the oedipal problem.
4. Latency stage—Crisis of industriousness versus feelings of inferiority and overconformity.
5. Adolescent stage—Crisis of identity adoption versus identity diffusion.
6. Genital stage—Crisis of gratification from intimacy and solidarity versus isolation and withdrawal from relationships.
7. Adulthood—Crisis of caring for others and being a contributor versus self-absorption, stagnation, and interpersonal impoverishment.
8. Senescence—Crisis of ego integration versus despair.

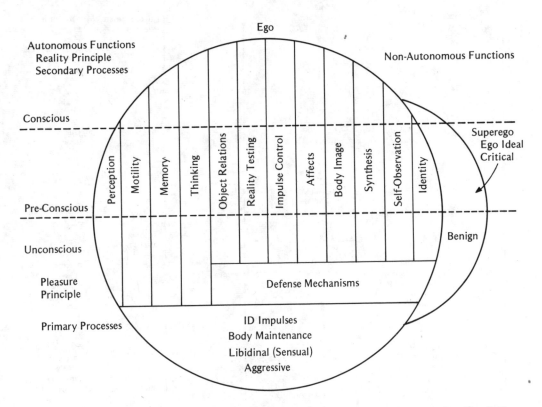

From a personal communication with Jack C. Westman, M.D., Professor of Psychiatry, University of Wisconsin. Used with permission.

EXHIBIT 5–2
Stages at a Glance

This chart is taken from notes from a lecture given by Dr. Mary Burns at the University of Michigan School of Social Work. It is an excellent summary of major stage theories, showing the relationship between physical and social development.

PSYCHOBIOLOGICAL DEVELOPMENT

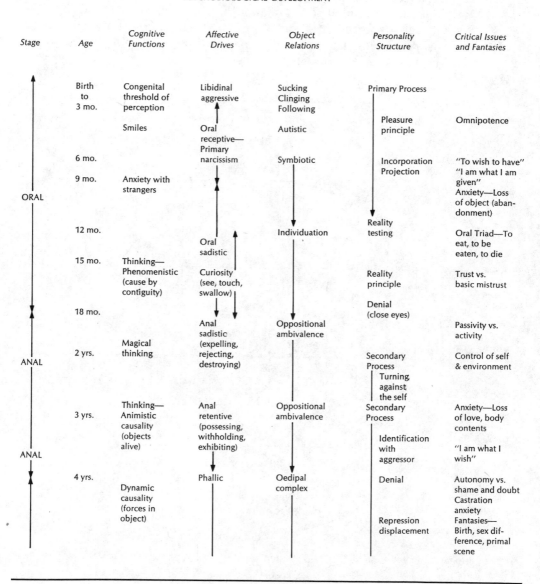

Stage	Age	Cognitive Functions	Affective Drives	Object Relations	Personality Structure	Critical Issues and Fantasies
ORAL	Birth to 3 mo.	Congenital threshold of perception	Libidinal aggressive	Sucking Clinging Following	Primary Process	
		Smiles	Oral receptive— Primary narcissism	Autistic	Pleasure principle	Omnipotence
	6 mo.			Symbiotic	Incorporation Projection	"To wish to have" "I am what I am given"
	9 mo.	Anxiety with strangers				Anxiety—Loss of object (abandonment)
	12 mo.		Oral sadistic	Individuation	Reality testing	Oral Triad—To eat, to be eaten, to die
	15 mo.	Thinking— Phenomenistic (cause by contiguity)	Curiosity (see, touch, swallow)		Reality principle	Trust vs. basic mistrust
	18 mo.		Anal sadistic (expelling, rejecting, destroying)	Oppositional ambivalence	Denial (close eyes)	Passivity vs. activity
ANAL	2 yrs.	Magical thinking			Secondary Process Turning against the self	Control of self & environment
ANAL	3 yrs.	Thinking— Animistic causality (objects alive)	Anal retentive (possessing, withholding, exhibiting)	Oppositional ambivalence	Secondary Process Identification with aggressor	Anxiety—Loss of love, body contents "I am what I wish"
	4 yrs.	Dynamic causality (forces in object)	Phallic	Oedipal complex	Denial Repression displacement	Autonomy vs. shame and doubt Castration anxiety Fantasies— Birth, sex difference, primal scene

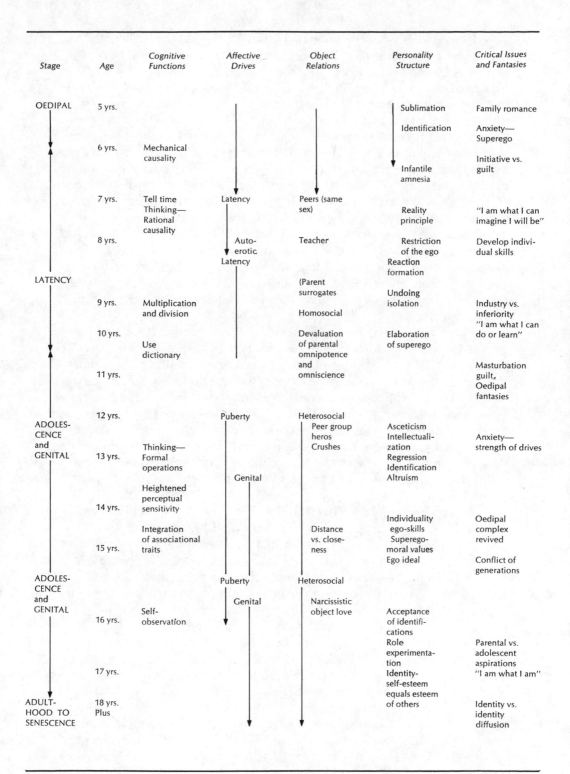

Stage	Age	Cognitive Functions	Affective Drives	Object Relations	Personality Structure	Critical Issues and Fantasies
OEDIPAL	5 yrs.				Sublimation	Family romance
					Identification	Anxiety—Superego
	6 yrs.	Mechanical causality				Initiative vs. guilt
					Infantile amnesia	
	7 yrs.	Tell time Thinking—Rational causality	Latency	Peers (same sex)	Reality principle	"I am what I can imagine I will be"
	8 yrs.		Auto-erotic Latency	Teacher	Restriction of the ego Reaction formation	Develop individual skills
LATENCY				(Parent surrogates	Undoing isolation	
	9 yrs.	Multiplication and division		Homosocial		Industry vs. inferiority "I am what I can do or learn"
	10 yrs.	Use dictionary		Devaluation of parental omnipotence and omniscience	Elaboration of superego	
	11 yrs.					Masturbation guilt, Oedipal fantasies
ADOLES-CENCE and GENITAL	12 yrs.		Puberty	Heterosocial Peer group heros Crushes	Asceticism Intellectualization	Anxiety—strength of drives
	13 yrs.	Thinking—Formal operations	Genital		Regression Identification Altruism	
		Heightened perceptual sensitivity				
	14 yrs.				Individuality ego-skills	Oedipal complex revived
	15 yrs.	Integration of associational traits		Distance vs. close-ness	Superego-moral values Ego ideal	Conflict of generations
ADOLES-CENCE and GENITAL			Puberty Genital	Heterosocial Narcissistic object love		
	16 yrs.	Self-observation			Acceptance of identifications Role experimentation	Parental vs. adolescent aspirations "I am what I am"
	17 yrs.				Identity-self-esteem equals esteem of others	
ADULT-HOOD TO SENESCENCE	18 yrs. Plus					Identity vs. identity diffusion

Having briefly reviewed the major outlines of psychoanalytic theory, it remains to evaluate its utility for social welfare practice contexts. The theory is basically historical in nature, focusing on the client's past life experiences and emphasizing his early childhood experiences. It asserts that there are universal life stages which everyone must traverse due to physiological needs and an epigenetic maturational plan. There is said to be a normal progression through the stages, with given physical and social skills developing in each. The mental structures which are assumed to be developing concurrently with the stage progression cannot be seen or directly measured. They must be inferred from behavior which is considered symptomatic. However, since the personality system is closed with respect to psychic energy available, changing symptoms may only produce another symptom rather than achieving a change in the underlying mental structures. The focus in using the theory is on identifying and ultimately overcoming those stage fixations which have prevented subsequent personality growth according to the ideal model. In other words, the view tends to be backward and inward rather than present or future and outward.

There are several problems with the theory which have important effects on attempts to translate the theory into social welfare practice principles. The first is the problem of empirical validity: "The primary findings obtained by the therapeutic method are rich verbal characterizations of the individual's uniqueness. Nevertheless, one is struck by how little such data have seemed either to test the validity of psychoanalytic assertions or to lead to revision of the theory as to the nature of psychosexual, psychosocial, and ego development."[14] Stated in another way, "the basic criticism to be made of psychoanalytic theory is that it focuses upon thoughts and feelings as the real data and these are relatively inaccessible."[15]

A second problem is that of objectivity: "The data are uniquely confounded with the therapist's interpretation, and therapists tend to interpret the same observations differently, that is, in accordance with different theoretical assumptions. Thus, not only are the data not reliable, but it is also not always certain which theoretical assertions they are relevant to."[16] The third problem is the inferential nature of the theory with respect to normal behavior: "Little is done to examine average or normally expectable psychological development directly. Rather, the initial and fundamental conceptualization of normal behavior is based upon extrapolations from abnormal behavior."[17] Fourth, the theory does not clearly specify the natures of the id, ego and superego at each stage of development: "It is therefore not clear what characteristic functional differences and causal or interactive functional relationships exist between the personality structures and psychosexual, psychosocial, perceptual, coping, and intellectual activity at each stage."[18] Finally, not all aspects of the theory have been equally developed, detracting from its logical consistency and explanatory power.[19]

Turning now to practice implications for social welfare contexts, the first is the caution that must be exercised in the use of a theory whose validity has not or cannot be proven. The social sciences are not presently at a stage in their development at which one can insist on such empirical proof before using potentially relevant social science theory. However, while one wants to use every logical possibility, one also wants to keep the possible risks in mind, especially with a theory that has resisted empirical validation as long as psychoanalytic theory has. A second implication is that a psychoanalytic approach takes three scarce resources: practitioners skilled in its considerable complexities, ample time to explore the client's early life history, and a verbal client. Until the amount of training necessary to become a certified, competent psychoanalyst is lessened, it seems unrealistic to anticipate larger numbers of them, thereby limiting the social welfare contexts in which psychotherapy can be used. As will be seen below, social welfare practitioners may make use of psychoanalytic theory in a variety of ways. However, they should not be thought of as junior psychotherapists since they do not have the skills to control all of the processes involved (transference and counter-transference, for example),

There have been recent attempts to reduce the length of time involved in the use of psychoanalytic theory in some contexts. For example, Phillips and Weiner talk of short-term psychotherapy; this includes several possible techniques, but requires a firm therapeutic structure to use in changing behavior as directly and efficiently as possible.[20] They also see a role for the psychotherapist as "directing the work of others who will help in accomplishing change and [not being limited to] the practice of psychotherapy in the consulting room."[21]

The ego psychologists' concern with rational processes and potential for coping with present problems has also tended to reduce the time spent in treatment.[22] The aim of ego psychologists

is to clarify how (a) the structure of the ego originates and develops, and (b) the adaptive, rational forms of the child's ego functioning develop. These theorists accept Freud's conceptualization of the child's personality as composed of id, ego and superego. Unlike Freud, however, they do not assume that the child's ego was ever part of his id; rather, both id and ego are personality structures that are present from birth and that gradually differentiate from each other. Consequently, the focus of analysis for ego psychologists has shifted from the defensive mechanisms to the adaptive, coping ones.[23]

This difference in theoretical explanation and consequent approach to achieving change reduces the backward and inward view of the theory.

One of the results of the ego psychology perspective is Maslow's work in self-actualization, where the focus is on helping the client achieve his maximum potential by working through a hierarchy of needs.[24] Here again, the focus becomes more present and future oriented, with less time and attention being devoted to the past. In spite of such attempts, however, the historical nature of psychoanalytic theory always exerts a push toward lengthy analysis, and this is impossible in many social welfare contexts (public assistance agencies with large caseloads, medical settings where contact with clients is often limited, police work, etc.).

The verbal nature of psychoanalytic theory raises two issues: many client groups are simply not verbally oriented, and many problems are concrete rather than attitudinal or emotional. There is evidence to indicate that some client groups, such as lower-class clients, are not accustomed to verbalizing, do not do so easily, and do not believe that talking about a problem solves it.[25] To some extent, clients skeptical of talking about problems are correct; poverty may be related to early childhood experiences, but talking about poverty or its origins early in life is not likely to solve the poverty problem. Hence, the verbal orientation of psychoanalytic theory runs the risk of elevating concrete problems to verbal abstractions, thereby rendering the professional-client relationship sterile.[26]

The whole concept of stages can also have its disadvantages. A stage theory posits a set developmental progression for everyone. This tends to minimize the focus on individual differences. It encourages the selective picking out of data indicating that a given stage was encountered and completed, or that there was an encounter and subsequent fixation. Since stage theories are sensitive to the unique experiences of each individual as these affect stage developments, a minimizing of differences need not occur. However, it becomes very easy to almost unknowingly select information that allows a tidy diagnosis rather than grappling with complexities that could otherwise resist therapeutic organization. The haste often created by too-large caseloads, and the somewhat inbred nature of professions also tend to foster a reliance on formulas rather than an open appraisal of each unique situation.

If one attempts to resolve the problem objectively, the nonempirical nature of the psychoanalytic system makes it difficult to "prove" the stages. On one hand there has been cross-cultural evidence to show that culturally determined child-rearing patterns tend to produce distinctive patterns of child development. This suggests that a formulation of universal stages may be at least partially inadequate. On the other hand it is clear that the child goes through a genetically patterned physical maturational sequence, and since the stages are related to physical development, there is some support for stage theories. The alert social welfare practitioner needs to be wary of premature categorization, and until the controversy is settled on the basis of empirical data, erring on the side of individual uniqueness minimizes chances of harming a client.

A final problem to consider with psychoanalytic theory is its non-behavioral nature. Given that its constructs are basically historical and nonvisible, the social welfare professional is in a difficult interventive position. Untrained for in-depth psychoanalysis, and lacking adequate time, the historical nature of the system tends to exclude his participation. Having to deal with internal personality constructs whose existence is inferred creates other barriers. Ego psychology's stress on ego strengths is probably the best solution to these problems. They provide a point from which to progressively test the individual's capacity to cope with present reality, using the internal and historical constructs as potentially useful tools to understand the individual's relevant life history.

In spite of the problems the psychoanalytic approach has for use in a variety of social welfare contexts, it does have real utility. As noted earlier, it is a total system to explain personality development, a crucial area of knowledge for the social welfare professional. We need only think how heavily we rely on such ideas as the influence of the social environment on an infant, the significance of parents and peers in human development, and the potential conflicts between physiological needs and wants and social norms and structures, to realize how much of what we know about human development comes from a psychoanalytic perspective. Further-more, although one may be primarily concerned with present functioning, few things and no people spring full-blown into the world: current levels of functioning must be at least partially understood with reference to past experiences. This time-experience continuum becomes especially impor-tant in future planning, where the social welfare practitioner attempts to find a social environment that will be related to past and present experi-ences in certain defined ways.

A related utility of the psychoanalytic system revolves around the concept of diagnosis. A person with a problem needs some help in under-standing what the problem is, how it occurred, and what the possible solutions are. The psychoanalytic approach can be helpful in understand-ing those problems that are strongly related to personal feelings and personality characteristics, and may be especially helpful in trying to under-stand how the problem occurred. This process of understanding the prob-lem and its causes is called diagnosis. Treatment usually refers to the planning for and carrying through of solutions to the problem.[27] The totality of the psychoanalytic system has also had the beneficial effect of balancing the view of the human personality as both a physical and social entity. Psychoanalytic theory is built on both physical and social matura-tion, and this rounded perspective can serve as a welcome antidote to more narrowly conceived attempts to understand and change human be-havior.[28]

Having briefly reviewed psychoanalytic theory and its implications for use in social welfare contexts, perhaps the best conclusion would be that it has its advantages and disadvantages. Yet its development has stagnated because it is subject to many interpretations which are not easy to verify empirically. This has stimulated a search for other psychological theories that avoid some of the problems of psychoanalytic theory. As a result, behavioristic psychological theories have been employed. Because these theories are primarily concerned with individual behaviors rather than internal states of the organism, they suggest a very different approach to behavior modification than does psychoanalytic theory.

Behavioral Perspectives

The social welfare practitioner wants to be able to modify given behavior according to the problem-solving plan worked out with the client. In order to do so, he must have some theoretical conception of how behavior is learned and maintained. Psychoanalytically oriented and behavioristically oriented practitioners are working toward the same goal of behavior modification, but have different theoretical conceptions of how behavior is learned and maintained. The psychoanalytically oriented practitioner focuses on the individual's early biological, psychological, and social experiences. The logical intervention point, then, is internal. The practitioner attempts to modify behavior by modifying the internal personality structure which is the source of behavior. As will be shown, the behaviorally oriented practitioner proceeds quite differently and from a rather different conception of personality structure and functioning.

Central to a behavioristic theory is the belief that behavior is learned in separate units (acts), that the units (acts) are related to each other, and that the units (acts) become established in the individual's behavior repertoire by means of external reinforcement.

Central to the [behavioristic] conception of growth is the environmentalistic assumption that the source of all psychological phenomena is stimulation from the outside world . . . [and] psychological phenomena, like all other natural occurrences, are really physical in quality, or, at least, reducible to characterization in physicalistic terms.[29]

In a behavioristic perspective, acts are stimulated by the environment, and are associated with each other into habits (or learned behavioral patterns). Since acts are associational, behavior already learned does affect future behavior. "Stored associations influence the child's responses to environmental stimulation. The major [behavioristic] developmental hypothesis is therefore that early conditioned associations affect the child's behavior later in life."[30] While the ideas of environmental influence on behavior, and early behavior affecting later behavior, are not incongruent with a psychoanalytic approach, the fact that no internal personality structure is specified is quite different from psychoanalytic theory. The focus on individual acts implies that they can be modified without a major realignment of the personality structure, a belief that is also quite divergent from psychoanalytic postulates.

There are three ways in which behavioral theorists assert that behavior may be learned: classical (or respondent) conditioning, operant (or instrumental) conditioning, and imitation. Conditioning is most simply defined as the association of stimuli with responses. Classical (or respondent) conditioning is built on the principles of the unconditioned reflex and contiguity. An unconditioned reflex is an "innate response to stimuli,"[31] while the contiguity principle specifies that "the contiguity of two stimuli tends to give one of them the ability to elicit responses previously made to the other."[32] Classical conditioning, then, involves stimulus substitution. An unconditioned stimulus (one that evokes an unconditioned reflex) is paired with a conditioned stimulus (one which would not normally evoke the unconditioned reflex). Eventually the conditioned stimulus evokes the behavior previously evoked by the unconditioned stimulus. The famous Pavlov experiment illustrates classical conditioning (see Exhibit 5–3).

Notice that there is a built-in limitation to the learning which may occur in classical conditioning. Since this type of conditioning depends on the existence of an unconditioned stimulus and response, only responses which already exist can be tied to different stimuli. Although

---

EXHIBIT 5–3
Classical Conditioning Illustrated: Pavlov's Dog

This excerpt is from Alfred Baldwin's Theories of Child Development. *For more detail, an original source is suggested: I. P. Pavlov,* Experimental Psychology and Other Essays *(New York: Philosophical Library, 1957).*

In his original experiments, Pavlov conditioned the salivary response in the dog. The dog was operated on, so that the secretion of the salivary gland could be measured accurately, ordinarily in drops of saliva. The dog salivated whenever a food powder was introduced into his mouth. This salivary response to the food powder occurred on the first trial, so the salivation is called the *unconditioned response,* and the food powder the *unconditioned stimulus.* The conditioning process consists of pairing some other stimulus with the unconditioned stimulus. In one of the famous Pavlovian experiments, a bell was rung slightly before the food stimulus was presented. After this combination of bell and food had been repeated a number of times, the dog began to salivate whenever the bell was rung, even if on that particular trial no food was given. So the bell is called the *conditioned stimulus* or *conditioning stimulus,* and the salivation to the bell the *conditioned response.*

From Alfred Baldwin, *Theories of Child Development,* p. 396. Copyright © 1967 by John Wiley & Sons, Inc. Used with permission.

---

classical conditioning is usable in social welfare contexts, a more flexible learning mechanism would clearly have greater utility.

Operant (or instrumental) conditioning is just such a tool. In operant conditioning, an individual's behavior is reacted to in some way by the environment (the individual can in some respects be his own environment). Behavior which is responded to in a reinforcing way has the probability of its repetition increased. If the behavior continues to be reinforced it can be established as a habit. Operant conditioning may occur for randomly performed behaviors, or it may be shaped. Shaping starts with randomly performed behavior, successively reinforcing it and eliminating it as new behaviors closer to the ultimately desired behavior occur and are in turn reinforced and eliminated.

There is one major difference between classical and instrumental (operant) conditioning. In classical conditioning, an action that is already a response to a stimulus can be put under the control of a stimulus by contiguity of the two stimuli. In instrumental conditioning, an action that is not tied to any specific stimulus can be put under the control of a stimulus by rewarding the action consistently when it is performed in the presence of the stimulus. Thus, randomly occurring actions can be made into reliable, controllable responses or regularly recurring actions.[33]

Two of the major issues to be faced in operant conditioning are the nature of the reinforcements and the schedule (frequency) of reinforcements. It is believed that individuals are ready to respond to stimuli in different ways at different times (called the drive state), and that different drive states have different drive stimuli. Therefore, there is not a general uniformity of conditioning states; what will be reinforcing will vary between individuals and by drive state of any given individual. While candy may be a generally effective reinforcer for the average child, it will not be for certain children, and will be less effective for any given child at some times than at others. Clearly the individual's past reinforcement history will be important in understanding the crucial question of what is reinforcing for that individual, and this in turn is tied to cultural values and behavior patterns. Without such knowledge, the practitioner's ability to control behavior in an operant context is limited. A further complication is that the frequency of reinforcement also affects the learning which occurs. It has been experimentally shown that the frequency and patterning of reinforcements produces different learning patterns, again suggesting that the operant conditioning context is more complicated than might at first be assumed.[34]

A third behavioristic learning device is observational learning, or, specifically, imitation. Observational learning "describes the fact that people can learn behavior patterns merely by watching other people perform them, that their own acts can be reinforced or inhibited by observing reinforcements and punishments to other people, and that they can acquire conditioned emotional responses to stimuli which accompany a painful stimulus to another person."[35] Whether observational learning occurs through imitation is affected by the individual's history of reward for imitation, his history of reward deprivation, his level of self-esteem and general dependency, and his drive state. Observational learning may occur in primary or secondary contexts (that is, direct viewing or via a mechanical medium).

Bandura and Walters suggest four major behavioral modification techniques based on behavioral principles.[36] Most directly related to conditioning as a learning process is positive reinforcement—the teaching of behavior through the manipulation of positive reinforcements (re-wards). The environment commonly dispenses rewards that enable social learning to occur in many societal contexts. Social welfare practitioners may manipulate rewards in purposeful ways to strengthen existing be-haviors that are rarely or randomly performed. For example, a common problem of many marginally employable persons is their lack of skill in job-interview situations. In such a case, the helping person could use positive reinforcements to strengthen those behaviors appropriate to the job-interview context, such as punctuality, style of dress, and so on.

Shaping is a particularly potent adjunct of positive reinforcement as a behavior changing technique because of its use in teaching behaviors that do not exist in the client's behavioral repertoire (in conjunction with extinction, discussed below). Social welfare practitioners are often in the situation of teaching new behaviors that are more socially acceptable

---

EXHIBIT 5–4
The Student's Revenge: Reinforcing the Instructor

The following incident is said to have happened at a large state university. It is an excellent example of positive reinforcement working without the knowledge of the person being re-inforced; student readers may also gain other satisfactions from this account.

In a course dealing with principles of behavioral modification, the students decided to band together to control the behavior of the instructor in the classroom. When the instructor lec-tured from one corner of the room, the students showed interest and enthusiasm; when he was in the other corner, they showed apathy and boredom. Soon they had the instructor confined to the corner in which he was rewarded by the students' interest. In this example, one notes that the instructor was responsive to student reaction, and found student interest rewarding. There may be instances, of course, where an instructor is unaware of student re-action, and is uninterested in student interest, in which case the students would have to find other rewards to manipulate.

---

ways to achieve client goals. A behavior modification technique which can capitalize on existing adaptive behavior and also teach new behavior is highly desirable. Positive reinforcement and shaping are especially de-sirable because they accentuate the positive. The positive reinforcement process is one which achieves change in a way that is likely to be ac-ceptable to the client and that does not require that he recognize his problems. The recognition by a client of problems in his functioning is often productive and important, but there are times when such recog-nition is itself part of the problem, and when the emphasis on problems can be destructive to the client's self-esteem.

The question of problem awareness raises the issue of morality in the use of behavior modification techniques. In a psychoanalytic ap-proach, the talking through of the individual's problems and social history presumably insures at least a minimal recognition and acceptance of the behavior change process by the client. In the behavioristic approach, since behavior modification occurs through the manipulation of stimuli, reinforcements, and models, it is entirely possible for an individual's behavior to be modified without his knowing it (see Exhibit 5–4).

Some have questioned the desirability of behavior modification techniques because of their obvious subversive potential. However, the resolution of the problem of misuse of a therapeutic tool does not lie in its abandonment. Doctors are known to occasionally misuse their techniques, but few would seriously propose that the techniques therefore be abandoned. The resolution of the issue in medicine lies in the strength of the profession to regulate member behavior, and this must be the solution in those professions using any form of behavior modification techniques.

It must be recognized that a common goal of social welfare professionals is to achieve behavior change. Such change may be the result of therapeutic intervention with individuals or groups, as with psychoanalytic and behavioral techniques. It may also result from social structural change which alters the environment in which individuals live, thereby facilitating individual and group behavior change. The social welfare practitioner cannot avoid the considerable responsibility entailed in behavior change. He must be certain that his efforts toward change are acceptable to the people who will be affected by them, and that he uses all the skill and knowledge at his disposal in planning and executing change.

Psychoanalytic and behavioral techniques are two possible approaches to achieving behavior change. In trying to decide which approach to use in any given problem situation, the practitioner will want to consider the empirical evidence relating to demonstrated effectiveness, and considerably more evidence exists for behaviorally based techniques than for psychoanalytically based ones. Such evidence must then be weighed in terms of the appropriateness of a behavioral approach, given the conditions under which the practitioner and client must work, and the acceptability of such an approach to the client. Ultimately it always comes down to a matter of individual judgement and conscience,[37] but these decisions should always rest on the evaluation of the behavior change desired by the practitioner and the client as well as a consideration of the demonstrated effectiveness and appropriateness of alternative behavior-change techniques.

Whereas positive reinforcement was shown to be a powerful tool in strengthening and maintaining behavior, extinction is a tool usable in weakening and eliminating behavior.[38] Thomas defines the use of extinction as "withholding the reinforcer when a response, previously reinforced by that reinforcer, is emitted."[39] In many respects, extinction is the reverse side of positive reinforcement, and is based on the same principle that behavior will be performed when it results in gratification for the actor.

Extinction is a planned process of making sure that the reinforcement that previously occurred (thereby maintaining the behavior) no longer occurs. Under such conditions, the basis for the future performance of the behavior will be eliminated and the probability of its future occurrence reduced until it is eliminated altogether.

Related to extinction, but distinct from it, is punishment. Thomas sees punishment as "being a consequence of responding that reduces the future rate of that response."[40] He goes on to say that "there are two operations following an operant response that may have this effect. One is the presentation of a stimulus that is usually 'aversive' [unpleasant], and the other is the removal of a positive reinforcing condition. . . ."[41] Clearly the removal of a positive reinforcement is closely related to extinction, which entails withholding such a reinforcement. However, the distinction between removing and withholding produces rather different results.

EXHIBIT 5–5
An Example of Extinction

. . . A twenty-one-month-old boy . . . engaged in tyrannical tantrum behavior. The child would scream and fuss when put to bed and his parents couldn't leave the bedroom until he was asleep. The parents generally spent one-half to two hours simply waiting in the room until the boy went to sleep.

After it was determined that the tantrum behavior was sustained by the attention provided by the parents at bedtime, it was decided to institute a regimen of extinction. The treatment program was based upon research indicating that by steadfastly withholding reinforcers that sustain the behavior, there will eventually be a diminution of the behavior in question. It was decided to put the child to bed in a leisurely and relaxed fashion. Then, following the usual pleasantries, the parent was to leave and the door to be left closed. On the first night, the child screamed for forty-five minutes; on the second, he did not fuss at all; on the third, he screamed for ten minutes; on the fourth, for six; on the fifth for three, on the sixth, for two; and, finally, after seven sessions, there was no screaming at all. In a follow-up, there were no side- or after-effects, and the child was found to be friendly, expressive, and outgoing.

From Edwin Thomas, ed., *The Socio-Behavioral Approach and Applications to Social Work* (New York: Council on Social Work Education, 1967), pp. 3–4. Used with permission.

Punishment as a technique has some potential side effects which can limit its effectiveness, while extinction does not. Before considering the use of punishment in behavior modification, the practitioner should consider the costs, alternatives, conditions for its use, and possible side effects (such as avoidance, aggression, or loss of control).[42]

A third behavioral technique is counter-conditioning, sometimes called reciprocal inhibition. "The fundamental principle in using counter-conditioning therapeutically, is to establish a response which is incompatible with a maladaptive response so the latter is eliminated."[43]

Counter-conditioning is a tool usable in eliminating undesirable behavior. It is based on the obvious fact that one cannot do two incompatible things at once. Rewards are provided to strengthen the desired behavior which are more attractive than the rewards maintaining the undesired behavior when the stimulus evoking the undesired behavior occurs. Counter-conditioning frequently includes desensitization, which involves the purposeful manipulation of the stimulus evoking the undesired behavior. It is first presented in mild forms so that the resulting undesired responses are relatively weak and thus readily extinguishable.[44] As the desired behavior is progressively more strongly established, the stimulus evoking the undesired behavior may be presented in its normal form. The undesired response will now be more weakly reinforced than the desired response and will therefore be extinguished.[45]

Most often one's goal is not simply to eliminate an undesired be-

---

EXHIBIT 5–6
An Example of Counter-Conditioning

A now classic example is the treatment of fear of rabbits, rats, and other furry objects, in a three-year-old child named Peter. . . . Feeding was used as an incompatible response, but if Peter was given sweets with a rabbit near him, his fear was so strong that he ignored them in favor of escaping from the animal. To overcome this difficulty, while Peter ate, a caged rabbit was first introduced into the far corner of the room, and then gradually over a number of sessions, it was released from the cage and brought nearer to him, until finally he quite happily held the animal on his lap and allowed it to nibble his fingers.

From Derek Jehu, *Learning Theory and Social Work* (London: Routledge & Kegan Paul; New York: Humanities Press Inc., 1967), p. 84.

---

havior. Techniques for eliminating an undesirable behavior are commonly used along with techniques to establish or maintain a desired behavior. In some cases, an individual knows an appropriate behavior, but is being rewarded for performing an inappropriate behavior rather than the appropriate one. In such cases, the undesired behavior may be eliminated and the desired behavior strengthened, through, for example, the simultaneous use of extinction and positive reinforcement. In other cases, an individual may not know an appropriate behavior, so that elimination of the undesired behavior could create a behavioral void. In such cases, a technique to establish a new behavior is required. Two such techniques will be presented below.

One technique used in establishing a new behavior is "shaping." It begins with a spontaneously emitted behavior and then uses differential reinforcement of selected responses to achieve closer approximations of the desired behavior.[46] However, shaping can be a long, complex procedure. It is best suited to teaching relatively simple behaviors when an approximation of that behavior is already being spontaneously performed. As Bandura has said,

Differential reinforcement alone can be employed to evoke new patterns of behavior under conditions where responses are composed of readily available elements, stimuli exist that are capable of arousing actions that resemble the desired pattern, erroneous responsiveness does not produce injurious consequences, and the learning agent possesses sufficient endurance.[47]

Shaping, then, is based on reinforcement and can be used to teach new behavior, but it is somewhat limited in the range of behaviors easily taught in this manner.

Modeling, on the other hand, offers a more flexible teaching technique. Modeling, or observational learning, results in new behavior when an observer faithfully reproduces a model's behavior that was not previously in the observer's behavioral repertoire. Observing a model can also serve to inhibit or disinhibit an observer's behavior, depending on the consequences to the model of his behavior. Inhibition, disinhibition, and response facilitation are not mechanisms for learning new behaviors. These involve already existing behaviors being performed more or less frequently as a result of exposure to a model.[48] Modeling may occur when the model is physically present or when the model is presented vicariously, and characteristics of the model will affect the amount of modeling which takes place (the model's prestige and power, age, consequences to the model of his behavior, etc.).

Having briefly reviewed some major behavioral concepts, and having seen some of the specific behavior modification techniques resulting from such theory, we can now examine some of the general considerations in the use of these techniques in social welfare settings. One is struck by the everyday nature of many of these techniques. Social welfare personnel frequently reward clients for desired behavior, as when a worker nods and smiles when a client tells him significant information. Similarly, one commonly withholds rewards in personal and professional settings when someone has not acted properly. This realization of the common usage of behavioral techniques reveals their strength in being usable in almost any situation. It also suggests that social welfare personnel must have a high level of self-awareness to use these common techniques in a planned way rather than inadvertently reinforcing or extinguishing behavior. For example, a doctor can easily extinguish preventative visits by patients if he fails to keep appointments, has unpleasant auxiliary staff, or has unreasonably high fees, even though he may actually want to encourage preventative medical practice. It is also evident that practitioners subscribing to nonbehavioral treatment approaches are, whether they realize it or like it, practicing behavioral modification techniques.[49]

A second implication of this approach is that behavior change must be carefully planned. A variety of techniques is available, selected according to the problem at hand. Each technique has its distinctive application requirements, and must be specifically applied in any given situation. As just one example, it has been noted that there is no such thing as a uniform reward; what is rewarding will vary from person to person and situation to situation. Once rewards have been selected, the schedule of their presentation must be determined as well as the specific behaviors to which they will be related. This approach is clearly contradictory to psychoanalytic approaches, which assume that any problem may be solved using one basic technique. The resolution of this confrontation between approaches is an individual decision, but it appears that the weight of empirical evidence is on the side of behavioral approaches.

A third issue in behavioral techniques is the control needed for effective use. Since reinforcers and stimuli must be manipulated, behavioral techniques can be most effectively used in settings allowing complete control of the client and his environment. Although this is possible in some social welfare settings, such as prisons and mental hospitals, many settings permit variable, partial control. Some behavior modification can occur under such conditions, and may then be generalized to situations not directly under the practitioner's control, as, for example, when a social worker positively reinforces promptness in keeping appointments. However, in many cases the lack of the practitioner's ability to control all the significant rewards or stimuli can seriously interfere in the behavior modification process. Lack of access to all controlling variables may also make it difficult to determine what the meaningful rewards and stimuli are, especially when there are socioeconomic and cultural differences between practitioners and clients.

A fourth point to consider about the utility of behavioral techniques is their close relationship to the social environment. Since behavior is seen as supported by rewards that are most often external to the individual, a behavioristic approach is quite social. This suggests that such techniques are very accessible to practitioners (with the limitations noted in the preceding paragraph). Behavior can be seen and directly manipulated, while internal processes can only be dealt with indirectly. On the other hand, it is obvious that social processes maintaining behavior may be very difficult to change, and, if individual change depends on social change, the prognosis for both may be poor. This serves to emphasize the important point that social welfare practitioners must function at both the individual and community levels to have maximum impact on the ability of individuals to function effectively in society.

Finally, there is the following point raised by Bandura:

Even if the traditional forms of psychotherapy had proved highly effective, they would still have limited social value. A method that requires extended and highly expensive training, that can be performed only by professional personnel, that must be continuously applied on a one-to-one basis over a prolonged period of time, and is most beneficial to self-selected highly suggestible persons cannot possibly have much impact on the countless social problems that demand psychological attention.[50]

These practical issues must be raised and faced, especially as social welfare services are called upon to justify their claim for social resources. In a mass society with mass problems, can we afford to restrict ourselves to one-to-one techniques practiced by an elite professional group?

Conclusion

Of the many psychological perspectives on behavior, the psychoanalytic and behavioral represent two of the most commonly used by social welfare professionals. Their basic orientations are quite different, as are their implications for practice. The task of translating them into practice principles is a difficult, on-going one, but one which is important for the continued development of social welfare practice. Both psychological perspectives help to understand the structure and functioning of the social system, and are thereby essential ingredients of the social welfare institution. However, any psychological perspective on social behavior concentrates on individual functioning rather than other levels of functioning. In the next chapter, selected sociological perspectives important to an understanding of the social welfare institution will be presented.

REFERENCES

1. Robert Merton, *Social Theory and Social Structure,* rev. ed. (New York: Free Press, 1957), pp. 85–117.
2. An overview of the different social science perspectives on human behavior may be found in Edward Norbeck et al., *The Study of Personality: An Interdisciplinary Appraisal* (New York: Holt, Rinehart, and Winston, 1968), pp. 88–100.
3. Alfred Baldwin, *Theories of Child Development* (New York: John Wiley, 1968), p. 375.
4. Arnold Rose, *Sociology: The Study of Human Relations,* 2nd rev. ed. (New York: Alfred Knopf, 1967), p. 729.
5. Baldwin, op. cit., p. 350.
6. For brief summaries of the Freudian system, the following can be recommended: developmental stages, Baldwin, op. cit., pp. 351–373; and Charles Brenner, *An Elementary Textbook of Psychoanalysis* (Garden City: Anchor, 1957), pp. 16–32; levels of consciousness, ibid., pp. 35–37; mental structures, ibid., pp. 37–140.
7. Baldwin, op. cit., p. 351.
8. A representative work is Otto Rank, *Will Therapy,* trans. Jessie Taft (New York: Alfred A. Knopf, 1968).
9. A representative work is C. G. Jung, *Analytical Psychology: Its Theory and Practice* (New York: Pantheon, 1968).
10. See C. H. Patterson, *Theories of Counseling and Psychotherapy* (New York: Harper & Row, 1966), pp. 403–439.
11. Jonas Langer, *Theories of Development* (New York: Holt, Rinehart, and Winston, 1969), p. 33.

12. Ibid., p. 34.
13. Ibid., pp. 36–46.
14. Ibid., p. 49. See also Alfred Baldwin, op. cit., pp. 374–384.
15. Baldwin, op. cit, p. 384
16. Langer, op. cit., p. 49.
17. Ibid.
18. Ibid., p. 50.
19. Baldwin, op. cit., p. 384.
20. E. Larkin Phillips and Daniel N. Wiener, *Short-term Psychotherapy and Structured Behavior Change* (New York: McGraw-Hill, 1966), pp. 1–10, esp. p. 9.
21. Ibid., p. 9.
22. A good discussion of the place of the ego in treatment may be found in Robert Roberts and Robert Nee, eds., *Theories of Social Casework* (Chicago: University of Chicago Press, 1970), pp. 129–179 and 265–311.
23. Langer, op. cit., p. 23.
24. A summary of Maslow's ideas may be found in Calvin Hall and Gardner Lindzey, *Theories of Personality* (New York: John Wiley, 1957), pp. 324–327.
25. The problems of using verbal techniques with certain socioeconomic groups is well illustrated in August Hollingshead and Frederick Redlich, *Social Class and Mental Illness* (New York: John Wiley, 1958).
26. A good example of this is in Phillips and Weiner, op. cit., pp. 159–185.
27. A thoughtful discussion of diagnosis as a concept and its utility in social welfare contexts may be found in Carol Meyer, *Social Work Practice* (New York: Free Press, 1970), pp. 110–115.
28. See Don Gibbons, *Society, Crime, and Criminal Careers* (Englewood Cliffs, N.J.: Prentice-Hall, 1968), pp. 139–170; and George Vold, *Theoretical Criminology* (New York: Oxford University Press, 1958), pp. 28–40.
29. Langer, op. cit., p. 52.
30. Ibid., p. 55.
31. Ibid., p. 56.
32. Baldwin, op. cit., p. 397.
33. Ibid., p. 398.
34. Albert Bandura and Richard Walters, *Social Learning and Personality Development* (New York: Holt, Rinehart and Winston, 1963), pp. 4–7.
35. Baldwin, op. cit., p. 428.
36. Bandura and Walters, op. cit., pp. 224–246; for applications of their theory, see Edwin Thomas, ed., *The Socio-Behavioral Approach and Applications to Social Work* (New York: Council on Social Work Education, 1967).
37. Albert Bandura, *Principles of Behavior Modification* (New York: Holt, Rinehart and Winston, 1969), pp. 70–112.
38. Edwin Thomas asserts that the objectives of socio-behavioral intervention are the acquisition, strengthening, maintenance, weakening, or elimination of behavior. See p. 12 of his "Selected Sociobehavioral Techniques and Principles: An Approach to Interpersonal Helping," *Social Work* 13 (January 1968): 12–26.
39. Ibid., p. 18.
40. Ibid., p. 23.
41. Ibid.
42. Ibid., pp. 23–24.

43. Derek Jehu, *Learning Theory and Social Work* (New York: Humanities Press, 1967), p. 84.
44. Ibid., p. 430.
45. Ibid., pp. 424–554.
46. Edwin Thomas, "Selected Sociobehavioral Techniques . . . ," op. cit., p. 21.
47. Bandura, op. cit., p 144.
48. Ibid., p. 120.
49. Ibid., pp. 52–112.
50. Bandura, op. cit., p. 60.

SELECTED READINGS

In reviewing major psychological theories, the Baldwin and Langer books are helpful in providing a comparative approach. Bandura, Walters, and Brenner are excellent summaries of specific theoretical approaches. Thomas' work focuses on problems of application.

Baldwin, Alfred. *Theories of Child Development.* New York: John Wiley, 1968.
Bandura, Albert. *Principles of Behavior Modification.* New York: Holt, Rinehart and Winston, 1969.
Bandura, Albert, and Richard Walters. *Social Learning and Personality Development.* New York: Holt, Rinehart and Winston, 1963.
Brenner, Charles. *An Elementary Textbook of Psychoanalysis.* Garden City: Doubleday, 1957.
Langer, Jonas. *Theories of Development.* New York: Holt, Rinehart and Winston, 1969.
Thomas, Edwin, ed. *The Socio-Behavioral Approach and Applications to Social Work.* New York: Council on Social Work Education, 1967.

SOCIOLOGICAL BASES

6

The cumulative impact of World War I and the Great Depression was a major stimulus to sociology taking its rightful place alongside psychological theory in understanding social welfare issues.[1] Sociology as a scientific discipline began to develop in a systematic way in the mid-1800s.[2] However, it took the major social upheavals of the period from 1915 to 1935 to make the sociological perspective seem appropriate in analyzing the social changes that had begun in the Industrial Revolution.[3]

The sociological perspective focuses on the major group contexts of human behavior. Freud rightly questioned the advantages and disadvantages of group life,[4] but the size, complexity, and productivity of contemporary social life would be impossible without the functional advantages of groups.[5] The group has its own structural needs, and each group member must learn the rules or culture of the group to which he belongs in order to function effectively.[6] Such learning is the process of socialization,[7] in which the norms of the group are taught as well as the consequences of not obeying the group's rules.* Socialization is necessary to develop the human being's social and biological potential, and it does so in a way specifically adapted to the groups in which the individual will be living.

Normative behavior helps to introduce stability into social life. Ideally each individual knows the behavior expected of him and others, and the group can plan its structure knowing what kinds of member behavior may be expected. Such social stability leads to the social psychological processes of identity and self-concept formation, in which the individual comes to perceive himself through interaction with others in socially defined contexts.[8] In reality, socialization is made difficult by the fact that in a large, complex society, we are all members of many groups. Appropriate behaviors must be learned for each, creating a complicated learning network, made even more so when rules of two or more groups conflict, or when group memberships are changed. The sociological perspective, then, sees the environment as the stimulus and context for individual behavior. Although this view focuses on group structures, rather than starting with the individual as the psychological perspective does, the sociological and psychological perspectives are closely related and complementary.

Sociological theory is particularly useful for understanding the structure and interaction of the major components of the social system. This

---

*Norms are rules for behavior defined by the group. The consequences of deviation from norms are called sanctions, which may be positive (rewarding normative behavior) or negative (punishing deviant behavior). The exercise of sanctions is the process of social control.

perspective involves considerably more variables affecting behavior than was true when reviewing psychological perspectives, and as a result some of the theory lacks precision and specific practice applications. However, the lack of theoretical sophistication of much sociological knowledge in no way reduces the importance of the social behavior studied by it. It simply magnifies the need for further theoretical development and its translation into practice principles.

Role Theory

Role theory is the study of how tasks are organized and distributed in society. Societies have tasks that must be performed in socially approved (normative) ways. These tasks are grouped into positions, which are named collections of persons performing similar functional behaviors. Examples of positions would be mother, social worker, physical therapist, etc. For each position, there are appropriate behaviors which occupants of that position are expected to perform; these expected behaviors are called roles. In the position of doctor, for example, each occupant is expected to treat patients, prescribe drugs, use medical instruments, keep abreast of new medical technology, and so on. Roles, then, are norms which are clustered around a certain position, and positions and roles together enable society to perform needed functional behaviors in normative ways.

Since roles are made up of norms, they are socially defined and functionally oriented, so they can and do change. Role behavior is behavior expected of a category of people, and sees the individual in the group context. The concept of role performance is used to refer to an individual's actual behavior in contrast to the expected behavior as objectively defined in the role definition. Role performance illustrates the fact that groups do permit some flexibility in individual member behavior, and such flexibility is one way in which individuals may initiate social change.[9] Although sociology normally studies group behavior, it does not ignore the effects of individuals on groups.

There are two significant areas of social functioning relevant to social welfare that role theory illuminates: role problems and the distribution of social positions. A variety of problems may be created by attempts to learn and act within roles.[10] In a large and complex society, positions are added and subtracted regularly. This requires appropriate role changes, but once role behavior has been learned it is not easily forgotten. Vestiges of old role behaviors that are inappropriate in new role contexts are often seen, creating one type of role problem. A second type of problem results from the lag in the societal definition of an appropriate role constellation for new positions. A contemporary example is the position of dissenting priests. One category of role problem, then, results from situations where obsolete behavior continues even though a position and role no longer exist. A second results when a new position and role have not yet been clearly defined.

A third category of role problem is role ambiguity, in which the role definition is unclear. Ambiguity may result from lack of clarity in the societal definition of the role, as with adolescence in the United States. It may also result from inadequate socialization, as when the lower-class child is unsure of how to behave in the middle-class school. A fourth type of role problem, role conflict, results when there are conflicting expectations existing in one or more positions at the same time. Role conflict is caused by the complexity of the role structure. We occupy many roles at the same time, and society has few methods of avoiding conflicting expectations between all possible role combinations. Role conflict may occur within one position, as when a college professor is expected to be an objective evaluator of students and at the same time

---

EXHIBIT 6–1
Where Does It Start?

The following is an excerpt from Oscar Lewis's La Vida. It expresses well the unequal conditions under which the achievement struggle occurs, and gives one pause when thinking about the magnitude of social change that would be needed to alter the conditions under which families such as this live in the future.

When I was a child my stepmother told me my *mamá* was a prostitute but I didn't believe her. I said I wanted to see my *mamá*, to know her and my stepmother would say that there was no reason for me to see that bitch because she was no mother, the way she treated us. She said that my *mamá* didn't want to cook for us and that she went out with men, carrying on and drinking and leaving us dirty and alone at all hours of the night.

I didn't care what my stepmother said. I was sad because my *mamá* and *papá* were living apart and the only thing I wished was that they'd get together again so they could be a good example to us.

My stepmother mistreated us kids and didn't want to cook for us or send us to school. According to my grandmother, Hortensia would throw our bread and food to us on the floor. She didn't want to buy us clothes, and would beat us if we sat down in the living room. Once Crucita was crying, and Hortensia went and grabbed her and threw her to the floor and that's why she is lame. But my stepmother says it was meningitis that made Cruz a cripple.

From Oscar Lewis, *La Vida* (New York: Random House, 1966), p. 299.

---

a counselor and friend. It may also occur between two or more positions, as when the demands of being an adequate mother conflict with the expectation to remain a physically attractive, sexually vital wife.

Two techniques society uses to minimize role conflicts are (1) role sets, where complementary roles are defined in relationship to each other; and (2) definitions specifying when given roles are manifest (to be acted upon) and when they are latent (not to be acted upon). However, such attempts are rarely completely successful, with the individual being left to try to solve his own particular problems. This he may do in the short run, such as compromising conflicting expectations, or in the long run by changing the role definitions or leaving the roles.[11] Another way in which role problems are resolved is through the welfare system, which may be seen as an institutionalized way to cope with role problems when they occur. For example, various social welfare structures are concerned with strengthening and supplementing socialization contexts to try to minimize problems resulting from inadequate socialization. To summarize, then, sociological role theory emphasizes the systematic, structured, categorical nature of social life, suggesting the need to assist individuals to function more adequately in such a structured setting. It also points out some of the foreseeable role difficulties that may occur, and suggests some possible solutions to these problems.

Social Stratification Theory

A basic concern in a social structure is the distribution of social positions, since power and influence are vested in positions. The mechanisms which society uses to define and allocate positions become extremely important in determining which groups will have access to which social rewards. Definitions of desirable social rewards and their accessibility to societal members is an ideological function in society,[12] and as such affects the actual distribution of positions. However, Marx noted long ago that the reverse is also true, since those having power will create social structures to maintain their privilege.[13]

Our conception of the possible and appropriate methods of achieving goals is dependent on the way in which we look at the world.[14] It is often assumed that there is common acceptance of the ideologies of capitalism and political pluralism, both of which would support a social welfare position that left primary responsibility for individual and social change in the hands of socially sanctioned welfare structures and political processes. However, Dolbeare notes that there are several contemporary ideologies which would lead to quite different assumptions concerning the proper functioning of the political, economic, and social welfare systems.[15] Many others have noted the failures of the American Dream ideology,[16] and have suggested that value readjustments are going to be necessary even if the processes used to achieve such changes are far from traditional or nonviolent. These theoretical considerations suggest that ideology is not an inappropriate concern for the social welfare practitioner.

Allocation of positions may be made on either of two bases: ascription, where positions are assigned without consideration of an individual's abilities; or achievement, where positions are assigned on the basis of ability.[17] Ascription characterizes caste societies, although every society uses ascription to the extent that positions are distributed according to age, sex, physical appearance, and so on. When ascription is the dominant allocation mechanism, one's life chances are determined from birth, and social welfare structures would seek to change behavior only within limits appropriate to one's caste position. In the United States, positions are said to be allocated on the basis of achievement, so that changes in positions and life patterns are possible. Achievement places a far greater emphasis on individual effort and responsibility. Lack of success or change can thereby easily be attributed to individual failure even if in fact caused by social conditions.

However positions are assigned, every society has a ranking system that defines some as being more desirable than others.[18] This indicates that a competition is established in society to obtain socially defined rewards, whether they be money, cows, or wives. Such competition is said by some to be functional for the society in that it motivates persons to seek difficult positions which offer great rewards.[19] Others point out that a conflict system is created which may have its own functions,[20] but which may also be disruptive to the social order.[21]

Regardless of societal functions, such competition practically guarantees that there will be losers, since individuals enter the competition with varying amounts of physiological and social resources. Parts of the professional social welfare role can be seen as attempts to equalize the competitive positions of all members of society as far as possible, as well as providing concrete and emotional help to those who are losers in the competition.

A stratification system obviously creates and perpetuates inequality, and institutionalizes its desirability in a society. There are haves and have nots, with the latter category clearly and systematically disadvantaged in its attempts to wrest power from the former group. To the extent that societal members are free to compete for societal positions, the successful can attribute their privileged social position to their own efforts and abilities and thereby justify their position regardless of the many problems it creates for the less successful. However, when ascription is built into the process by which positions are allocated in a systematic but unacknowledged way, the assertion that everyone can succeed if he tries is simply untenable. It is clear that race, sex, and socioeconomic background are commonly used in an ascriptive manner, so that many kinds of opportunity are quite unequally distributed. Under such conditions, competition creates frustration rather than incentive.[22]

Social welfare as an institution must insure that it is not being used to perpetuate such inequality.[23] In many respects, social welfare values conflict with societal values which support inequality of opportunity and inequality of life chances. Being committed to helping all persons achieve their highest potential and a satisfying life, social welfare values cannot accept the inevitability of a competitive system which by its nature generates disadvantaged persons. This is not to suggest that everyone must be equal. Persons have widely differing potential, and the magnitude of their achievement must recognize such differences. Nevertheless, social welfare is committed to achieving a social system which gives everyone an equal opportunity to attain his or her potential, as well as developing a service structure providing needed services in an adequate and equal manner.[24] An achievement orientation in society has many advantages, but if they are to be realized, then the struggle for achievement must be under rules which do not automatically handicap certain groups. Role and stratification theory, then, indicate that many major problems are generated by the social structure rather than by individual malfunctioning. The long-run solutions to these problems are to be sought in the structure, although short-run intervention at the individual level may reduce the pain and disruption experienced.

EXHIBIT 6–2
Sex, Physical Appearance and Ascription

The following letter written to Ann Landers is a pathetic reminder of how sex and physical appearance continue to be used as a basis for ascription in the United States.

Dear Ann Landers:
    I could never talk to anyone about this problem and I must tell it to somebody. It is getting me down.
    My husband and I have been married 10 years. Our son, who is now 8, is a very handsome boy. He has my husband's eyes and smile, my nose, a great shaped head and strong jaw-line. Everyone remarks on his good looks.
    Our daughter is 2 years old, and I am sorry to say she is the homeliest child I have ever seen. Nature really played a dirty trick on us. It would have been much better if the boy had been homely and the girl had been good looking. A girl needs beauty—a boy doesn't.
    Our daughter inherited the worst features of both my husband and me. When people see her they don't know what to say. Occasionally someone will ask, "Is that your child, or is she adopted?" I know what they are driving at.
    When our daughter is older we can have her protruding ears fixed, her chin built up and her nose remolded. Hopefully she will have a good figure. If she doesn't, there are several things a girl can do. But the growing up years are going to be very hard on this pathetic child. Please tell me how to face the future cheerfully. If you could name some movie stars who were homely youngsters, it would help a lot.—Star Crossed

From Ann Landers, in the *Washington Post*, April 15, 1971. Used by permission of Publishers Hall Syndicate.

Small-Group Theory

People live in groups of various sizes, ranging from the largest societal contexts to the small groups in which everyday tasks are commonly performed. Group dynamics refers to behavior in small-group contexts. Such behavior must be understood by any social welfare practitioner if he is to have a conceptual and practical base for intervention in the many kinds of groups he is likely to confront. The family will be the first small group analyzed, since it occupies an important mediating function between large societal groups and smaller group contexts.

It has been seen that socialization is an essential part of the humanizing process, serving to liberate the potential of the human animal and establish social control boundaries which allow men to live together in relative harmony and productive order. At the same time, we have seen that socialization can stifle human growth and lead to ethnocentrism, the culture blindness that tends to restrict our ability to openly accept other cultures and persons. The socialization process, in its good and bad aspects, is entrusted by society to a variety of small-group contexts, of which the family is the earliest and in some ways the most important. The family as a social institution is clearly undergoing change, and in that sense is a dynamic, flexible group structure not easily described. However, some major functions of the family in American society may still be noted.[25] (1) The family is the approved social context for reproduction and sex behavior. To the extent that homosexual behavior is accepted, and as reproduction is shifted toward a zero-population growth concept, this function of the family may be modified in the future. (2) The family serves as a mechanism for the transmission of family name and resources. This makes the family one of the very important institutional supports for a system of social stratification, since regardless of equality of opportunity, family inheritance gives persons differential starting points in life. (3) The family is a major context of primary-group satisfaction, whereby its members can interact as total human beings rather than as role performers acting in socially circumscribed ways. As society becomes increasingly complex and secondary relationships predominate, this function of the family assumes increasing importance in the maintenance of stable individual personalities. The fourth and fifth major functions of the family, education and economic functioning, have been profoundly affected by changes in the societal structure. (4) As specialized educational structures have grown, they have taken over many educational functions previously performed in the family. This progressive differentiation of function has been accelerated by the society's emphasis on formal certification of competence (test scores, academic degrees, etc.) and the proliferation of the knowledge base to the point that the family cannot hope to encompass extant knowledge. Nevertheless, the family still serves as an education context, especially in such areas as learning appropriate sex roles and informal skills, although the progressive reduction of the educational function has no doubt contributed to the decreasing authority of adults in the family context. (5) The economic function has shifted from a primarily productive function to a consumption function. The family rarely produces its own basic needs, but does serve as an important context in which consumption decisions are made. The family is still productive in that the adults in the family typically work for wages which then make consumption possible.

From birth until death, the individual usually lives in a family, a group of biologically and legally related persons. This group transmits values and concrete objects, and affects personality development and the possession of necessary social skills. In the family, then, we begin to see that small groups have several possible functions. Some are primarily task oriented and others primarily socio-emotional in nature. We can also see that small groups have distinctive internal structures, with leadership roles, power relationships, norms, and distinguishable roles. In some ways, the small group can be seen as a microcosm of general societal group processes, and much social science research has been done in small groups in the hopes of more clearly understanding such processes.[26]

Robert Bales, in attempting to conceptualize small-group structure and dynamics, proposes four main problems confronting a small group: adaptation to outside forces that affect the group; instrumental control over the performance of group tasks; the expression and management of the feelings of group members; and group integration.[27] Bales' conceptualization is useful because it highlights several significant factors in small-group structure and behavior, especially the social context of the group, the group's purpose, and leadership in the group. Like any other facet of social life, a group exists in a larger social system and is affected by its social environment, making knowledge of the relevant environment essential. In cases where the environment is hostile to the group, the hostility can help the group to achieve cohesion with which to preserve itself. It is also possible for such hostility to ultimately destroy the group.

Group purpose may be seen in several ways, but perhaps the most generally usable perspective is to draw a distinction between task-oriented and process-oriented groups. In the former, the main focus of the group is on the achievement of a task, such as fund-raising. In the latter, the primary emphasis is on the pleasure derivable from the interaction of group members, as in various kinds of social groups. In social welfare one often hears the term *therapeutic group,* which is generally task focused in attempting to achieve a specified therapeutic goal, but which may also try to maximize member interaction as part of the therapeutic environment. The conditions under which interaction occurs in task-oriented groups is also significant. Conditions in which cooperation is possible and encouraged tend to lessen hostility and dissatisfaction with the group, although task performance is not necessarily maximal. Competitive conditions in which one member's goal attainment will hinder the goal attainment of others tend to have opposite effects.[28]

A consideration of group purpose leads naturally into the issue of leadership in small groups, since the consensus of relevant research is that most groups have at least two leaders. The task leader is effective primarily in helping the group to achieve its goals, especially when the group is task oriented. The socio-emotional leader promotes group interaction (process) and helps to maintain a cohesive interpersonal network within the group. Therefore, the typical task leader is respected, while the socio-emotional leader is more personally popular.[29] Leadership is a complex issue, especially as it relates to task performance or process attainment. In particular, it has been found that authoritarian leadership maximizes task achievement but minimizes member satisfaction, that laissez-faire leadership leads to both low task attainment and low member satisfaction, and democratic leadership has limited task attainment but high member satisfaction.[30] Clearly the most desirable type of leadership depends on group purpose, which in turn can have value-based foundations.

The ways in which leadership can be attained is another important aspect of small-group leadership, and relates to the bases of power in a group. Power may be defined as the ability of one person to influence others regardless of the wishes of the persons being influenced.[31] Five bases of power have been formulated, and are very relevant to task and socio-emotional leadership. Reward is the ability of the influencer to control items desirable to the influencee. Reward as a basis of power may be used by a task leader because task attainment is commonly perceived as rewarding. A socio-emotional leader can use reward to the extent that pleasant interpersonal relations are rewarding. Punishment is the ability of the influencer to prevent goal attainment of the influencee, a basis of power typically more feasible for a task leader. Reward and punishment are directly related to the behavioral theory discussed earlier. Consistent with that theory, both reward and punishment tend to operate only as long as control is maintained, although reward tends to generalize to identification (discussed below), while punishment tends to generate evasion, resentment, and resistance.

A third basis of power is legitimacy, the ability of the influencer to claim the right to influence others and have the influencee agree. This base of power tends to be restricted to specified areas of legitimacy and may be hampered by conflicting definitions of legitimacy. Expertise as a basis of power refers to the ability of the influencer to influence others because of his recognized superior knowledge. There are also limits to the areas of one's claimed expertise, and it is a power base more feasible for a task leader than a socio-emotional leader. Finally, identification is the ability of the influencer to win the affection of the influencee, a basis of power slow to develop but very durable once achieved. Identification frequently leads to modeling behavior, and is most usable by a socio-emotional leader in his facilitation of interpersonal contacts and member satisfaction within the group. The bases of power are not conceptually clear in some areas, and will be very dependent on the group and external environments. Even so, they are suggestive of some of the ways in which group leadership occurs and is maintained.

A knowledge of small-group functioning enables the social welfare professional to understand the effect of group dynamics on behavior, and to use the group to attain social welfare goals. Since most behavior occurs in ongoing groups, the worker must be able to understand the dynamics of individual personality functioning as they interact with the dynamics of a group's structure. When the professional believes that modification of a group's structure would help to attain goals for one or more group members, he must have an adequate understanding of group principles to attain the desired changes. In some cases, new groups may need to be formed to attain specific objectives, in which case the worker would have to understand the possible group structures for the purpose desired, and then how to build such structures. In conclusion, the sociological perspective emphasizes the effect of group structures on human behavior, and such structures range from large-scale organizations to smaller group contexts.

Community Theory

Dentler notes that "the main feature in the setting of a community is this: It is of a size and design that allows a great range of functions to be car-

---

EXHIBIT 6–3
Public Assistance in the United States: Some Illustrative Data

The societal demographic shift of population from rural to urban areas has created many social problems—unemployment, overcrowding, inadequate housing and public services, emotional tension and breakdown, etc. These societal processes, when centered in urban areas, create a need for appropriate welfare services. The data presented in the table (opposite) indicate the magnitude of the problems in selected United States cities and the magnitude of the task for the welfare system.

Source: *Public Assistance Statistics, February 1971* (NCSS Report A-2 [2/71]), U.S. Department of Health, Education, and Welfare, Social and Rehabilitation Service, Program Statistics and Data Systems, National Center for Social Statistics, p. 4.

---

ried out within its boundaries . . . ; a community supplies a geographical and psychological focus for institutional arrangements. A community is a place within which one finds all or most of the economic, political, religious, and familial institutions around which people group to cooperate, compete, or conflict."[32] In other words, communities have the important characteristics of spatial boundaries within which there is social interdependence and relative autonomy. The concept of community, then, is a study in ecology, the way in which the physical environment affects human behavior and organization. In our world of resource pollution, resource destruction, and overcrowding, ecology is a vital area of study for all Americans, not just social welfare professionals and social scientists.

Communities have traditionally been conceptualized as urban or rural. Urban communities have recently received major attention to the neglect of rural communities, since urban communities have been rapidly developing at the expense of their rural counterparts:

The result of a great cityward migration from Europe, from the American Deep South, and from the rural hinterland, and a great suburban dispersion that has occurred at the same time, is the formation of the metropolitan-area community. The Census Bureau of the United States calls these standard metropolitan areas. As of 1960, there were 212 such areas. Each contained one or more cities of fifty thousand or more residents plus surrounding localities. The areas accounted for 70 percent of the national population but less than 10 percent of the nation's land area. Within each metropolitan area, there exist satellite cities and suburbs and a kind of rural residue, or urban fringe residents.[33]

Given the tremendous surge in urbanization, it is natural for urban communities to be the focus of most study. But there is also recent recognition that rural communities have problems, which, though perhaps different from those of urban communities, are no less difficult to solve.

A major problem in the concept of community has traditionally been the diversity of social units encompassed by it. Not only are rural and

Recipients of Public Assistance Money Payments* by Selected Cities (February 1971)

City	Number	% Increase from 1/70	% of City's Population
New York	1,181,310	12.6	15.0
Philadelphia	288,297	29.8	14.8
Baltimore	137,793	20.1	15.2
District of Columbia	79,412	58.6	10.5
San Francisco	101,710	23.1	14.2
St. Louis	91,665	20.6	14.7
New Orleans	88,018	19.2	14.8
Denver	51,825	23.1	10.1

*Includes old-age assistance, aid to the blind, aid to the permanently and totally disabled, aid to families with dependent children, and general assistance.

urban communities quite different from each other, but so are such communities as metropolitan areas, neighborhoods, regions, and megalopolises. Each of these units has spatial boundaries, interdependence within the boundaries, and some degree of autonomy; yet each is also quite different. Traditionally, major attention was paid to what can be called center cities, the major downtown areas. Louis Wirth, for example, cited large size, high population density, and population heterogeneity as characteristic of such communities, and noted how they led to social problems.[34] However, Wirth could not foresee the growth of suburbs as a way to mitigate these problems, nor did he emphasize the effect of urban neighborhoods in providing smaller community units within larger ones.[35] To further complicate community theory, Gans asserts that urban slums may be quite cohesive and village-like,[36] while Dobriner[37] notes that suburbs are not nearly as homogeneous and personal as had been assumed by such writers as Whyte.[38]

Warren has made an attempt to organize the tremendous diversity of phenomena subsumed under the concept of community by noting four ways in which communities differ from each other.[39] The first is the degree of autonomy in the performance of what he considers to be the five main functions of a community: production-distribution-consumption, socialization, social control, social participation, and mutual support. Obviously a metropolitan region would be quite different from a neighborhood in autonomy, with the former having greater autonomy in production-distribution-consumption, but the latter more autonomous with respect to the other functions. A second difference is the extent to which service areas in local units coincide and form a cohesive whole. Third, there are differences in the extent of psychological identification with a common locality. The last difference is in the community's horizontal pattern, or the structural and functional relation of the various units to each other.

EXHIBIT 6–4
Three Theories of Urban Ecology

There have been many attempts to understand the way in which urban areas develop. Three of the best-known theories are presented here (opposite), and while each varies in its details, all show how urban communities are comprised of several types of smaller communities. These diagrams are taken from Melvin De Fleur, William D'Antonio, and Lois De Fleur, Sociology: Man in Society *(Glenview: Scott, Foresman, 1971), p. 291.*

Communities, then, will vary in their size, degree of internal interdependence, and their autonomy, and these differences will be significant in understanding and ultimately intervening in community life.

As a context for social behavior, a community is very complex; to paraphrase Dobriner, the community is a microcosm of larger societal processes.[40] As such, to understand a community, one must understand several levels of social functioning, brought together in a geographical area that has its own distinctive social organization. Naturally a community must first reflect its environment—other communities, larger political entities (such as counties and states), and societal values and structures. Warren states "that many of the problems which are confronted on the community level simply are not solvable on that level at all, but are *problems of the larger society of which the community is a part.*"[41] Within the community, there is a multitude of groups, organizations, and subcommunities which must be understood, and whose interaction is essential to the functioning of the community being studied. An understanding of small-group processes, formal organizational principles, and basic processes of social organization (social integration, conflict, deviance, etc.) is essential to an understanding of the structure, functioning, and change of a community.

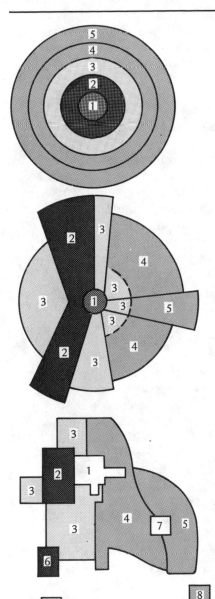

A. *Concentric Zone Theory**
1. Central business district
2. Zone in transition
3. Zone of workingmen's homes
4. Residential zone
5. Commuter zone

B. *Sector Theory†*
1. Central business district
2. Wholesale, light manufacturing
3. Low-class residential
4. Medium-class residential
5. High-class residential

C. *Multiple Nuclei Theory‡*
1. Central business district
2. Wholesale, light manufacturing
3. Low-class residential
4. Medium-class residential
5. High-class residential
6. Heavy manufacturing
7. Outlying business district
8. Residential suburb
9. Industrial suburb

*Source: Adapted from Ernest W. Burgess, "The Growth of the City," in *The City*, ed. R. E. Park et al. Copyright © 1925 by the University of Chicago.

†Source: Homer Hoyt, *The Structure and Growth of Residential Neighborhoods in American Cities* (Washington, D. C.: Federal Housing Administration, 1939); drawing adapted from Chauncy D. Harris and Edward L. Ullman, "The Nature of Cities," *Annals of the American Academy of Political and Social Science* 242 (November 1945).

‡Source: Adapted from Chauncy D. Harris and Edward L. Ullman, "The Nature of Cities," *Annals of the American Academy of Political and Social Science* 242 (November 1945).

Urban communities have been the geographical units developing most rapidly as contexts for human activity, and have been subject to tremendous stress. A brief look at some of the major contemporary urban community problems can therefore provide an additional community perspective. As Wirth noted years ago, a major problem is size and density, or what Dentler calls "problems of scale": "A major source of urban community problems is rapid escalation—that is, swift increases in environmental range, population, and technology—rather than population massing or some less precise process called urbanization."[42] An increase in scale creates problems because of the changes required to adapt to the changed scale, "all of them involving an increased scale of population, organization, service requirements, and institutional complexity."[43] A second problem, related to Wirth's heterogeneity, is the residental segregation of ethnic and racial groups in the typical urban community.[44] This creates a condition of distinctive cultural groups existing in close geographical proximity but with little cooperative interaction. Such conditions foster the development of prejudicial attitudes, discriminatory behavior, and intergroup conflict.[45]

A third problem area revolves around the maintenance of boundaries and internal power structures.[46] The definition of a community is often vague enough to create ambiguity about the geographical area involved, and yet extensive enough to encompass a variety of quasi-autonomous political and social units. With unclear boundaries, it is difficult to identify important community resources, and the uncertainty may create chronic conflict. These difficulties exacerbate the problem of uniting diverse community elements into a coherent, democratic community power structure that minimizes discrimination and political disenfranchisement for any group in the community. A fourth and related problem is community autonomy, or what Dentler calls "growth in *vertical aspects* of social structure: . . . the ever-elaborating ties between local agencies, institutions and services, and their counterpart units in society."[47] Here one sees that any community is deeply tied to its larger social environment, making community autonomy more difficult to achieve. The community must have its own decision-making structures and service outlets, yet it must also relate to those extra-community forces that ultimately affect its ability to exist as a political and service entity.

This discussion of community theory will conclude with a summary of its relevance for the social welfare professional. One major utility is its sensitizing function, highlighting the basic coherence of social science theory in the areas of individual development, group functioning, societal processes, and political and economic concepts to be discussed in the next chapter. Since community theory builds on these other theories, it facilitates their integration into a comprehensive social science view of human behavior. Although any individual social welfare practitioner may wish to specialize in a given area of the social welfare system, the integrated perspective helps to more fully understand each part. Second, community theory sensitizes us to areas of theoretical and practical concern previously overlooked. For example, a community cannot be adequately understood without understanding its political structure and power relationships, two areas commonly omitted in earlier, more psychologically oriented approaches to social welfare needs and functioning. Finally, the community is at the same time traditional and contemporary in its relevance. Many of the major societal changes of our time (industrialization, urbanization, migration, etc.) have had their major impact on individuals through communities, and many major social welfare programs are organized for delivery at the community level. In a very basic way, then, the community forms a central core in understanding human needs and the social welfare system.

Social Change Theory

There are few phenomena of greater interest to social welfare personnel than social change, and yet few areas of theory are less helpful in understanding actual behavior. One reason for the discrepancy between theory and reality is the traditional concentration in sociological theory on macrosociological change.[48] Social welfare practitioners are typically more directly concerned with microsociological change, especially at the individual, organizational, and community levels. Yet the social system is so interlocking that macro and micro phenomena are related, and theories at each level should have some applicability at the other. In this section a brief review of theory at both levels will be undertaken, and then some ideas on their interrelationship will be presented.

An immediate problem arises in the definition of social change. Nisbet's definition as "change within a persisting identity" seems to be a simple, usable one if it is modified slightly.[49] Nisbet's definition affirms the basic point that change is most commonly measured with respect to a given function. For example, the political structure of a society may change from democratic to autocratic, but one is still talking about a political structure and the change is described with reference to the performance of political activities. However, on some occasions one may also wish to speak of change as occurring in the elimination of a function or the creation of a new one. For example, some occupations have disappeared, while new ones have appeared, and it is questionable whether there are persisting identities in these cases. Here one is directly into the macro-micro issue, since perhaps on the macrosociological level the disappearance of an occupation may simply be a change in the overall productive function of society, while at the micro level within the given occupation there is no persisting identity. Although seemingly a semantic problem, it is this basic lack of clarity in social-change theory that underlies many problems in attempts to identify change and its causes.

Moore suggests that there are several things one needs to know in order to talk about change: the structure that is changing, the source of the change, the direction of change, and the time period in which the change occurs.[50] While it would seem relatively easy to identify the characteristics of change, it is frustratingly difficult. For example, Moore asserts that change is occurring constantly,[51] while Nisbet and Swanson suggest that persistence is the rule rather than the exception.[52] The fact that social structures are so closely interwoven creates difficulties in identifying the sources and targets of change—if one wanted to assert that the hippie phenomenon is a change, what structure or structures would one identify? The point is, then, that social science theories of social change are still evolving and need to be approached with some care.

Out of the many conflicting theories, the following seems to be a useful perspective on change. Change may be stimulated by external or internal forces. However, persistence is more likely than change, simply because any social structure is a complex system which generates vested interests in terms of psychological security and concrete advantages. Change will occur when the structure involved reaches a point of crisis, which Nisbet defines as a point at which the traditional solutions to problems are no longer effective.[53] Alternatives are needed, and they may be of several kinds. Among the internal sources of alternatives are what Moore calls flexibilities built into a social system, including variability in socialization, deviance caused by the imperfect operation of social control mechanisms, and the variability in individual role performance. Moore also sees the aggregate of small-scale changes (population size, composition, and distribution) and the inconsistency between societal values and concrete reality as additional internal sources of change.[54] Note that in some cases change is being used to explain change; nevertheless, Moore's ideas are useful.

A second source of innovation is external sources of change. These include, according to Moore, borrowing from other cultures (diffusion) and environmental changes, which stimulate social adaptation.[55] Extending Moore's ideas, Lenski suggests that further sources of internal innovation are inventions (useful combinations of already existing information) and discoveries (innovations providing completely new information).[56] Moore notes that whether or not the potential sources of internal and external change actually do generate innovative ideas will depend on five factors: (1) the size of the culture base, which is the number of ideas existing in the social system that can be combined in new ways to generate new ideas; (2) the number of people looking for a solution, which is normally related to the population size; (3) the extent of contact with other cultures from which ideas may be borrowed; (4) environmental stability, which allows the search for innovations to proceed; and (5) the degree to which the values of the social system encourage innovation.[57]

In addition to a crisis and available alternatives, social change seems to require a change agent or advocate who will push for the selection and adoption of one of the alternatives. The characteristics of a change agent are not well understood, although charisma is commonly thought to be one of them.[58] The general framework of change presented above seems applicable to either the macro or micro level, although clearly the focus has been mainly macrosociological. The compatibility of this framework at the micro level can be seen by looking at Swanson's discussion of routinized change in organizations.[59] He says that the organization must first have a "generalized objective" against which all changes will be planned and evaluated—here one sees the similarity with a need or desire for innovations. Then there must be standards to select innovations, which he feels must include continuous evaluation of the operation of the organization. Innovations should be evaluated heuristically, with alternatives being selected when they are satisfactory rather than necessarily perfect (called "satisficing"). In Swanson's analysis of organizational change, then, he is basically concerned with the perceived need for change, the availability of alternatives, and, elsewhere in his analysis, the institutionalization of the change in the organization.[60]

Conclusion

Social welfare personnel are by definition agents of social change at some level, whether it be changing individual behavior or affecting social policy. Sociological social change theory addresses itself to changes in social structures, which then can have relevance to individual change; psychological theories of personality change are more directly focused on individual change. In spite of some ambiguities and gaps, sociological social change theory does attempt to explicate the way in which social structural change occurs. As is often the case, the theory does not directly suggest actual techniques for change. However, the specific intervention techniques discussed later inevitably grow out of the social science theories discussed in Chapter 5, this chapter, and Chapter 7.

REFERENCES

1. Robert Nisbet, *The Social Bond* (New York: Alfred A. Knopf, 1950), pp. 5–20.
2. Ibid., pp. 21–42.
3. An excellent summary of history, characteristics, and effects of the industrialization process may be found in William Faunce, *Problems of an Industrial Society* (New York: McGraw-Hill, 1968).
4. Sigmund Freud, *Civilization and Its Discontents* (New York: Norton, 1961).
5. A classic work addressing this question is Emile Durkheim, *The Division of Labor in Society* (New York: Free Press, 1964).
6. See Talcott Parsons, *The Social System* (New York: Free Press, 1964), pp. 26–36.
7. An excellent account of socialization and institutionalization is in Peter

Berger and Thomas Luckmann, *The Social Construction of Reality* (Garden City: Anchor, 1967).

8. See Berger and Luckmann, op. cit.; and Tamotsu Shibutani, *Society and Personality* (Englewood Cliffs, N.J.: Prentice-Hall, 1961), pp. 491–594. See also Anselm Strauss, ed., *George Herbert Mead: On Social Psychology* (Chicago: Phoenix, 1965), pp. 19–42.

9. See the discussion of social structural flexibility as a source of change in Wilbert Moore, *Social Change* (Englewood Cliffs, N.J.: Prentice-Hall, 1963), pp. 52–68.

10. A good summary of role theory and its applications may be found in Edwin Thomas, ed., *Behavioral Science for Social Workers* (New York: Free Press, 1967), pp. 15–50 and 59–77.

11. Ibid.

12. See Berger and Luckmann, op. cit.; and Kenneth Dolbeare and Patricia Dolbeare, *American Ideologies* (Chicago: Markham, 1971), pp. 1–21.

13. Karl Marx and Friedrich Engels, *Basic Writings on Politics and Philosophy*, ed. Lewis Feuer (Garden City: Anchor, 1959), pp. 26–30, 263–266.

14. Kenneth and Patricia Dolbeare, op. cit.

15. An interesting discussion of this point in terms of domain assumptions is Alvin Gouldner, *The Coming Crisis of Western Sociology* (New York: Basic Books, 1970), pp. 3–87.

16. There is a wealth of literature on this subject. A few of them are Elliot Liebow, *Talley's Corner* (Boston: Little, Brown, 1967); Martin Rein, *Social Policy: Issues of Choice and Change* (New York: Random House, 1970); President's Commission on Income Maintenance Programs, *Poverty Amid Plenty* (Washington: Government Printing Office, 1969); Ben Seligman, *Permanent Poverty* (Chicago: Quadrangle, 1970); and the extensive literature by blacks on their place in American society, such as William Grier and Price Cobbs, *Black Rage* (New York: Basic Books, 1968).

17. John L. Roach et al., *Social Stratification in the United States* (Englewood Cliffs, N.J.: Prentice-Hall, 1969), pp. 20ff., 225–233, 537–552.

18. Ibid., pp. 11ff., 32–33, 596–597.

19. Ibid., pp. 13–20, 32–44.

20. See Lewis Coser, *The Functions of Social Conflict* (New York: Free Press, 1956).

21. Roach et al., op. cit., 54–60.

22. For example, see Liebow, op. cit.; Oscar Lewis, *La Vida* (New York: Random House, 1966); and Robin Morgan, ed., *Sisterhood is Powerful* (New York: Vintage, 1970).

23. Rein, op. cit., pp. 26–27, 249–270, 353–373.

24. A useful compendium of such techniques is Si Kahn, *How People Get Power* (New York: McGraw-Hill, 1970).

25. See Bernard Berelson and Gary Steiner, *Human Behavior: An Inventory of Scientific Findings* (New York: Harcourt, Brace, and World, 1964), pp. 297–323.

26. See Dorwin Cartwright and Alvin Zander, *Group Dynamics: Research and Theory* (Evanston: Row, Peterson, 1960).

27. Clovis Shepherd, *Small Groups: Some Sociological Perspectives* (San Francisco: Chandler, 1964), p. 28.

28. Ibid., pp. 58–99. This chapter summarizes some of the enormous literature

related to the issues involved in task and process groups, as well as presenting a useful selected bibliography.

29. An excellent example of the factors involved in task and socio-emotional leadership and their interplay is William F. Whyte's classic *Street Corner Society* (Chicago: University of Chicago Press, 1943).

30. Cartwright and Zander, op. cit., pp. 512–519, 586–605.

31. John French, Jr., and Bertram Raven, "The Bases of Social Power," in Cartwright and Zander, op. cit., pp. 607–622.

32. Robert Dentler, *American Community Problems* (New York: McGraw-Hill, 1968), p. 16.

33. Ibid., pp. 24–25.

34. See Louis Wirth, *On Cities and Social Life* (Chicago: University of Chicago Press, 1964), pp. 165–178, 229–270.

35. See Suzanne Keller, *The Urban Neighborhood: A Sociological Perspective* (New York: Random House, 1968).

36. Herbert Gans, *The Urban Villagers* (New York: Free Press, 1962).

37. William Dobriner, *Class in Suburbia* (Englewood Cliffs, N.J.: Prentice-Hall, 1963), pp. 85–126.

38. William H. Whyte, Jr., *The Organization Man* (Garden City: Anchor, 1956), pp. 295–434.

39. Roland Warren, "A Community Model," in Ralph Kramer and Harry Specht, eds., *Readings in Community Organization Practice* (Englewood Cliffs, N.J.: Prentice-Hall, 1969), pp. 43–44.

40. William Dobriner, *Social Structures and Systems* (Pacific Palisades: Goodyear, 1969), pp. 206–210.

41. Warren, op. cit., p. 45.

42. Dentler, op. cit., p. 33.

43. Ibid., p. 37.

44. Ibid., pp. 37–38.

45. Raymond Mack, "The Components of Social Conflict," in Kramer and Specht, op. cit., pp. 327–337.

46. Dentler, op. cit., pp. 41–54.

47. Ibid., p. 38.

48. A concise review of sociological theories of change may be found in Richard Applebaum, *Theories of Social Change* (Chicago: Markham, 1970).

49. See Robert Nisbet, *Social Change and History* (New York: Oxford University Press, 1969), p. 168.

50. Moore, op. cit.

51. Ibid., pp. 1–21.

52. Guy Swanson, *Social Change* (Glenview: Scott, Foresman, 1971).

53. Nisbet, op. cit., pp. 282–283.

54. Moore, op. cit., pp. 45–68.

55. Ibid., pp. 77–80, 85–88.

56. Gerhard Lenski, *Human Societies* (New York: McGraw-Hill, 1970), pp. 48–94.

57. Moore, op. cit., pp. 27–44.

58. Swanson, op. cit., pp. 140–141; and Everett E. Hagen, *On the Theory of Social Change* (Homewood: Dorsey, 1962), pp. 55–182.

59. Swanson, op. cit., pp. 148–170.

60. Ibid., pp. 112–135.

SELECTED READINGS

The diversity of sociological theories pertinent to social welfare creates an enormous body of potentially relevant theory. The following are of interest in and of themselves, but also have excellent bibliographies for those wishing to pursue any given area in greater depth.

Dentler, Robert. *American Community Problems.* New York: McGraw-Hill, 1968.

Knowles, Lewis, and Kenneth Prewitt. *Institutional Racism in America.* Englewood Cliffs, N.J.: Prentice-Hall (Spectrum), 1969.

Lewis, Oscar. *La Vida.* New York: Random House, 1965.

Liebow, Elliot. *Talley's Corner.* Boston: Little, Brown, 1967.

McGee, Reece. *Social Disorganization in America.* San Francisco: Chandler, 1962.

Shepherd, Clovis. *Small Groups: Some Sociological Perspectives.* San Francisco: Chandler, 1964.

Stein, Herman, and Richard Cloward, eds. *Social Perspectives on Behavior.* New York: Free Press, 1958.

Thomas, Edwin. *Behavioral Science for Social Workers.* New York: Free Press, 1967.

POLITICAL AND ECONOMIC BASES

BASES

To conclude this review of the social science foundations of the social welfare institution, selected economic and political concepts will now be presented. As in the previous two chapters, the relevance of the concepts discussed to an understanding of the structure and functioning of the social welfare institution will be emphasized.

The economic system of any society is concerned with the distribution of scarce resources, the fact of scarcity suggesting that there is always a competitive element in the economic system. The political system also is concerned with a scarce resource—power. The economic and political systems are related in that the distribution of economic resources is affected by the power structure, while the possession of economic resources is a source of power. However, methods of obtaining economic and political power are varied, and to be an effective change agent, the social welfare professional must understand all of the possibilities open to him.

Economic Perspectives

In theory, the American economic system is based on a free-enterprise market. Economic resources are offered to consumers by producers, and it is the combination of attractiveness of product, price of product, utility of product, and availability of competing products which will determine consumer response. In the free-enterprise market, then, producers compete for the purchasing power of consumers, the assumption being that the producer with the best product (as defined by consumers) at the best price will flourish. The federal government has increasingly imposed limitations on the freedom of the market mechanism as it became evident that there were many intervening conditions that prevented the ideal interaction between producer and consumer from occurring. For example, producers could attempt to lower costs by exploiting their employees,[1] or by using inferior quality components whose true worth could be hidden from the consumer.* Producers could also enter into a variety of collusive arrangements among themselves to artificially fix prices at higher levels than would occur if the market was free in its operation.† It also became evident that in a mass society consumers could be manipulated through mass advertising,‡ through lack of access to competing products,[2] and through lack of information.[3]

---

*This practice led to the development of special government agencies, such as the Pure Food and Drug Administration.

† Such collusion led to much of the United States' antitrust legislation, especially relevant today with the growth of many quasi-legal conglomerates.

‡ The image manipulation used in the advertising of cigarettes is an excellent example. Cigarette smoking was related to such desirable characteristics as physical attractiveness

In spite of governmental intervention in the marketplace, the United States continues to rely on a modified market economy, with several important effects on the social welfare system. A public welfare system interferes with the operation of the market, and as such is counter to society's modified free-enterprise economic values. This leads to attempts to minimize the disruption of the market by welfare, thereby preserving the market as far as possible, and presumably minimizing resentment against welfare recipients. Such attempts include making welfare services either combinations of public and private services, publicly subsidizing private services, or specifically designing services so that they minimize interference with the market's operation. Health care for the aged is an excellent example of a welfare service provided partly publicly (Veterans Administration hospitals and other public hospitals), and partly privately (doctor's care, clinics in private hospitals, nursing homes, etc.). It also includes public subsidy for privately provided services (Medicare payments to doctors and hospitals, public-assistance vendor payments to nursing homes, etc.).

The food stamp and surplus commodities programs illustrate attempts to minimize interference in the marketplace, as well as the complexity and illogic of subsidizing such divergent groups as farmers and the poor with the same programs. Surplus commodities provide a way to dispose of excess food produced by farmers who, rather than operating in a free market, are subsidized for producing excess food. Since data show that the majority of subsidies go to relatively affluent farmers with large farms,[4] the willingness to interfere in the marketplace for the relatively wealthy is apparent. The fact that similar interference is begrudged the poor serves to highlight the importance of values in the social welfare institution. However, surplus commodities are bulky, difficult to prepare,[5] and directly competitive with retail food producers. Therefore, their utility is limited, and food stamps have become a more popular solution to the food problem. They can be used in the regular marketplace, thereby protecting normal channels of distribution. They can, however, be used only to purchase food (not household supplies, cigarettes, liquor, etc.), a type of paternalism that protects both the market and morality. Proposed legislation for welfare reform would translate food stamps into a direct cash grant, which could then be spent in the marketplace as one wished.

The whole area of food purchasing is an excellent example of the difficulties involved in trying to preserve a market system along with a welfare system. Jones and Caplovitz have poignantly documented the fact that the poor and disadvantaged are chronically exploited in the market by paying more for inferior products.[6] The market is by definition not set

and sexual prowess, and was very successful in spite of growing evidence that cigarette smoking caused lung cancer. The eventual elimination of cigarette advertising from radio and television and the placing of a health warning on each package of cigarettes were imposed by the government as ways of trying to counteract the power of mass advertising.

up to protect those in need. It is a mockery of societal values to continue to believe that those who need extensive welfare assistance are able to be self-reliant, informed consumers in a free enterprise system.

The clash of free market and social welfare values inevitably creates resentment and discrimination against welfare recipients. Public monies spent on welfare must necessarily reduce the amount of such monies available for other purposes. The market model suggests that the same criteria used to evaluate private programs can and should be used to evaluate public programs. In one sense this is perfectly logical, since the public does have the right to get value for money spent. However, the difficulty of measuring human needs and appropriate services creates a tendency to concentrate on those services and persons most easily proved successful, a practice called "creaming."[7] Furthermore, the pursuit of efficiency tends to reduce complex problem clusters to simplified problems whose "solution" lies in a combination of money and chasing those needy persons alleged to be shiftless welfare exploiters from the rolls.[8] This is accentuated by societal values that stress individual achievement. They make it easy to believe that those who are in need have not tried hard enough, and need a combination of opportunity and incentive. It becomes difficult to popularize the fact that data show the great majority of welfare recipients to be multi-problem persons with enormous disadvantages and obstacles to self-sufficiency.[9] The institutional inequality built into the market system makes it extremely difficult for the person discriminated against to find a toe-hold, but this, too, is easily ignored in a competitive market system.

Further problems associated with a quasi-market oriented welfare system include funding and political problems. Although the government has been given the power to tax in order to provide welfare services, there are clearly limits to this ability if the public is to continue to determine tax policies. The problem is most readily visible at local levels, with many large cities claiming that their tax base is inadequate to support the services needed.[10] This condition is accentuated by the rapid migration of affluent taxpayers to the suburbs. The inner city is left with those needing help but with few taxable resources.[11] The stress in the Nixon administration on revenue sharing is an attempt to make the greater tax-generating power of the federal government available to local governments, a system very supportive of a sharing of power and decision-making.[12]

Deciding on the allocation of political power between the federal, state, and local levels is difficult, and points out several of the inconsistencies and problems with this society's political system. The massive scale at which the federal government operates allows fairly open participation by various interest groups, but realistically the costs of such participation favor those groups with substantial economic and organizational resources.[13] Furthermore, the enormously complex bureaucracy that is the federal government appears to make it relatively easy to hide potentially significant processes and documents (the Pentagon Papers leaked by Daniel Ellsberg is a case in point). The state and local political levels are more accessible to small groups, and encourage individual participation in the political process. However, political power is somewhat more limited at these levels, and local compromises may be made to obtain access to higher political levels. Nevertheless, in spite of limited political power and control over economic resources, local decision-making is more easily controlled by the average citizen. As such, it provides a valuable source of individual participation in the political process and an important opportunity for local groups to develop political expertise that may then be used at higher levels in the political process. The federal and local levels of the political system offer rather different opportunities and problems, and both are important for the attainment of needed social welfare resources.

Political Perspectives

Moving more directly into political concepts, political pluralism is of great importance. Pluralism is based on three major societal values: (1) sociocultural diversity; (2) freedom of expression; and (3) the melting-pot nature of the society. It creates a system in which the many groups comprising society can freely compete in the political process. It is assumed that coalitions will be formed, creating a majority enabling elections to occur and legislation to be enacted. In this way, the majority opinion has presumably found expression, and the defeated minority accepts this opinion until the next voting opportunity when it may again have a chance to enact its wishes. Our political system, then, is a competitive one, but one which provides a structured opportunity for all groups to fight for their own particular interests.

Competition in the political process turns out to be an unequal struggle. First, the majority in power has a built-in advantage in subsequent competition, since it has access to a variety of legal and illegal powers to preserve itself. Political patronage is one such power; those in power have various political appointments to make and can otherwise legally take advantage of the opportunities for popularizing its own interests and beliefs. Among the illegal techniques, gerrymandering of political boundaries has been popular and often quite effective. A second reason why political competition is unequal is the cost of espousing a cause. Although anyone can write to his elected representative as an individual, to go out and mobilize a large number of people to a cause is expensive. The wealthy can thereby afford to gain support for their interests. Lobbies exist to provide a voice for virtually every interest group, but some have more resources than others. The National Association of Social Workers employs two people as lobbyists in Washington, a far cry from the enormous staff of union lobbyists or an organization such as the American Medical Association. The National Welfare Rights

Organization was organized relatively recently as a lobby group for welfare recipients, and has become a meaningful force.[14] But welfare recipients comprise one of many groups whose resources are pitifully small compared to other lobbies.

A third inequity is the complexity of the political system. It is so complex that one has to have some sophistication to be able to understand its operation. To work within it, one must progress up through the political ranks, a process that frequently requires money or obligations to those who can provide the money. Such an apprenticeship commonly leads to a changing frame of reference as one works through the system. When a position of some power is reached, the politician may be quite detached from the powerless people of his constituency. The average citizen in turn has little opportunity to learn about the political system in any practical way, and may be either frightened or cynical when con-

---

EXHIBIT 7–1
The Legislative Process—Learning to Participate

Although virtually all of us learned it in high school, can you recount the process involved in a bill becoming law? Do you know who your elected representatives are? Do you know how to effectively write them to express your wishes? The answer to the second question can be found in a publication such as the Congressional Quarterly's Guide to Current American Government (issued twice yearly at $3.00 an issue, available from the Congressional Quarterly, 1735 K St., N.W., Washington, D.C. 20006, and full of much more valuable information about our government). Summary answers to the first and third questions are given in the illustration (opposite) and below, and are taken from pp. 89 and 99 of the Spring 1971 Guide, respectively. Another valuable reference for understanding the political system is Donald Herzberg and J. W. Peltason, A Student Guide to Campaign Politics (New York: McGraw-Hill, 1970).

   Writing to your Government: Tips

1. Write to your own Senators or Representatives. Letters sent to other Congressmen will end up on the desk of Congressmen from your state.
2. Write at the proper time, when a bill is being discussed in committee or on the floor.
3. Use your own words and your own stationery. Avoid signing and sending a form or mimeographed letter.
4. Don't be a pen pal. Don't try to instruct the Representative or Senator on every issue that comes up.
5. Don't demand a commitment before all the facts are in. Bills rarely become law in the same form as introduced.
6. Whenever possible, identify all bills by their number.
7. If possible, include pertinent editorials from local papers.
8. Be constructive. If a bill deals with a problem you admit exists but you believe the bill is the wrong approach, tell what you think the right approach is.
9. If you have expert knowledge or wide experience in particular areas, share it with the Congressman. But don't pretend to wield vast political influence.

sidering an attempt to express himself politically—"You can't fight city hall." Exposure to the issues themselves is likely to be very limited, so that the average citizen may be unaware of proposed legislation of vital importance to his interests. If aware, knowledge about the details of the legislative process may be so meager that effective political debate with major political figures is unrealistic. Even if one is aware and knowledgeable, access to the major centers of government can be a problem. Certainly at the national level Washington, D.C. is quite remote from the majority of the country. Some states are geographically so large that it is prohibitively expensive for concerned citizens to appear personally at the state capitol to support their cause. It is simply unrealistic to think that Spanish-speaking welfare mothers in New York City are going to have the knowledge and the resources to go to Albany to fight for badly needed welfare reforms at the state level.

How a Bill Becomes Law

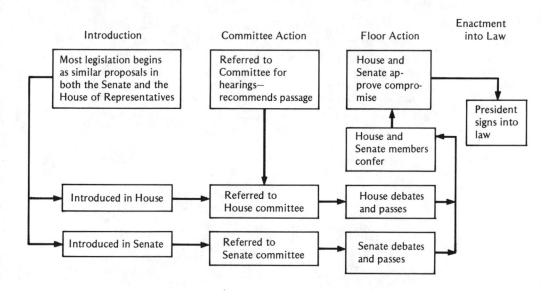

10. Write to the Congressman when he does something you approve of. A note of appreciation will make him remember you more favorably next time.
11. Feel free to write when you have a question or problem dealing with procedures of government departments.
12. Be brief, write legibly, and be sure to use the proper form of address.

A 15-word telegram called a Public-Opinion Message (POM) can be sent to the President, Vice President or a member of Congress from anywhere in the United States for $1. Name and address are not counted as part of the message unless there are additional signers.

The government often operates very slowly. The process by which a bill becomes law is a long and tedious one, made more so by the fact that most bills never complete the process, for a variety of reasons. Understanding the reasons for the slow progress, and being able to maintain the necessary persistence are formidable problems which greatly weights the struggle on the side of the knowledgeable, powerful, and wealthy. A final problem lies in the weaknesses of minorities. The system assumes that minority groups will ultimately form coalitions to pool whatever knowledge and power each group possesses. However, these minority groups may be characterized by different racial and ethnic backgrounds, different norms and languages, and different income and educational levels. Therefore, the basis for coalitions may be submerged under a variety of seemingly insurmountable differences. Experience has shown that the ability to form coalitions is itself a skill that is learned. It requires

---

EXHIBIT 7–2
HR 1—A Complex Bill

HR 1 (House of Representatives bill number 1), was the Nixon administration's proposed welfare reform bill introduced in the 92nd Congress (1971). It was hotly contested and was not enacted into law. A modified version was introduced the following year, parts of which were enacted into law. To illustrate the complexity of this kind of legislation, the table of contents from a press release summary of provisions of the 1971 HR 1 is given below, and on the next five pages. When looking at this table of contents, it becomes clear how well-informed the politically active welfare practitioner must be. It is easy to understand why such a bill would be fought over by many interest groups that would be affected in one way or another.

Contents

a level of sophistication in the political process learned slowly and pain-fully by many minority groups.[15]

Having noted the several problems in the operation of America's pluralistic, competitive political system, the relatively new ombudsman concept must be mentioned as a way to overcome some of these prob-lems.[16] American society today is so complex that many persons are un-aware of services available, the structure of services, the political process, their rights as citizens, and so on. In the attempt to provide a link between the individual, with all of his lack of knowledge, fears, and prejudices, and the political and service structures that exist to serve him, the ombudsman concept was developed. The ombudsman is a person or group whose presence is made popularly known and whose purpose is to provide the information to help individuals find what they seek. Ideally, the ombuds-man also seeks out problems in the provision of services or the involvement of citizens in the political process. Whether or not new problems are identified, the ombudsman helps the citizen obtain what he wishes in a system that is meant to serve him but which by its very scope may dwarf him instead.

It is easy to talk about the political structure and note its effects on the average citizen without realizing that the political system has important effects on social welfare professionals and their work. In a very basic sense, welfare professionals are dependent on the political system for their jobs, since the decisions made in that system determine the need for welfare practitioners. For example, recent decisions to separate social services from financial payments is having an important impact on the number of social welfare professionals and the training they require.[17] Political decisions may create service delivery systems that conflict in whole or in part with professional values. While it is clear that the fragmented public welfare structure that currently exists as an outgrowth of the 1935 Social Security Act is ineffective and financially untenable in many cases, family assistance legislation proposed in 1970 and still not passed at the end of 1972 has some professionally unacceptable components. Optional state residence requirements, enforced work provisions, and level of state payments are examples. It is difficult indeed to decide whether to try to defeat proposed legislation and live with the present toppling structure until more successful legislation is passed, or to support the proposed legislation and then hope to be able to modify it to achieve professional goals.** The implications of this decision are enormous for the role of professional social welfare in the future.

**The National Association of Social Workers' decision has been not to support the family assistance legislation proposed in 1971.

Unfortunately, many social welfare professionals are poorly equipped to participate in the political process. Some fear that their jobs will be jeopardized if they participate, a fear that in some cases is very realistic. However, the alternative of having decisions made for the profession, which then may seriously weaken its ability to provide services, is not very attractive either. Even given the perceived desirability of participating, the problems which the average citizen faces also confront the typical social welfare professional. Social welfare education has rarely included political action, and although this gap is being somewhat lessened today, the political action that is undertaken tends to be at the local level. Although very important, it must also be bolstered by national political action. A third factor is the current complexity of the welfare structure even for the professional welfare practitioner. The typical worker has limited tasks to perform, and rarely has the opportunity to study the total welfare picture. Yet when welfare reform legislation is proposed, it is comprehensive and complex, leaving the practitioner uninformed about many details easily overlooked but of great significance. The fact that welfare professionals are often unable to see beyond their specialized interest to combine into a unified, more powerful social welfare lobby accentuates the problems the professions have in being active, effective political forces.

A final problem in the way of welfare professionals being politically active is again related to political sophistication. It is the lack of tenacity required to see legislation enacted and then implemented. Wilbur Cohen has well expressed the false optimism that can develop when working for legislation, and the crushing disappointment when one's efforts fail. He also realistically discusses the need to accept such defeats and continue to work for change.[18] Even beyond the tenacity to get legislation passed, however, is the sophistication to know that legislation is only as good as the provisions for its enforcement. Wilcox repeatedly makes the point that so much good legislation has been relatively ineffective because of inadequate implementation provisions—lack of funds, lack of structures for enforcement and supervision, lack of legal support to untangle legal problems, and so on.[19] This helps to explain why, in spite of so much legislation in areas such as school desegregation, inequities still exist. Obviously, then, political tenacity has to go much further than simply the enactment of legislation, as difficult as that may be to achieve successfully.

Conclusion

It is apparent that an understanding of the economic and political processes are essential to an understanding of the nature of the social order and avenues of change. Competition is a basic part of the American system. Nevertheless, the economic and political systems must be modified so that all citizens can find their satisfactions. The best way in which the total system can be modified has not yet been found, and the needy continue to suffer as a result. As social welfare personnel gain greater expertise in economic and political participation, and assuming that American society continues to claim a respect for the rights of the needy, the economic and political systems will ultimately help the welfare structure function more effectively.

The eclectic scope of social welfare concerns has created a vast body of knowledge with which the social welfare professional should be familiar. The preceding three-chapter overview of selected social science knowledge, specifically relevant to a more adequate understanding of the social welfare institution, indicates this is true. Rarely can all of the relevant knowledge pertaining to a specific social welfare area be mastered by a practitioner. Yet a conception of the richness of material available can help the practitioner to satisfy his interests and practice needs in an intelligent and productive way. The next two chapters deal specifically with practice principles and the utility of social science knowledge.

REFERENCES

1. Excellent examples of early worker exploitation may be found in the writings of early "muckrakers." A classic is Upton Sinclair's *The Jungle* (New York: Doubleday, Page, 1906), concerning conditions in the meatpacking industry at the turn of the century. The growth of unions helped to reduce such exploitation, although it is by no means absent today (migrant farm workers, for example).
2. Lack of equal access has been frequently demonstrated, especially in areas where low-income people are presented with low-quality products at inflated prices in food stores. See W. Ron Jones et al., *Finding Community* (Palo Alto: James Freel, 1970), pp. 3–37; and David Caplovitz, *The Poor Pay More* (New York: Free Press, 1967).
3. The current use of unit pricing is an attempt to overcome this in food purchasing. See Jones, op. cit., pp. 3–15.
4. President's Commission on Income Maintenance Programs, *Working Papers* (Washington, D.C.: Government Printing Office, 1969), pp. 285–290.
5. Ibid., pp. 351–356.
6. Jones, op. cit.; and Caplovitz, op. cit.
7. Martin Rein, *Social Policy: Issues of Choice and Change* (New York: Random House, 1970), pp. 53–67.

8. Excellent discussions of moral perspectives used in evaluating the worth of recipients of public assistance may be found in John Romanyshyn, *Social Welfare: From Charity to Justice* (New York: Random House, 1971), pp. 41–46; and Gilbert Y. Steiner, *Social Insecurity: The Politics of Welfare* (Chicago: Rand McNally, 1966), pp. 108–140.

9. A good survey of some of the major contemporary problems in welfare is "The Welfare Industrial Complex," *The Nation,* June 28, 1971, pp. 808–811. See also President's Commission on Income Maintenance Programs, op. cit., pp. 13–41.

10. See Bill Kovach, "States Move to Reverse Wide Welfare Expansion," *New York Times,* August 16, 1971, p. 1.

11. "State, Local Tax Loads: Why No Relief in Sight," *U.S. News and World Report,* June 7, 1971, pp. 59–61.

12. Congressional Quarterly, *Guide to Current American Government* (Washington, D.C.: Congressional Quarterly, Spring 1971), pp. 139–149.

13. Ibid., pp. 127–130.

14. Jones, op. cit., pp. 51–52.

15. Excellent examples are provided in Ralph Kramer, *Participation of the Poor* (Englewood Cliffs, N.J.: Prentice-Hall, 1969).

16. "An Educational Ombudsman for New York City," *School and Society* 99 (March 1971): 168–170.

17. See United States Department of Health, Education, and Welfare, *The Separation of Services from the Determination of Eligibility for Assistance Payments* (Washington, D.C.: Government Printing Office, 1970).

18. Wilbur Cohen, "What Every Social Worker Should Know about Political Action," in Robert Klenk and Robert Ryan, eds., *The Practice of Social Work* (Belmont, Cal.: Wadsworth, 1970), pp. 334–346.

19. Clair Wilcox, *Toward Social Welfare* (Homewood, Ill.: Richard D. Irwin, 1969), esp. pp. 159–208. He notes the distinction between legislation and its implementation in looking at the difference between de jure and de facto segregation.

SELECTED READINGS

The political and economic realities of social welfare in American society have been among the most ignored aspects of social welfare as a social institution. The readings suggested here attempt to persuade you of the need for greater political and economic awareness, as well as some of the ways such awareness can be obtained.

Alinsky, Saul. *Reveille for Radicals*. Chicago: University of Chicago Press, 1946.

Caplovitz, David. *The Poor Pay More*. New York: Free Press, 1967.

Cohen, Wilbur. "What Every Social Worker Should Know about Political Action," in Robert Klenk and Robert Ryan, eds., *The Practice of Social Work*. Belmont, Cal.: Wadsworth, 1970, pp. 334–346.

Congressional Quarterly. *Guide to Current American Government*. Issued twice yearly. Weekly guide of current legislation may be obtained from Congressional Quarterly, 1735 K Street, N.W., Washington, D.C. 20006.

Herzberg, Donald, and J. W. Peltason. *A Student Guide to Campaign Politics.*
    New York: McGraw-Hill, 1970.
Theobold, Robert. *Free Men and Free Markets.* Garden City: Anchor, 1965.
Titmuss, Richard. *Commitment to Welfare.* New York: Pantheon, 1968.

III

INTERVENTIVE METHODS

TRADITIONAL PRACTICE PERSPECTIVES

The social welfare institution has been seen as a complex group of values, structures, and programs, all closely interlocked with the larger social system. All of the characteristics of the institution discussed so far have great importance for the way in which services are offered. However, they do not deal with the actual practice techniques which social welfare practitioners use to achieve change in individual, group, or societal behavior patterns. Over time, such techniques became broadly categorized into those for individuals (casework), those for small groups of individuals (group work), and those for large groups concerned with social policy (community organization).[1] The focus will be on the basic generic practice methods commonly used to solve specific problems. The application of these generic methods in specialized practice contexts is the function of specialized practice courses and on-the-job training.

Methods of practice have changed to adapt to new societal needs and professional values. The traditional distinctions between casework, group work, and community organization helped define the various behavior contexts for which practice principles had to be developed. These distinctions continue to dominate social welfare professions, and are discussed in this chapter. Yet increasing practice experience and social science knowledge have suggested that the traditional distinctions can be dysfunctional in hiding commonalities between methods, and in creating service gaps and redundancies. Attempts to reexamine basic practice needs and principles have resulted in some new perspectives on practice. These will be the focus of the next chapter, and, together with this chapter, should provide a reasonably complete view of present and future practice trends.

Interviewing

Any practice method depends on communication. Underlying casework, group work, and community organization is interviewing, the skill which facilitates productive communication. Interviewing is focused communication, aimed at informing, explaining, and collecting relevant facts essential to understanding issues and problems objectively and completely.[2] Interviewing is a natural part of social interaction, and all of us have been interviewers and interviewees on numerous occasions.

In social welfare, interviewing is a professional skill used in a planned way. De Schweinitz distinguishes two types of interviews: objective, which are goal and task oriented (as when interviewing to determine eligibility for receipt of services); and therapeutic, which are more subjective and introspective (as when allowing a client to express his feelings).[3] Most interviews have elements of each, but to maintain an interview's focus it is often helpful to keep the distinction in mind.

It was seen earlier that values are an extremely important part of social welfare practice. This is especially so in interviewing, where they become part of the interviewing process. De Schweinitz presents what he calls "axioms" about human behavior which an interviewer must understand.[4] These are some basic human values which must be accepted and used in the interviewing situation and, indeed, in all social welfare practice. The first axiom is that people are alike in some ways and different in others. While theory and experience can help to establish a framework to understand and predict behavior, there must always be a basic respect for the uniqueness of each individual. Although one may expect certain behavior, and feel such expectations are justifiable or "natural," they must never be allowed to interfere with being nonjudgemental and nonauthoritarian. The second axiom is that feeling often outweighs reason. As professionals, it is the social welfare worker's task to remain as objective and oriented toward rational problem-solving as possible. This does not mean that the client will have such an orientation. Human behavior has many motivations, some objective and some subjective, some understood and many not understood by the actor himself. The ambivalence, conflict, and indecision that often accompanies behavior must be accepted as part of the totality that is the client. It would be foolish to expect that such feelings can be ignored or will not be present, no matter how rational the client may seem to be.

Third, there is the basic call to know oneself. A social welfare professional works with every aspect of himself, and he must make every reasonable effort to understand himself. It was once common for social welfare workers to go through psychoanalysis as a means of increasing their self-knowledge—an expensive, lengthy, and sometimes destructive procedure used much less frequently today. Every person has his own particular problems, strengths, and weaknesses he lives with every day, and to which he makes adjustments. Perfection is not required in social welfare. What is needed is an ability to look at oneself to identify the weaknesses, strengths, and problems so that they may be recognized, accepted, and controlled in the professional context. People who seek help from welfare professionals have problems they do not want exacerbated by the worker's intolerance, prejudices, or defenses. Our own problems tend to block communication with others in many ways, and since our goal in interviewing is to maximize profitable communication, it is a professional obligation to be in control of one's own weaknesses and problems.

With the above as a base for professional behavior, three major parts of the interviewing process may be identified: (1) conditions of good interviewing; (2) the interview itself, including the beginning, the main part of the interview, and the end; and (3) post-interview activity.[5] There are at least four conditions maximizing the chances for a successful interview. First, there is the physical setting for the interview. This pertains to the actual place where the person is interviewed, including comfortable seating arrangements, privacy, visual attractiveness, and comfort items such as a coat rack, ashtrays, and so on. The physical setting also includes the convenience of the location for the client, whether there is a long wait before the interview, degrading reception procedures, and the presence of a place for children to stay during the interview. It is remarkable how common it is for clients to have to travel some distance, often by public transportation with children, wait if the worker is busy, be gruffly received by a receptionist who obviously feels her position is degraded by dealing with clients, and then sit in a large, bare waiting room in full view of everyone. When the interview finally begins, it should be no surprise if the client is tired, nervous, and sullen. Frequently a practitioner plans interviews in the client's home or other community setting. In such instances, interviewing conditions may be less than ideal and not easily manipulated by the practitioner, but using the client's natural environment can be a convenience for him that results in greater cooperation. Interviewing in the home or community context can also be an aid in understanding the client's social environment.

A second element of the physical setting is confidentiality. People are often quite upset by their problems, and sensitive about discussing them. They rarely appreciate having to discuss problems where others can overhear, and commonly interpret privacy as an indication of a worker's respect. Third, the worker has a professional obligation to have obtained as much background information as possible. This includes studying any case records that are available from previous contacts, and includes basic knowledge of community and agency resources. Having this information at hand enables the worker to avoid repetition in the interview, which most clients appreciate. It also makes maximum use of available time, and draws upon other community resources as appropriate. It is sound practice to refer a client to another agency if it is likely to be better able to work with him and his particular problem. Fourth, note-taking, for the purpose of recording the content of the interview, must be planned. Too much note-taking can distract a client and impede communication. On the other hand, it has to be adequate to record significant facts. A workable compromise is to take notes on factual information, with minimal notes on other content. Mechanical recording devices can sometimes be used, but the client's permission must always be sought first, and such equipment should be as unobtrusive as possible.

Beginning the interview has at least five relevant factors.[6] First, the client has a right to know the realities of the interviewing context, such as the time period likely to be involved, costs involved if any, limits to confidentiality, the client's responsibilities, psychological investment, etc.[7] Second, one should be particularly aware of the physical conditions at the beginning of the interview to establish an obstacle-free context as quickly as possible. A third concern is to try to make one's genuine interest in the client as explicit as possible by paying complete attention to what the client has to say. Fourth, it is important to begin where the client wishes. The worker may have his own ideas about the problems involved, and may want to begin exploring those areas right away. The client, however, must have the freedom to tell his story in his own way, talking about the things he is feeling and thinking, and having a chance to find a comfortable method of expressing himself to the worker. The worker can always channel the interview at a later time, but at the beginning one does not want to risk stopping communication. Finally, it is important to be especially sensitive to clues the client gives that indicate areas of special meaning and feeling at the beginning of the interview. These clues guide a worker in his further approach to the individual, and suggest areas for further exploration.

The main body of the interview uses five rather specific techniques: listening, observation, questioning, responding, and guiding. Information will be obtained by listening and observing, and these are crucial to the flow of communication. Listening must be done with understanding, accepting silences naturally and allowing the client to find his own means of expression. There are few better ways to stifle communication than breaking in prematurely, keeping up a constant chatter that makes it impossible for anyone to collect his thoughts, or only half-listening, indicating to the speaker that his conversation is not really of interest. Observation is another form of listening, since everyone also speaks nonverbally through his actions.[8] Nonverbal communication often indicates the feeling behind the words, one of the many ways it can supplement verbal communication. Nonverbal communication can be especially valuable in indicating the client's feelings about the interview context itself, as when someone is excessively tense or refuses all offers of hospitality.

A third technique is concerned with questioning. The worker may need to obtain information not spontaneously offered, clarify a point, or probe beyond the point at which the client stopped talking. Questioning should be done sensitively and questions formulated carefully, since harsh questioning into overly sensitive areas can either stop communication or evoke information neither desired nor easily handled. Responding is a way to maintain communication, to put the client at ease, and, where appropriate, to begin to move toward behavior modification. Everyone wants some assurance that his communication has been received, so some small sign indicating that the worker is following what the client is saying is appropriate: perhaps a nod, a word or two, or a request for clarification. In this regard, the worker must be aware of his own nonverbal communication, since wandering eyes, doodling, and yawning are responses which the client is likely to understand all too well.

The client may ask personal questions about the worker, quite natural behavior given the importance the worker may assume in his life. Such questions should be answered simply and honestly, but at the same time the focus should be redirected back to the client.

Responding establishes the give and take through which the client gets the benefit of the worker's skill and professional experience. The worker expresses his feelings, provides information, gives advice, and provides a behavioral model. Responses, however, should not be too quick or too autocratic. The worker must be cautious and flexible in interpreting interview content, careful not to make promises that are unrealistic, and watchful not to eliminate the client's participation.

The last technique, guiding the interview, grows out of the previous four. On the basis of information already given, the worker's interpretation of it, and the need for further information, the interview should remain focused on the problems at hand as seen by the worker and the

---

EXHIBIT 8–1
An Outline of the Interviewing Process

Below is an outline of the interviewing process used in the Social Worker Technician program of the U.S. Army Medical Field Service School at Ft. Sam Houston, San Antonio, Texas. Although it differs in a few details from the above discussion, it is an excellent summary of the major components of interviewing.

A. *Interviewing Concepts*
  1. *Beginning of interview*
    a. Begin where the patient is
    b. Attempt to set patient at ease
    c. Attention to patient's comforts
    d. Efforts to establish rapport

  2. *Interest in patient*
    a. Courtesy
    b. Treating the patient with dignity
    c. Individualize patient
    d. Warmth
    e. Tone of voice
    f. Demonstrated sincerity of involvement
    g. Attentiveness and eye contact
    h. Remaining patient-centered, not note-centered

  3. *Drawing out affect*
    Encourage patient to express feelings, i.e., anger, sadness, warmth, joy, despair, hostility, and others

  4. *Skill in responding to patient's behavior*
    a. Recognition and appropriate use of verbal communication
    b. Recognition and appropriate use of non-verbal behavior

  5. *Clarification and consistency of role*
    a. Self-control of stress, prejudice, and judgmental feelings
    b. Appropriate appearance
    c. Conveying one's purpose in the interview

  6. *Questioning technique*
    a. Proper balance between general and specific questions
    b. Questions which guide the patient in telling story in his own words
    c. Transitions

  7. *Listening techniques*
    Proper use of silence which encourages the patient

  8. *Ending*
    a. Brief summarization of interview content
    b. Opportunity for patient feedback on interview
    c. Proper explanation of future plan/view in regard to the patient

client. Here one must remember the dual components of feeling and objective content, since "facts" should not dominate the feelings that give the facts meaning. Often, for example, a client seems to return again and again to the same point or recount the same story. This makes the maintenance of focus difficult, but it also indicates an area of great importance to the client.

In ending the interview, there are several points to keep in mind. Usually time is limited, and the interview must be ended when the time is up. At the same time, one should try to find a natural stopping point rather than abruptly terminating the interview. It is usually helpful to summarize the progress made in the interview so that the client feels some satisfaction that progress is being made, and gets some indication of the worker's interpretation of the content discussed. So far as possible, the worker should try to insure that the client leaves composed and in good spirits, with some guidelines for handling himself in difficult situations that may arise before the next interview. And finally, the arrangements for the next interview should be clarified, with due care for the convenience of the client (i.e., conditions of good interviewing), assuming that there will be further interviews.

After the interview, the worker should elaborate on any notes taken, making them complete enough to enable him to record accurately the interview's content at the appropriate time. He may also want to fill in some of his own reactions and thoughts by taking a moment after the interview to review it, thinking about meaning and interviewing technique. Diagnosis is the process of interpreting information and developing tentative approaches to solutions. This important step in problem-solving can best be done when the relevant material is fresh in one's mind.

Casework as a Practice Method

Having looked at some of the major points involved in interviewing, each of the major traditional interventive methods in social welfare will be explored, beginning with casework. There are many definitions of casework, reflecting the diversity of approaches possible. The Council on Social Work Education's definition is a concise summary of the basic approach: "a method of social work which intervenes in the psychosocial aspects of a person's life to improve, restore, maintain, or enhance his social functioning by improving his role performance."[9] Florence Hollis has said, "Central to casework is the notion of the person in his situation,"[10] while Helen Harris Perlman talks of a "biopsychosocial whole"[11] providing the focus in casework. Perlman further explains that casework involves a person with a problem coming to a place where a professional uses a method to help him.[12]

Thus it can be seen that casework embodies the goal of improving social functioning, which characterizes social welfare as a whole. It does so by concentrating on one person in some depth, looking at his biological-psychological-social behavior, and looking at the individual in his social context. The caseworker, then, has the client's biological capacity, personality strengths, and social environmental context as possible resources to work with in developing a problem-solving plan.

Before delving into some of the specific parts of the casework method, a look at the pre-casework process, explicated by David Landy, is important.[13] Landy noted that while caseworkers (and social welfare practitioners in general) are intent on the perfection of their practice techniques, they neglect the factors impinging on the client that influence whether or not he will ever get to the agency, and in what state he will arrive, when and if he does. Landy points out that the process of seeking

---

EXHIBIT 8–2
Problem-Solving in Social Welfare

Social welfare basically deals with people with problems coming to skilled professionals who attempt to solve the problems in cooperation with the client—note Perlman's person-problem-place-professional-process description in the text. Problem-solving is not confined to social welfare, of course, and there are many approaches ranging from the most scientific to the most idiosyncratic.* Below is an adaptation of a problem-solving approach used in a training manual for para-professionals in the human services. It is a good summary of the basic principles involved, and may be used by individuals or groups.

1. Define what your problem is. What is your goal and what do you want to accomplish in relation to the situation from which one is starting? Make sure there is agreement on what the problem is before attempting to solve it.

2. Probe for what makes it a problem. Study the obstacles to the attainment of the goals by specifying the causes underlying each obstacle, and by getting all relevant facts.

3. Search for all possible solutions, even unlikely looking ones. Reserve judgment and criticism until the next step.

4. Test the potential solutions. If you understand your problem well, you can now begin to pick out the most promising solutions. Weigh them carefully in the light of the facts, not prejudices.

5. Choose the best solution. In groups, it should be an informed, democratic decision.

6. Map out a plan of action to put your solution to work. You may have to develop a comprehensive or long-range plan, with "easy stages." It should be a realistic plan with a good chance of successful execution. In groups, make use of the potential contributions of all members.

7. Take a pause for appraisal and evaluation, which may bring out new facts that alter the solution or possibly cause you to set new goals. Problem-solving is a continuous process.

From Janet Rosenberg, *Breakfast: Two Jars of Paste* (Cleveland: Case Western Reserve University, 1969), p. 28. Used by permission of Community Development Institute of Southern Illinois University.
*Guy Swanson, *Social Change* (Glenview, Ill.: Scott, Foresman, 1971), pp. 150–153.

help is often difficult and complex. It begins with a recognition that some-thing is wrong, but such recognition is hampered by the common ten-dency to deny failing in some aspect of our lives. This is encouraged by a societal value system that preaches self-reliance and the belief that in-dividuals can and should solve their own problems. Under these circum-stances, it is not surprising that people often seek help only when they are desperate, and when the problems are so complex that they are very difficult to solve. Seeking help is admitting that one has "failed" in coping with his problems, a situation others may also become aware of. The stigma attached to seeking help is one reason why people tend to turn first to those in their indigenous environment for help: family, friends, or clergy. Here, problems can be discussed informally. Entry into the professional social service network implies that the problem is serious.

Landy also notes that the act of seeking help places the applicant in a dependent position and requires that he relinquish some autonomy (answering endless questions, having to travel to an inconvenient agency location, keeping appointments, etc.). The role of the helped is often an uncomfortable one, involving the confrontation with painful memories, unpleasant insights into oneself and others, and emotional stress. A person with problems may not be at all eager to temporarily endure more stress in order to achieve ultimate solutions. Talcott Parsons, a sociologist, has analyzed the role of those having a physical illness. It seems very relevant in understanding the problems of the person seeking help in our culture, emphasizing the rights and obligations incurred in the process.[14] Landy's point, then, is to remind the social welfare practitioner that ask-ing for help is a major step, and one that is likely to be stressful for a client. He suggests that the casework process ought to include the pre-casework experience in a planned way.*

Scott Briar notes three basic components of the casework process: a therapeutic (clinical) function; a social broker function; and an advocacy function (including social policy formulation).[15] The therapeutic approach in casework has traditionally had a one worker–one client focus. The worker helps the client to interpret and classify his problems, and then explore possible ways to solve or adapt to them. The one-to-one inter-action in casework is thought to lead to a "relationship," which Rapoport notes "is a rather fuzzy concept."[16] A meaningful relationship was com-monly defined rather psychoanalytically, including the presence of trans-ference and a "corrective emotional experience."[17]

More recently, casework has shifted toward a more crisis-intervention approach. This has led to a reexamination of the meaning of the relation-ship, and Rapoport's statement reflects a new perspective. "Perhaps the component of attachment in relationship is less crucial than the degree of involvement . . . ," with more stress on "cognitive restructuring and un-

---

*The outreach role (discussed in the next chapter) and the concept of neighborhood ser-vice centers attempt to deal with this.

linking the present context from past concerns."[18] Rapoport is supported by Meyer, who sees casework as being primarily concerned with the crises commonly occurring at transition points in the life cycle.[19] The concept of the relationship is founded in a psychoanalytic approach to human behavior, but a variety of power bases for a relationship may also be empirically identified, each quite different in its effects and uses. The traditional view of the casework relationship relies on identification as its main power base, although such bases of power as legitimacy, expertise, and even reward and punishment are also pertinent.

The therapeutic component of casework has focused on the behavior change that would eliminate a problem, as well as the counseling to help a client adapt to his problem if it could not be solved. Some have criticized casework for helping people to adapt to problems,[20] yet it seems realistic to see some problems as essentially unsolvable. A crippled person cannot regain his original capacities, and this kind of problem must be accepted. Casework would include getting such a person to realistically accept his limitations as well as positive efforts to minimize the range of such limitations through physical therapy and vocational rehabilitation. Casework should reach for as many problem solutions as possible, but there will always be persons who, unfortunately, have no choice but to accept certain problem conditions.

Recognizing the caseworker's responsibilities for achieving behavior change as far as possible, the social broker and advocacy functions have been increasingly stressed. Social brokerage entails serving as an intermediary between the client and existing services he needs; Meyer feels this will be the major function of the caseworker of the future.[21] Brokerage facilitates change by maximizing the resources the client has available for use, and implicitly recognizes the dependence of the individual on his social environment. A mother whose children manifest behavior problems may be faced with inadequate housing, no husband and father, lack of protection from criminal influences in the neighborhood, and so on. In such a situation, the caseworker may wish to review the mother's personality resources and child-rearing techniques. However, he would also want to explore more adequate housing resources, such as public housing; possible resources to provide a male influence for the children, such as Big Brothers or the Police Athletic League; recreational facilities to offer the children a wholesome play environment, such as the "Y" or a settlement house; etc. Here the caseworker is attacking a problem by tying his client into the full range of resources available to help solve her problem.

In cases where adequate resources simply do not exist, the caseworker may need to assume an advocacy role. As an advocate, he is concerned with "uncovering both incipient and unmet needs and blazing a trail of advocacy toward new methods of meeting those needs."[22] The advocacy role acknowledges that each individual is dependent on his social environment even more than the broker role does. The advocate

EXHIBIT 8–3
The Advocate and Social Policy Formulation

Harry Specht talks of the formulation of social policy as one part of the caseworker-advocate's task. He summarizes his discussion in the chart reproduced here, which shows how the advocate role can proceed from a perceived need to an institutional solution, and how this role relates to professional roles, tasks, and institutional resources.

Stages of Policy Formulation

Stage	Tasks	Institutional Resources	Professional Roles
1. Identification of problem	1. Case-finding, recording, discovery of gaps in service	1. Agency	1. Practitioner
2. Analysis	2. Data-gathering, analysis	2. Research organization	2. Researcher
3. Informing the public	3. Dramatization, public relations, communications (writing, speaking)	3. Public relations unit, communications media, voluntary organization	3. Muckraker, community organizer, public relations man
4. Development of policy goals (involvement of other agencies)	4. Creating strategy, program analysis	4. Planning bodies, voluntary associations	4. Planner, community organizer, administrator
5. Building public support	5. Developing leadership, achieving consensus	5. Voluntary associations, political parties, legislative and agency committees	5. Lobbyist, community organizer, public relations man
6. Legislation	6. Drafting legislation, program design	6. Legislative bodies, agency boards	6. Legislative analyst, planner
7. Implementation	7. Programs-organizing, administration	7. Courts, agencies	7. Administrator, practitioner, lawyer
8. Evaluation, assessment	8. Case-finding, recording, discovery of gaps in service, gathering data	8. Agency, research organization	8. Practitioner

From Harry Specht, "Casework Practice and Social Policy Formulation," *Social Work* 13 (January 1968): 44. Used with permission of National Association of Social Workers.

believes that some individual change can only be accomplished by changing the environment that is creating the problems or inhibiting constructive change. For example, when unemployment rates are high, and when a society has moved beyond the need for extensive unskilled labor, the two forces combine to push a large number of unskilled persons into involuntary unemployment and poverty. The solutions lie in changes in societal values regarding work, in alleviating those conditions that create unskilled persons, and in a public assistance system whose level of payments keeps people from living in poverty. These are changes that cannot be accomplished by talking to those with the problems. They must be solved by an advocate willing to work in the appropriate economic and political systems.

Group Work as a Practice Method

"When one gets down to the central core of what really happens that makes the group experience so meaningful and so useful, one discovers the simple truth that people with similar interests, similar concerns, or similar problems can help each other in ways that are significantly different from the ways in which a worker can help them in a one-to-one relationship. This is not to say that the group method is better—simply that it is different."[23] Put another way, "the group is the mediator between the individual and society. . . . Man can join with others in an effort to control what is happening to him."[24] The differences between casework and group work begin to emerge: (1) casework is usually a one-to-one relationship, while group work involves a worker and a small group of clients; (2) the worker-client relationship is the important process in casework, while in group work the group itself is the context and the process through which change occurs; and (3) casework and group work are methods with different requirements, and are most effective in the solution of different types of problems.

Group work builds on casework in that the group worker uses casework skills in relating to individual group members. It goes beyond casework when such relationships are supplemented by the interaction between group members, and as the structure of group activity generates social resources much greater than those available in a two-person group. Casework is more suited to problems involving extensive data-gathering, the discussion of strongly held feelings, and individual resource utilization. Group work is particularly effective in teaching interaction skills, achieving group goals, and providing recreation opportunities.

The American Association of Group Workers defines group work as follows:

The group worker enables various groups to function in such a way that both group interaction and program activities contribute to the growth of the individual and the achievement of desirable social goals.[25]

The basic professional goal of group work is helping people function, and many aspects of the group process may be used to attain this goal. Wilson draws a distinction between groups with two distinct purposes:

in [the task-oriented group], the group-enabler's primary responsibility is to support the group to accomplish its task; in [the growth-oriented group], the enabler's primary responsibility is to help members to use the group experience to resolve problems which are interfering with their personal growth and their social adjustment.[26]

Groups may exist, then, to accomplish group goal attainment or the social enjoyment and enrichment of its members. Wilson's emphasis on primary function suggests that one function may be dominant at any given time. However, she also implicitly recognizes that there are elements of both goals in all groups, as one would expect from the small-group literature reviewed earlier. Wilson also speaks of the professional person as an enabler in the group process. This concept is of great importance in interventive methods, and grows out of the professional value of client self-determination. Rather than imposing his judgment on the client, be it an individual or group, the worker helps the client identify and develop knowledge and skills appropriate for the attainment of his goals.

Elaborating somewhat on Wilson, groups may be seen as focusing around member enjoyment (interest), the attainment of a specific goal through concerted group organization (concerns), or the use of the group as a therapeutic milieu (problems). As would be expected on the basis of small-group theory, different kinds of groups will have different structural characteristics. Vinter suggests that one needs to examine the following structural properties of a group to be aware of its purpose and potential: the social organization of the group patterns, roles, and statuses; activities, tasks, and operative processes; group culture, norms, and values; and the group's relationship to its external environment.[27] An example of the utility of this kind of analysis is Rapoport's identification of the following structural characteristics of therapeutic (problem-oriented) groups: democratization of decision-making; permissiveness in the discussion of behavioral problems; communalistic, tight-knit, intimate relationships; and confrontation, the use of the group as social reality.[28]

Such a structural analysis helps to understand how the group affects individual behavior, and helps identify goals consistent with the group's structure. In both Vinter and Rapoport the importance of external reality for the group is emphasized. No matter how significant the group may become for its members, they ultimately must transfer their new-found skills to the larger social world beyond the group. Even the group itself is affected by the environment in which it exists. For example, there may be organizational restraints in therapeutic groups, limited recreational facilities for pleasure groups, and a lack of appropriate community structures for groups seeking to achieve goals.[29]

Tropp attempts to integrate these elements of group structure and functioning into an analytical framework that focuses on group purpose ("why it is formed"), group function ("what the group members are supposed to do to carry out the purpose"), and group structure (how the group will do what it is supposed to be doing).[30] He proposes that purpose, function, and structure be used as tools with which to evaluate interventive approaches in group work. The approaches that Tropp considers the most common in contemporary practice are: group education, including orientation and information programs aimed at a group of people with a common interest (such as informing parents about adolescent drug use); group counseling, where a group discusses a problem common to all its members (as when parents of retarded children meet to discuss ways of coping with their special childrearing problems); group psychotherapy, which is "a group method for the treatment of individuals with psychiatric disorders, and . . . aims at achieving basic personality change, which none of the other group approaches attempts"[31] (a very specialized therapeutic approach); group recreation, where group members enjoy informal, play-oriented interaction; and social group work, defined as "the process known as group-goal achieving . . . , [which] aims at the full utilization of forces in group life to bring about social growth in individual members."[32] Tropp concludes with the following: "The group work method thus includes, in addition to goal-achieving by the group, the dimensions of group recreation, group education, and group counseling, but any of these methods can be used separately."[33] In concluding this brief discussion of group work, the range of goals this method may be used to attain is worthy of emphasis, as is the relationship of group work to many of the skills discussed under casework. However, in addition to casework skills, the group worker must deal with the many social processes involved in group structure and interaction.[34]

Community Organization as a Practice Method

Since communities are types of groups, community organization may be seen as an expanded form of group work. The latter typically deals with groups of fifteen and under, and the former with larger groups functioning in community contexts. This size distinction has inevitable implications: therapeutic goals are more difficult to attain, while task-oriented goals are more feasible. However, the attainment of goals assumes that a structure exists through which such goals may be sought, and this may not be the case in many communities. This gives rise to two major thrusts in community organization: (1) a task focus, in which the attainment of a community need is emphasized (a new playground, more social service agencies, political redistricting, etc.); and (2) a process focus, where the emphasis is on the building of viable, effective community structures in which people can work to accomplish their goals.[35] This latter focus is sometimes called "community development" in an effort to distinguish between the two major parts of community organization.[36] Actually the task and process distinctions which tend to surface in community organization underlie all social welfare practice. Any interventive method attempts to solve specific problems while also trying to make it possible for the individual or individuals involved to be better able to solve the problems of the future.

Murray Ross's definition can be used to summarize community organization. He sees it as "a process by which a community identifies its needs or objectives, orders (or ranks) these needs or objectives, develops the confidence and will to work at these needs or objectives, finds the resources (internal and/or external) to deal with these needs or objectives, takes action in respect to them, and in so doing extends and develops cooperative and collaborative attitudes and practices in the community."[37] In discussing the nature of communities in an earlier chapter, it was seen that community organization actually involves working with shifting population groups. Their basis of organization may be of many kinds, or nonexistent, and they may be strongly influenced by forces outside the community. These factors intimate that the tranquility of Ross's definition of community organization may be unrealistic, although the general goals of identifying problems and resources for purposes of community action are sound.

There are many ways to approach the process of community organization; the following is comprehensive enough to encompass most others. First, the community must be identified. Drawing on earlier content, this must include geographical as well as functional dimensions. Second, community resources need to be identified; they may be of many kinds.[38] The groups within the community have their own social, physical, and organizational resources, which may be of potential use to the community at large. The geographical characteristics of the community create certain kinds of potential for recreation, industry, services, and so on. The physical organization is also crucial for the juxtaposition of various kinds of resources with the needs that may exist in the community. The community power structure can be a functional resource usable by social welfare practitioners, although the relationship of social welfare agencies to the community structure is an important intervening consideration.[39] The question of types of community power structures is a hotly debated one in the social science literature, but whatever the structure in a given community, those individuals who have leadership positions or potential can be of great utility to the community organizer.[40]

A third step in the community organization process is identifying the problems that exist and for which there is a realistic chance of solution using community organization principles. Given that communities are commonly diverse in social composition, the various community components are likely to have their own definitions of existing problems, as well as their own order of priority for problem solution. In assessing stated problems, one wants to be sure to give all community groups a chance to express their views. The extent to which there is uniformity or competing views on significant problems (and the order of priority in their solution) can then be assessed. After having done this, the practitioner will want to: (1) examine the extent to which there may be unexpressed problems which must be confronted before the expressed problems can be solved; and (2) the possible existence of problems ignored by the community. The question of problems ignored by the community can be a delicate one, since the worker should not try to force his views on a community. However, he may also recognize the potential impact of existing behavior and organization more fully than community members, he is less bound by community and subgroup values that may block community recognition of certain problems, and he is more likely to be concerned with the effects of community functioning on individuals and groups with no avenue of self-expression. The degree to which the worker chooses to introduce his perception of existing problems is part of his strategy (discussed below), although he can always try to get the community to recognize a previously unrecognized problem, without his direct intervention.

Having studied the community, the worker begins the actual organization process. It is common to begin with a clearly specified task that has a high probability of successful accomplishment. This helps establish the belief that change is possible, and draws people onto a "winning team."[41] In some respects, this can be seen as a community-level expression of the value "start where the client is." Then one must begin with a workable group, those who are willing to participate and who have relevance to the tasks at hand. It is important not to alienate those not participating at the outset. The initial organization should be as nonantagonistic as possible, and leave the way open for the participation of others at a later time as that becomes feasible and desirable. With a task set and a working group organized, the strategy for attainment of the established goal becomes crucial. For some time community organizers automatically tended to think in terms of cooperative and conciliatory strategies that were clearly within the established community power structures. Rocking the boat was to be avoided for several reasons: fear that insurgent groups did not have the power to force the power structure to change; fear that the social welfare agencies involved in power tactics would be punished through withdrawal of community sanction and funds; and an ingrained respect for due process of law.

Several significant events changed these perceptions, and helped to make Ross's view of community organization as a tranquil, orderly process somewhat limited. First, as Michael Harrington and others pointed out, after decades of sporadic social reform, major social problems remained. Second, the black revolution made it abundantly clear that aggressive community organization brought results that more passive, agreeable methods did not. Third, the black experience also stimulated more direct federal involvement in what were essentially community organization activities so that the participants would be given some protection from local community power structure retribution. Fourth, the swelling magnitude of need threatened to topple many existing programs unless newer programs, more efficient and more acceptable to the recipients, were developed. Finally, the social welfare professions recognized that human need transcended job security, so that the risk of retribution against agencies and practitioners had to be run if programs consonant with professional values were to be obtained.[42] Community organization thus rapidly expanded its range of possible strategies to adapt to a variety of new community conditions and needs.

Ralph Kramer, in his *Participation of the Poor,* examines the experiences of several San Francisco Bay area communities in promoting maximum feasible participation of the poor in community action.[43] Out of these experiences, he develops three strategies: collaboration, cam-

---

EXHIBIT 8–4
Strategies and Tactics

Specht presents the following chart in his article on "Disruptive Tactics." It relates strategies (each of which he calls a "mode of intervention") with specific behavioral tactics. It gives a concrete idea of the actual practitioner behaviors one could use.

Mode of Intervention	Tactics	Mode of Intervention	Tactics
1. Collaborative	a. joint action	3. Contest or Disruption	a. clash of position within accepted norms
	b. cooperation		
	c. education		b. violation of normative behavior (manners)
2. Campaign	a. compromise		
	b. arbitration		c. violation of legal norms
	c. negotiation		
	d. bargaining	4. Violence	a. deliberate attempts to harm
	e. mild coercion		
			b. guerilla warfare
			c. deliberate attempts to take over government by force

From Harry Specht, "Disruptive Tactics," *Social Work* 14 (April 1969): 9. Used with permission of National Association of Social Workers.

paign, and contest,[44] which Specht extends to include violence.[45] (1) Collaboration is rational and democratic, with an attempt made to get the facts and reconcile viewpoints. Common interests are assumed, and a problem-solving model is appropriate. This strategy clearly falls within Ross's definition, and is usable in many instances where it is simply a matter of getting a community to make choices about common goals and means. (2) A campaign is a planned effort to overcome apathy and moderate opposition when there is a difference of opinion on issues. It is assumed that agreement is possible, but that its attainment will involve an exchange of valued resources in return for concessions, rather than just calling for discussion. (3) The contest involves the temporary abandonment of the quest for consensus in order to further one's own side of an issue, despite opposition of other groups. This is accomplished by coercive threats of disruption, and the pressure of public support and attention. It is used when there is dissent (no congruence on values or interests), and agreement is not expected. (4) Specht sees violence as a relevant strategy when there is a need for the reconstruction of the entire system.

Important parts of the strategy decision concern the worker's role and the social welfare agency's organizational goals. Rein and Morris look at the latter,[46] while Grosser examines the former.[47] Grosser sees four possible worker roles: enabler, broker, advocate, and activist. The enabler role is "the traditional stance of the community organizer,"[48] recognizing that the community organization practitioner avoids imposing his ideas on the community. Self-help is emphasized instead. As a role it is limited in its activism, and seems to be most compatible with a collaborative strategy. The broker role sees the worker as an intermediary between service structures and their users. In community organization contexts, the community is both service structure and user, with brokerage also needed between the community and external structures. The advocate role is described as "a partisan in a social conflict, and his expertise is available exclusively to serve client interests. The impartiality of the enabler and the functionalism of the broker are absent here."[49] The broker and advocate roles seem most compatible with a campaign strategy. The activist encourages client groups to take direct action to attain their goals, and is most compatible with a contest strategy. For agencies, workers, and communities, then, appropriate roles and strategies must reflect community organization goals.[50]

The fifth and final community organization technique is to follow through to make sure that the community neither becomes too easily satisfied nor prematurely discouraged. When some goals have been attained, there is a tendency to relax and feel that the battle has been won. Lack of goal attainment may lead to discouragement and lack of interest. In both cases momentum is lost, and the community organization enterprise put in jeopardy. Once momentum is lost, it may be doubly hard to regain in the future, so the practitioner needs to be especially sensitive to premature cessation of effort and momentum. Rosenberg notes at least eleven barriers to success of which the community organization worker must be aware.[51] They are:

1. Passivity, whereby the brains, decisions, or influence of others are relied on.

2. Apathy, when people feel that they don't belong and nobody cares about them.

3. Prestige-seekers, where self-glorification is more important than the end result.

4. Superiority complex, in which groups refuse to cooperate with others said to be inferior in some way.

5. Vested interests, when change is resisted because it might be personally disadvantageous.

6. Intense specialization, leading to fragmented tasks, specialists, and overadministration.

7. Time shortage, in which responsibility is avoided due to other commitments.

8. Autocratic approach, where democracy is spoken but not enacted.

9. Inferiority complexes, lack of confidence by an individual or a community.

10. No skills, so basic information is lacking.

11. Dreamless peace, the obstacle of no vision of a better community.

Hopefully at this point several ways of avoiding these problems occur to the reader on the basis of previously discussed theory and interventive methods.

Conclusion

Concluding this discussion of community organization as an interventive method, it is ultimately a combination of casework, group work, and larger group processes. It is similar to casework in its focus on behavior change, and the necessity of dealing with the individuals who make up the community. It is like group work in its use of group processes, and its focus on the group as a context that can change individual behavior. Yet it is beyond either casework or group work in its involvement in large social structures and policy-making. It may be said, then, that the scope of community organization is greater than either one of the other two methods discussed, but that the basic interaction skills are similar. Seeing the caseworker and group worker roles as reaching out into the client's environment inevitably includes some type of community involvement. It is precisely this overlap between casework, group work, and community organization that has led professionals to rethink the whole field of interventive methods, raising the basic question of whether there might not be a set of skills that all social welfare practitioners use regardless of their context. Some of the current thinking along these lines is the concern of the next chapter.

REFERENCES

1. Additional methods, such as research and supervision, are discussed in Ruth Smalley, *Theory for Social Work Practice* (New York: Columbia University Press, 1967).
2. Basic references for interviewing in social welfare are Annette Garrett, *Interviewing: Its Principles and Methods* (New York: Family Service Association of America, 1942); and Elizabeth de Schweinitz and Karl de Schweinitz, *Interviewing in the Social Services* (London: National Institute for Social Work Training, 1962).
3. Elizabeth and Karl de Schweinitz, op. cit., pp. 9–11.
4. Ibid., pp. 18–23.
5. This discussion of interviewing principles draws heavily on ideas in Garrett, op. cit.
6. Ibid.
7. See Lydia Rapoport, "Crisis-Oriented Short-Term Casework," in Klenk and Ryan, *The Practice of Social Work* (Belmont, Cal.: Wadsworth, 1970), p. 108.
8. A good reference for nonverbal communication is Edward T. Hall, *The Silent Language* (Garden City: Doubleday, 1959).
9. Russell Smith and Dorothy Zeitz, *American Social Welfare Institutions* (New York: John Wiley, 1970), p. 249.
10. Ibid.
11. Helen Harris Perlman, *Social Casework: A Problem-Solving Process* (Chicago: University of Chicago Press, 1957), pp. 6–7.
12. Ibid.
13. David Landy, "Problems of the Person Seeking Help in our Culture," in Mayer Zald, *Social Welfare Institutions* (New York: John Wiley, 1965).
14. Talcott Parsons, *The Social System* (New York: Free Press, 1951), pp. 285–291, 476.
15. Scott Briar, "The Current Crisis in Social Work," in Klenk and Ryan, op. cit., pp. 91–97.
16. Lydia Rapoport, op. cit., p. 112.
17. Ibid.
18. Ibid.
19. Carol Meyer, *Social Work Practice* (New York: Free Press, 1970), pp. 87–90.
20. Scott Briar, "The Current Crisis in Social Casework," in Klenk and Ryan, op. cit., p. 91.
21. Meyer, op. cit., pp. 83–104.
22. Harry Specht, "Casework Practice and Social Policy Formulation," in Klenk and Ryan, op. cit., p. 131.

23. Emanuel Tropp, "The Group: In Life and in Social Work," in Klenk and Ryan, op. cit., pp. 176–177.
24. Janet Rosenberg, *Breakfast: Two Jars of Paste* (Cleveland: Case-Western Reserve University, 1969), p. 93.
25. Reproduced in Gisela Konopka, *Social Group Work: A Helping Process* (Englewood Cliffs, N.J.: Prentice-Hall, 1963), p. 14.
26. Gertrude Wilson, "Social Group Work: Trends and Developments," in Klenk and Ryan, op. cit., p. 170.
27. Smith and Zeitz, op. cit., pp. 253–254.
28. Ibid., p. 255.
29. The effect of the group's environment on its functioning is discussed in Lawrence Shulman, *A Casebook of Social Work with Groups: The Mediating Model* (New York: Council on Social Work Education, 1968), esp. pp. 23–30.
30. Emanuel Tropp, "The Group: In Life and in Social Work," in Klenk and Ryan, op. cit., p. 179.
31. Ibid., p. 182.
32. Ibid, p. 183. This total discussion is based on pp. 180–183.
33. Ibid., p. 183.
34. See Robert Vinter, "The Essential Components of Group Work Practice," in Paul Weinberger, *Perspectives on Social Welfare: An Introductory Anthology* (New York: Macmillan, 1969).
35. See Arthur Dunham, *The New Community Organization* (New York: Thomas Y. Crowell, 1970), pp. 4, 86. His relationship goals would be included under process goals in the framework being used here.
36. For a more detailed discussion of the distinction between community organization and community development, see ibid., pp. 175–179.
37. Murray Ross, *Community Organization: Theory and Principles* (New York: Harper & Row, 1955), p. 39.
38. An excellent discussion of practical approaches to identifying community resources appears in Sy Kahn, *How People Get Power* (New York: McGraw-Hill, 1970), pp. 11–20.
39. See Mayer Zald, "Organizations as Politics: An Analysis of Community Organization Agencies," in Ralph Kramer and Harry Specht, *Readings in Community Organization Practice* (Englewood Cliffs, N.J.: Prentice-Hall, 1969), pp. 143–154.
40. Kahn, op. cit., pp. 21–38. See also Richard Edgar, *Urban Power and Social Welfare* (Beverly Hills: Sage, 1970).
41. Ibid., pp. 57–67, esp. p. 62.
42. See Irwin Saunders, "Professional Roles in Planned Change," in Kramer and Specht, pp. 269–284, esp. p. 277.
43. Ralph Kramer, *Participation of the Poor* (Englewood Cliffs, N.J.: Prentice-Hall, 1969), op. cit., pp. 182–186.
44. Ibid., p. 184.
45. Harry Specht, "Disruptive Tactics," in Kramer and Specht, op. cit., pp. 372–386.
46. Martin Rein and Robert Morris, "Goals, Structures, and Strategies for Community Change," in Kramer and Specht, op. cit., pp. 188–200.
47. Charles Grosser, "Community Development Programs Serving the Urban Poor," in Klenk and Ryan, op. cit., pp. 266–275.

48. Ibid., p. 269.
49. Ibid., p. 271.
50. For further elaboration, see Kahn, op. cit., pp. 69–113.
51. Rosenberg, op. cit., pp. 115–116.

SELECTED READINGS

There is a huge body of literature on traditional interventive methods. Much of it is vague and ideological. Among the clearest and most seminal in my opinion are the following:

Banaka, William. *Training in Depth Interviewing.* New York: Harper & Row, 1971.
Combs, Arthur et al. *Helping Relationships: Basic Concepts for the Helping Professions.* Boston: Allyn and Bacon, 1971.
Frank, Jerome. *Persuasion and Healing.* Baltimore: Johns Hopkins Press, 1961.
Garrett, Annette. *Interviewing: Its Principles and Methods.* New York: Family Service Association of America, 1942.
Hollis, Florence. *Casework: A Psychosocial Therapy.* 2nd ed. New York: Random House, 1972.
Klenk, Robert, and Robert Ryan, eds. *The Practice of Social Work.* Belmont, Cal.: Wadsworth, 1970.
Konopka, Gisela. *Social Group Work: A Helping Process.* Englewood Cliffs, N.J.: Prentice-Hall, 1963.
Landy, David. "Problems of the Person Seeking Help in Our Culture," in Mayer Zald, ed., *Social Welfare Institutions.* New York: John Wiley, 1965.
Smalley, Ruth. *Theory for Social Work Practice.* New York: Columbia University Press, 1967.
Kramer, Ralph, and Harry Specht, eds. *Readings in Community Organization Practice.* Englewood Cliffs, N.J.: Prentice-Hall, 1969.

NEW PRACTICE PERSPECTIVES

The need for more effective practice methods will be explored in this chapter. New approaches to methods may be of two kinds. One seeks to reformulate the way in which problems and practice techniques are related. This draws heavily on three areas: (1) the theory underlying the causes of personal and social problems; (2) matching job tasks with client needs; and (3) the specification of levels of professional training that are needed to produce practitioners competent to perform the tasks that have been identified. The second approach focuses on the actual practice techniques themselves—how to achieve more effectively a given practice goal. Much of this chapter will be devoted to the first task, a fundamental reexamination of the way in which practice tasks are defined, and how practitioners are prepared to perform them. The second task—finding more effective practice skills—will receive somewhat less attention. This is partly because solutions are still few in number. It is also because many of the practice skills being proposed are not really new. Much of the traditional practice approach is being modified and broken down into more logically consistent and empirically verifiable components. What makes the use of these components new is the way in which they are conceptualized and juxtaposed, and that is a function of the first task of reconceptualizing the whole structure of social welfare tasks and the training to perform them.

Nowhere is the need for a future orientation more necessary than in the area of practice methods. The changes in the social welfare institution discussed earlier present the welfare practitioner with an unprecedented demand for practice competence and flexibility. The problems of contemporary society, the resources available to solve them, and the organization of professional activity are creating major changes in the dimensions of the welfare practitioner's role, changes that are likely to continue for some time. The traditional practice methods must be mastered, since new practice techniques will build solidly upon them. However, new methods must also be sought, as well as new ways to organize methods to more effectively perform the tasks that comprise the work of social welfare. This chapter, then, is an attempt to ease the transition into the new training and work contexts that are likely to confront the social welfare professional of the future.

New Practice Perspectives

Teare and McPheeters,[1] and Bisno,[2] have cogently discussed the problems of the traditional approach to interventive methods. They note that focusing on methods encourages a restricted view of problems and solutions, and tends to lead the worker to be more concerned with his own methodical and bureaucratic problems than with the needs of the people he is trying to help. Bisno emphasizes these problems in the traditional approach by quoting Kaplan on the "law of the instrument":

I call it the law of the instrument, *and it may be formulated as follows: Give a small boy a hammer, and he will find that everything he encounters needs pounding. It comes as no particular surprise to discover that a scientist formulates problems in a way which requires for their solution just those techniques in which he himself is especially skilled.*[3]

Bisno, in suggesting that the "law of the instrument" is applicable to social welfare practice, is saying that a worker's identification with one interventive method tends to limit his view of appropriate intervention techniques to that method. He feels that it would be more productive to begin with an analysis of the problem, and include all the possible ways to solve such a problem. Aside from the practical limitations of the "law of the instrument," Bisno also provides a thoughtful analysis of some of the theoretical problems growing out of the traditional approach.[4]

In developing a new perspective on interventive methods, Teare and McPheeters begin with the problem rather than the job. Once the problems have been defined and categorized, they focus on the tasks that could help to solve these problems. Then a rational way to group the designated tasks is developed.[5] This approach focuses on client needs, and allows the professional to clearly distinguish between the needs of the client, the professional, and the organization, all of which are important in the interventive process. The difference in approach, then, between the traditional and the newer perspectives on interventive methods lies in the fact that the former often forces a problem into the method, while the latter tries to shape a method to solve any given problem.

Traditional marital counseling, for example, is commonly done by psychiatrically oriented professionals who talk to the couple and possibly their children in an office setting. The newer approch might try to identify the components of the marital problem and use a range of approaches. These could include psychiatric counseling, reaching out into the community to find or develop recreational outlets for the children, helping the husband find job training or better employment to ease financial burdens, or mobilizing the couple and their neighbors to improve housing, since these issues can all be components of what is termed a marital problem. This comparison does not imply that traditional methods have been ineffective, but it does suggest that in many cases new perspectives can approach intervention in a more task-focused, flexible, creative manner than traditional approaches.

In attempting to identify the major problem areas requiring social welfare intervention, Teare and McPheeters list the following: health, education, employment, integrity of the family, money and financial resources, and integrity of the neighborhood and community.[6] The obstacles creating problems in these areas can be any of the following: deficiencies within individuals ("lack of education or training, inappropriate values, personal instability, poor physical health"); environmental deficiencies ("lack of resources or lack of access to them"); rigid or inequitable laws, regulations, policies, and practices (discriminatory practices, restrictive eligibility requirements, fraudulent contracts); and results of catastrophes.[7] Given these major problem areas and obstacles, four general functions of social welfare for meeting the identified needs are suggested by Teare and McPheeters: (1) promoting positive social functioning (promoting self-actualization); (2) preventing problems from occurring (providing accessible resources and developing skills in using these resources); (3) providing treatment (helping persons solve their problems); and (4) providing maintenance support for those unable to solve their problems.[8]

With the major problem areas, obstacles, and general goals of intervention specified, Teare and McPheeters develop nine "major objectives to social welfare activity," which can in turn be translated into specific tasks and ultimately clusters of tasks:[9]

1. Detection—"to identify the individuals or groups who are experiencing difficulty [at crisis] or who are in danger of becoming vulnerable [at risk] . . . [and] to detect and identify conditions in the environment that are contributing to the problems or are raising the level of risk."[10]

2. Linkage or connection—"to steer people toward the existing services which can be of benefit to them. . . . A further objective is to link elements of the service system with one another."[11]

3. Advocacy—"to fight for the rights and dignity of people in need of help . . . [including] fighting for services on behalf of a single client, and . . . fighting for changes in laws, regulations, etc. on behalf of a whole class of persons or segment of the society. Therefore, advocacy aims at removing the obstacles or barriers that prevent people from exercising their rights or receiving the benefits and using the resources they need."[12]

4. Mobilization—"to assemble and energize existing groups, resources, organizations, and structures, or to create new groups, organizations or resources and bring them to bear to deal with problems that exist, or to prevent problems from developing."[13]

5. Instruction-Education—"to convey and impart information and knowledge and to develop various kinds of skills."[14]

6. Behavior Change and Modification—"to bring about change in the behavior patterns, habits and perceptions of individuals or groups."[15]

7. Information Processing—"the collection, classification, and analysis of data generated within the social welfare environment."[16]

8. *Administration*—"the management of a facility, an organization, a program, or a service unit."[17]

9. *Continuing Care*—"to provide for persons who need on-going support or care on an extended and continuing basis . . . in an institutional setting or on an out-patient basis."[18]

In looking at the problem areas of concern to social welfare practitioners, and some of the obstacles commonly encountered in dealing with them, Teare and McPheeters set the parameters within which interventive methods must be effective. They then go on to discuss general functions of social welfare within these parameters, and finally the specific objectives of interventive methods. It should be clear that they have not yet spoken of actual methods to be used in achieving the objectives, although by looking at the objectives one can see that a social welfare practitioner's tools must give him the following skills: (1) to identify needs in the community; (2) to link those in need with services available; (3) to insure that services are accessible to those in need; (4) to utilize all possible community resources; (5) to participate in the development of new services; (6) to administer and monitor services; and (7) to change or support behavior as appropriate. Since these objectives are not mutually exclusive (e.g., a social welfare practitioner may change behavior by helping a client find and use available services), the specific methods used to achieve these objectives may be grouped into varying combinations, depending on the objectives being sought. This introduces the need not only to specify the methods necessary to attain professional objectives, but also the need to consider ways in which objectives and methods may be grouped into clusters.

Teare and McPheeters identify twelve "roles," which will be referred to here as methods since they are essentially types of intervention. These methods include the following:[19]

1. *Outreach worker*—reaching out into the community to identify need and follow up referrals to service contexts.

2. *Broker*—knowing services available and making sure those in need reach the appropriate services.

3. *Advocate*—helping specific clients obtain services when they might otherwise be rejected, and helping to expand services to cover more needy persons.

4. *Evaluation*—evaluation of needs and resources, generating alternatives for meeting needs, and making decisions between alternatives.

5. *Teacher*—teaching facts and skills.

6. *Mobilizer*—helping to develop new services.

7. *Behavior changer*—changing specific parts of a client's behavior.

8. *Consultant*—working with other professionals to help them be more effective in providing services.

9. *Community planner*—helping community groups to plan effectively for the community's social welfare needs.

10. *Care giver*—providing supportive services to those who cannot fully solve their problems and meet their own needs.

11. *Data manager*—collection and analysis of data for decision-making purposes.

12. *Administrator*—the activities necessary to plan and implement a program of services.

Having developed the above roles or methods, Teare and McPheeters do not suggest clusters of methods to achieve any of their earlier noted objectives. They do note that in general a practitioner would use several of these methods (a generalist) rather than specializing in only one (a specialist).[20] They seem to intend that their method clusters remain flexible, consistent with their assertion that an interventive plan must be built around the desired objectives. In their words, "the rationale for grouping roles into single jobs will depend to some degree on client needs and to some degree on agency goals."[21]

As much as Teare and McPheeters' methods should remain closely related to objectives, there is both theoretical and practical justification for looking at some of the method clusters that could be expected to occur with some frequency. From a theoretical perspective, the methods clearly grow out of the objectives sought, so any time a specified type of objective is sought, the methods appropriate to that objective will be used. For example, the use of the behavior changer role will normally be used to alter self-destructive behavior of many types (i.e., a behavior changer role to achieve a behavior change objective). Practically speaking, bureaucratically organized welfare structures require some consistency in objectives and methods for purposes of program planning, recruitment, resource utilization, and so forth. In practice, then, any given service structure is likely to deal with a limited range of problems, objectives, and methods, with somewhat standard method clusters resulting. For purposes of rethinking the whole purpose and nature of therapeutic intervention in social welfare, Teare and McPheeters' work is extremely important. However, its implementation requires attempts to organize their ideas into patterns that have theoretical and practical utility.[22] Two men have recently attempted to do this.

Ralph Dolgoff has built on the work of Teare and McPheeters in his discussion of "modes of strategic intervention."[23] He develops seven social welfare practice objectives, and then relates specific method clusters to them as follows:

Objectives	Method Clusters
1. Facilitating linkages and communication	Mediator, conciliator, broker
2. Rehabilitative and developmental	Enabler, helper, therapist, mobilizer
3. Supportive	Provider, care-giver
4. Instructional	Teacher, guide, expert
5. Detection and problem-finding	Initiator and outreach
6. Confrontation and social action	Advocate, adversary, activist, organizer
7. Research and disseminator of information	None specified

EXHIBIT 9–1
Bisno's Theoretical Framework

Problem	Method	Techniques
1. Actual or potential conflict of interest or purpose	Adversary	Negotiation, bargaining, conflict generation through articulation and advocacy of competing interests
2. Lessen or eliminate conflict or competition	Conciliatory	Compromise, maximize similarities and minimize differences, accept a subordinate position, clarify misinterpretation
3. Lack of resources or the desire to mobilize those that exist or are potentially usable	Developmental	Role-playing, coordination and establishment of new power centers in the community
4. Transmit professional skill and knowledge to others	Facilitative-Interactional	Advice-giving, lectures, staging, role-playing, serving as role model, giving performance evaluation

---

Although different in some details, Dolgoff's objectives and methods are quite closely related to those of Teare and McPheeters. For example, Dolgoff talks of an instructional objective and teacher, guide, and expert methods, while Teare and McPheeters think in terms of an instruction-education objective with, presumably, their methods of teacher, consultant, administrator, and community planner being appropriate methods. Dolgoff, then, suggests some appropriate method clusters for given service objectives.

In the works of Teare and McPheeters as well as Dolgoff, methods are listed, but the exact skills needed to operationalize these methods are not specified.[24] Herbert Bisno has attempted to unify these separate strands to develop a unified framework which relates objectives, methods, and skills.[25] His framework begins with a problem, which is quite similar to Teare and McPheeters' objective. He then proceeds to look at the method best suited to the solution of the problem, as well as some of the specific interventive techniques of which the method is comprised. A summary of Bisno's theoretical framework is illustrated in Exhibit 9–1.

Having summarized interventive methods as formulated by Teare and McPheeters, Dolgoff, and Bisno, it is important to recognize that there is a basic similarity among the three. Making allowances for minor variations in language and conceptualization, Exhibit 9–2 compares the three perspectives on interventive methods in social welfare. It becomes clear in this exhibit (p. 150) that the three perspectives generate a considerable degree of uniformity in their assessment of the significant

	Problem	Method	Techniques
5.	Lack of professional knowledge and need for evaluation	Knowledge Development & Testing	Theory-building and research skills
6.	Restore a given level of social functioning	Restorative	Counseling, sensitivity training, provision of material resources
7.	Need for regulation of behavior	Regulatory	Conditioning techniques, analysis, provision of information
8.	Implementation of laws, policies, programs, procedures	Rule-Implementing	Administration, policy interpretation, translation of policy into programs
9.	Formulate new rules, policies, laws	Rule-making	Legislative lobbying, debates, policy briefs, public statements

Based on material in Herbert Bisno, "A Theoretical Framework for Teaching Social Work Methods and Skills, with Particular Reference to Undergraduate Social Welfare Education," in Frank Loewenberg and Ralph Dolgoff, eds., Teaching of Practice Skills in Undergraduate Programs in Social Welfare and Other Helping Services (New York: Council on Social Work Education, 1971), pp. 78–82.

elements of social welfare interventive methods. First, they take a task approach, whereby the method is selected on the basis of the task to be performed, rather than starting with a method and fitting the task into it. Second, they suggest that specific methods must and should be combined, as necessary, to deal with the dimensions of the task at hand. Third, one can deduce from the first two points that social welfare training in the area of interventive methods should be generic. Every social welfare practitioner should have basic competence in these methods, rather than being trained only in one method or cluster.

EXHIBIT 9–2
A Comparison of Teare and McPheeters, Dolgoff, and Bisno: Their Frameworks for Analyzing Interventive Methods in Social Welfare

Teare-McPheeters	OBJECTIVES-PROBLEMS		METHODS			TECHNIQUES
	Dolgoff	Bisno	Teare-McPheeters	Dolgoff	Bisno	Bisno
Detection	Detection and Problem finding	None specified	Outreach	Initiator-Outreach	None specified	None specified
Linkage or Connection	Facilitating linkages and communication	Eliminate conflict	Broker-Outreach	Mediator-Conciliator, Broker	Conciliatory	Compromise, clarification, minimize differences, be subordinate
Advocacy	Confrontation and social action	Potential conflict, new policy	Advocate, Community planner	Advocate-Adversary-Activist-Organizer	Adversary, rule-making	Negotiation, bargaining, conflict generation, lobbying, debates
Mobilization	None specified	Lack of resources, use of those existing	Mobilizer-Broker	None specified	Developmental	Role-playing, coordinate and establish new power centers
Instruction-Education	Instructional	Transmit knowledge and skills	Teacher-Consultant, Community planner	Teacher-Guide-Expert	Facilitative-Interactional	Role-playing, lectures, role-modeling, advice, performance evaluation
Behavior change	Rehabilitative and Developmental	Restore given level of functioning, regulative behavior	Behavior-changer	Enabler-Helper-Therapist-Mobilizer	Restorative, Regulatory	Counseling, conditioning, material resource use, provision of information, sensitivity use, analysis
Information processing	Research and Dissemination of information	Need for knowledge, evaluation	Evaluator-Data manager	None specified	Knowledge development and Testing	Theory-building and research skills
Administration		Implementing policy	Administrator-Consultant	None specified	Rule implementing	Administration, policy-planning and interpretation
Continuing care	Supportive	None specified	Care-giver	Provider-Care-giver	None specified	None specified

The basic idea of generic training is not new in social welfare education. Traditional interventive methods have been taught so that every student had basic exposure to casework, group work, and community organization. However, each student also chose his specialization, and developed his professional identity as a specialized practitioner. The new perspectives summarized in Exhibit 9–2 do not solve this problem, since it is not at all certain how these methods can all be taught and how much expertise is needed in each. Yet it is clear that a great deal of methodological flexibility will be required in a practice environment in which methods adapt to problems. Even considering that agencies tend to specialize in certain problems or problem groups (unwed mothers, marital problems, crime, etc.), problems often come in multiproblem clusters, and workers do move to different agencies. Because the task approach in interventive methods is relatively new, details need to be worked out; however, the concepts underlying the task approach are important.

The work of Teare and McPheeters, Dolgoff, and Bisno suggests a general overview of the interventive process. First, problems must be identified, requiring one to reach out into communities to find the problems with which people are struggling, individually and collectively. This can be accomplished by actually seeking out people in their environment, or by using the power of statistical fact to document need. Second, an evaluation of resources at all levels—individual, community, social welfare agencies, and society as a whole—must be accomplished to understand when needs can be met with existing resources and when new resources are necessary. This requires a diagnostic ability to understand individuals and groups, a sound knowledge of the social welfare service structure, and a grasp of the effects of societal values and structures on various types of problems. After evaluating resources and needs, the third and fourth steps are the joining of those in need with those who can meet the need, and then working to establish ways in which the unmet needs of the present can be met in the future.

A fifth step entails working with an individual or group to locate the best resource once the problem is identified. This may involve considerable behavior change, or it may be a long-term dependency on the resource. In either case it requires that the practitioner has considerable knowledge of psychological, biological, and personality variables and processes. A sixth and final part of the interventive process is the recognition that every practitioner has the responsibility for generating support for new and better resources, sharing his skills with others, cooperating with other professionals and nonprofessionals, and enhancing his own personal self-awareness and growth. The great value of the new perspectives on interventive methods discussed in this chapter is not only the explication of these basic interventive procedures in some detail, but also the assertion that every professional is involved to some extent in all of them.

EXHIBIT 9–3
An Approach to New Interventive Methods

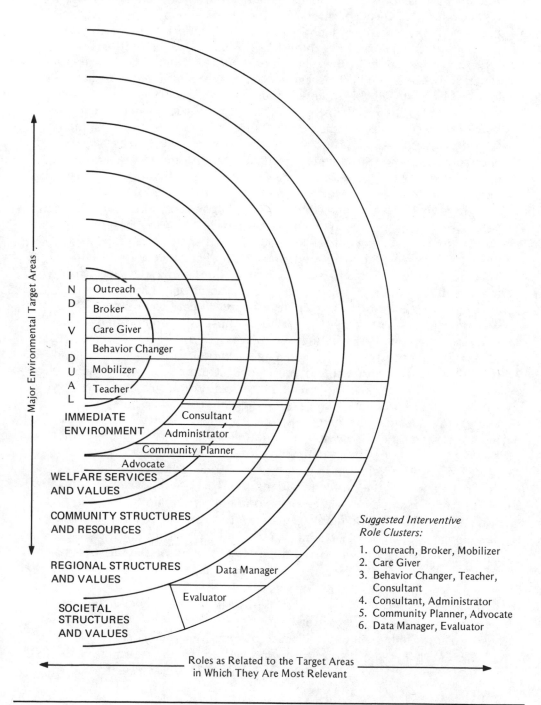

Major Environmental Target Areas

I
N
D
I
V
I
D
U
A
L

Outreach

Broker

Care Giver

Behavior Changer

Mobilizer

Teacher

IMMEDIATE
ENVIRONMENT

Consultant

Administrator

Community Planner

Advocate

WELFARE SERVICES
AND VALUES

COMMUNITY STRUCTURES
AND RESOURCES

REGIONAL STRUCTURES
AND VALUES

Data Manager

Evaluator

SOCIETAL
STRUCTURES
AND VALUES

*Suggested Interventive
Role Clusters:*

1. Outreach, Broker, Mobilizer
2. Care Giver
3. Behavior Changer, Teacher,
   Consultant
4. Consultant, Administrator
5. Community Planner, Advocate
6. Data Manager, Evaluator

Roles as Related to the Target Areas
in Which They Are Most Relevant

The one area in which there is still considerable lack of development in these new perspectives is the area of techniques. Bisno addresses himself somewhat to this question, as do Dolgoff and Teare and McPheeters to a lesser extent. However, substantial work needs to be done before a more adequate conceptualization can be achieved. One should recognize that the techniques Bisno presents are not startlingly new (with a few exceptions noted below) from those used in traditional methods. They are organized very differently in Bisno's work, but role-playing, theory-building, research, administration, counseling, conditioning, and policy-planning are all integral parts of traditional methods. Bisno does suggest that their traditionally fragmented, ideological organization minimizes their effectiveness in many cases, but he does not suggest that they are inappropriate or useless. The areas in which the traditional methods are broadened are those of conflict, legislation, and outreach, to some extent. Even though there is an old tradition of social action in social welfare work, for decades methods have been intellectualized and rather detached from legislative and conflict contexts. There has also been some middle-class withdrawal from the horrible conditions under which many needy persons live their lives. Bisno and others are again supporting the use of conflict, when necessary, to insure the rights of the needy; they are reaffirming the need to organize, and to make the legislative process as responsive to the needs of those who have *not* as well as those who *have;* and they are reaffirming the basic humanity of all. The social welfare practitioner struggles with the needs of anyone who has need, rather than moving away from the unpleasant, the different, and the seemingly hopeless.

Conclusion

Given the early stage of development of these new perspectives on interventive methods, they cannot be definitively stated. At this point each person has to struggle with them individually to find effective or promising uses, ideas, and solutions to problems. This chapter has been an attempt to relate Teare and McPheeters' methods to the major components making up the social welfare system, using this as a way of developing logical methodological clusters. Exhibit 9-3 shows the result of such preliminary thought.[26] It illustrates the way in which these new perspectives can be used, yet not giving any kind of definitive conclusions.

REFERENCES

1. Robert Teare and Harold McPheeters, *Manpower Utilization in Social Welfare* (Atlanta: Southern Regional Education Board, 1970), pp. 4–8.

2. Herbert Bisno, "A Theoretical Framework for Teaching Social Work Methods and Skills, with Particular Reference to Undergraduate Social Welfare Education," in Frank Loewenberg and Ralph Dolgoff, eds., *Teaching of Practice Skills in Undergraduate Programs in Social Welfare and Other Helping Services* (New York: Council on Social Work Education, 1971), pp. 72–78, 84–85.

3. Ibid., p. 84.

4. Ibid., pp. 75–77.

5. Teare and McPheeters, op. cit., pp. 7–8.

6. Ibid., pp. 11, 66–70.

7. Ibid., p. 12.

8. Ibid., pp. 17–18.

9. Ibid., pp. 19–21.

10. Ibid., p. 20.

11. Ibid.

12. Ibid.

13. Ibid.

14. Ibid.

15. Ibid., pp. 20–21.

16. Ibid., p. 21.

17. Ibid,

18. Ibid.

19. Ibid., pp. 34–35.

20. Ibid., p. 37.

21. Ibid., p. 36.

22. Teare and McPheeters are emphatic in noting that their work is just a beginning, which will ultimately be developed in theory-building and practice contexts.

23. Ralph Dolgoff, "Basic Skills for Practice in the Human Services: A Curriculum Guide," in Loewenberg and Dolgoff, op. cit., p. 25.

24. Teare and McPheeters analyze specific behaviors for each method on pp. 42–51. Their focus is on work activities rather than the skills underlying them, although in some cases the two areas are closely related.

25. Bisno, op cit., pp. 78–82.

26. These ideas grew out of discussions with Winifred Thomet and a workshop operated by the Southern Regional Education Board (SREB), for whose help I am deeply grateful. Exhibit 9-3 was originally done in a slightly modified form for a paper entitled "Theoretical Bases for Interventive Methods," written as part of the SREB workshop mentioned above.

SELECTED READINGS

New perspectives by their very nature are not elaborately documented in print. By the time they are, they have become accepted. Nevertheless, a few sources are available which suggest some of the new approaches to interventive methods.

Levin, Lester, ed. *Teaching Social Welfare*. 3 vols. Atlanta: Southern Regional Education Board, 1971.

Loewenberg, Frank, and Ralph Dolgoff. *Teaching of Practice Skills in Under-graduate Programs in Social Welfare and Other Helping Services.* New York: Council on Social Work Education, 1971.

Meyer, Carol. *Social Work Practice.* New York: Free Press, 1970.

Teare, Robert, and Harold McPheeters. *Manpower Utilization in Social Welfare.* Atlanta: Southern Regional Education Board, 1970.

OCCUPATIONAL CONTEXTS

10

No text introducing a student to social welfare as a social institution can ignore the nature of social welfare occupations. It has special practical relevance to students faced with a career decision and appropriate planning, and actual contexts of practice can help a student of social welfare see how the many areas of theory become translated into concrete service structures, including their problems, potential, strengths, and weaknesses. In this brief introduction to contexts of practice, four rather diverse contexts will be examined: work in a public assistance context; work in the public school system; work in medical contexts; and work in neighborhood settlement houses. Although far from exhaustive, these areas are diverse enough to illustrate some of the different work contexts available to the social welfare professional. In the discussion of these contexts, three areas of concern will be stressed: (1) the interaction of welfare professions and contexts; (2) the major objectives of each work context; and (3) some of the major problems and potential inherent in each context.

Before looking at these contexts of practice, briefly considering educational preparation for various types of positions will be helpful. There are four basic educational levels to which jobs are related: high school, Associate of Arts (junior college), Bachelor's degree (four years of college), and Master's degree (graduate study). There are no countrywide, uniform standards governing the educational level required for particular jobs, but there are some generalizations that are more or less commonly accepted. Jobs requiring only a high school degree are few and tend to be those that utilize the worker's actual life experience in a certain social context. For example, a streetcorner worker who has contacts in a target neighborhood could be hired with only a high school degree (sometimes even less). Opportunities for advancement are quite limited, and pay scales generally low, although the New Careers Program is an attempt at the federal and state levels to provide high school graduates with reasonable career opportunities. At the Associate of Arts (AA) level, there is generally a technician focus. Such persons do relatively routine work requiring few decisions, freeing people with higher levels of training to perform more complex tasks requiring judgement and depth knowledge. There are increasing numbers of technician programs at the AA level in such areas as mental health, social work, and nursing, but actual jobs available are lagging behind the proliferation of such programs.

The Bachelors (BSW) level has traditionally been the one from which most social welfare personnel are recruited. The BSW-level practioner usually has a mixture of routine and judgement-type work, and in some cases carries the major part of an agency's workload. In the past, the BA graduate with any major could move relatively easily into social welfare related jobs. Specialized Bachelor's-level programs, in such areas as social work, criminology and law enforcement, and counseling, are now developing. As they develop, educators, practitioners, and students have begun to exert pressure on social welfare agencies to give preference in hiring and salary level to graduates of such programs. The Master's-level people typically hold the positions of most responsibility, authority, and pay, and have the greatest choice of positions. The majority of the professional leaders in such social service professions as social work, teaching, and criminology will no doubt continue to have Master's-level training. Naturally, this simple breakdown of educational levels does not easily accommodate some specialized training programs, such as medicine and law, but has general applicability to the social welfare field.

EXHIBIT 10–1
The Maryland Social Welfare Picture—January 30, 1971

To give some idea of a typical proportion of jobs at various educational levels in major social welfare professions, below are the results of a census of social welfare jobs, undertaken by the Health and Welfare Council of Baltimore, Maryland.

Categories of Social Welfare Jobs by Level of Education Required,

Occupational Category	Less Than High School		High School Diploma		Special Training		Some College (No Degree)	
	No. of jobs	Percent of category	No. of jobs	Percent of category	No. of jobs	Percent of category	No. of jobs	Percent of category
Supportive Aides	2638	83.6%	400	12.6%	72	2.3%	17	0.5%
Social Workers	—	—	—	—	1	—	2	.1
Correctional Workers	1	—	1876	74.6	—	—	—	—
Employment Workers	3	.3	158	14.8	—	—	22	2.1
Community Workers	46	5.7	243	30.2	122	15.1	64	7.9
Fin. Asst. and Ben. Workers	—	—	98	16.6	—	—	278	47.8
Administrators	2	.4	7	1.3	—	—	5	.9
Youth and Recreation Workers	6	1.2	12	2.5	—	—	135	28.0
Health Related Workers	3	2.1	7	5.0	1	.7	1	.7
College Teachers of Social Welfare Subjects	—	—	—	—	—	—	—	—
Total	2,699	22.1%	2,800	22.9%	196	1.6%	523	4.3%

From Health and Welfare Council of the Baltimore Area, *12,000 Social Welfare Jobs: A One-Day Census of Social Welfare Jobs in Maryland, January 30, 1971—Part I* (Baltimore, Maryland: June 1971), pp. 24–25.

Public Assistance

Public assistance is a diverse collection of social welfare services, usually located in government departments of social service, and drawing upon resources of the health department and the department of agriculture. In Maryland, for example, there is a state department of social services that sets policy, and also supervises a system of county departments of social service that provides concrete services to applicants (i.e., state-wide policies locally administered). In some states, social service departments may also operate mental health clinics, detention facilities, or residential facilities. The federal government is currently encouraging states to separate financial aid from the provision of other types of service, such as

from Less Than High School Diploma through the Doctor's Degree

Associate Degree		Bachelor's Degree		Master of Social Work Degree		Any Other Master's Degree		Doctor's Degree	
No. of jobs	Percent of category	No. of jobs	Percent of category	No. of jobs	Percent of category	No. of jobs	Percent of category	No. of jobs	Percent of category
10	0.3%	11	0.3%	4	0.1%	—	—	—	—
10	.3	1900	65.6	834	28.8	148	5.1%	—	—
—	—	639	25.4	—	—	—	—	—	—
—	—	864	81.2	—	—	17	1.6	—	—
9	1.1	249	31.0	46	5.7	27	3.3	—	—
—	—	208	35.6	—	—	—	—	—	—
2	.4	257	50.0	170	32.7	72	13.9	2	0.4
8	1.7	311	64.6	1	.2	8	1.7	—	—
15	10.7	113	80.7	—	—	—	—	—	—
—	—	—	—	31	50.0	2	3.2	29	46.8
54	0.1%	4,551	37.3%	1,087	8.9%	274	2.2%	31	0.3%

counseling, follow-up, child care, and others. There is also a concerted effort to allocate tasks according to levels of education and experience. Routine tasks, such as the calculation of eligibility for money payments, are being separated from those requiring professional judgement, such as abortion counseling.

The public assistance agency provides the most diversified experience possible in one agency structure, and therefore is an excellent work context in which to become exposed to a variety of social welfare activities. It is unfortunate that many young people see public assistance as a purely financial service. It is a good deal more than that, despite the problems encountered in trying to operationalize its mandate. The typical social service agency is divided into two major parts: adult services and child welfare services. Under adult services there are eight major programs:

1. *Old Age Assistance*—aid to needy persons over age 65, including medical care, financial assistance, counseling, and rehabilitation.

2. *Aid to the Blind*—aid to needy blind persons, including medical care, financial assistance, counseling, and rehabilitation.

3. *Aid to Families with Dependent Children*—aid to needy families with children under eighteen, including medical care, financial assistance, counseling, recreation, and housing.

4. *General Public Assistance*—a residual program to care for emergency need and those not falling in other categories.

5. *Medical Assistance*—financial assistance to those not receiving public assistance but unable to meet specific medical costs.

6. *Food Stamp Program*—provision of food stamps to public welfare recipients to enable them to increase the food purchasing power of each dollar spent (in some areas, this is replaced by a commodity distribution program).

7. *Homemaker Service*—assistance in managing a home in cases of illness or lack of skill or knowledge.

8. *Aid to the Permanently and Totally Disabled*—aid to the needy disabled, including medical care, financial assistance, counseling, and rehabilitation.

Under child welfare services there are five major programs:

1. *Foster Care*—placing a child in a foster home when he cannot remain in his own home, and including medical care for the child, counseling for the child and natural and foster parents, and licensing of the foster home.

2. *Adoption*—legal transfer of a child from his natural parents to adopting

parents, including investigation of the adoptive family, counseling for the natural and adoptive parents, medical care for the natural mother and the child, and completing the legal aspects of the adoption.

3. *Protective Care*—investigating reports of child neglect or abuse, obtaining legal custody when appropriate, and providing counseling for the child and the parents when possible.

4. *Day Care*—day care services for children whose mothers work or are in school or training.

5. *Aid to Families with Dependent Children*—can also be seen in this category to the extent that it maintains households that might otherwise deteriorate.

It should be evident from the above summary that public assistance work offers a variety of interesting, challenging jobs for those interested in counseling, social work, legal aid, child care and education, consumer and homemaker services, geriatric care, physical and occupational therapy and rehabilitation, mental and emotional retardation, and a variety of other medical helping services.

Despite the excellent opportunities, however, public assistance work has several problems. A worker faces the frustrations of a paper bureaucracy, since there are many rules and forms that govern each service. Often there is a depressing work environment. Public assistance agencies are frequently located in run-down or industrial areas, in buildings that are overcrowded and physically deteriorated. The worker deals with socially stigmatized and disadvantaged client groups who can be physically unattractive, socially inept, and at times abusive. A further depressing feature of public assistance work is the hard-core, multi-faceted nature of the problems encountered, since public assistance is often the social service of last resort. To add to the above problems, caseloads are commonly very large, making it difficult to achieve the level of service one might wish. Public assistance frequently has high personnel turnover. Manpower shortages have in the past led to the hiring of persons with minimal skill and commitment, who left as soon as there was a better opportunity. The highly skilled and motivated practitioner frequently leaves because of the frustrations he encounters in trying to accomplish his goals. He is likely to move on to other settings where the problems are less overwhelming. This shifting personnel scene makes it difficult to establish meaningful personal and professional ties for those motivated enough to stay.

Although there are considerable problems in public assistance, there are obvious advantages. The public assistance worker interacts with a number of other social welfare professionals in such places as clinics, schools, courts, and residential treatment centers. Public assistance has the basic public mandate to develop a viable, effective network of services, and it forms the backbone around which all other social services are built. Struggles to work out a better system of social welfare revolve around the present public assistance system, and all other services will inevitably have to adapt to changes in this basic system. If this country ultimately gets a family allowance, guaranteed annual income, negative income tax, or some other plan, it will be in response to the need to unify the present patchwork of services, which is administratively awkward and costly, and which permits serious gaps and duplication. The separation of financial aid programs from social services and the differential use of personnel according to their level of training are moves in this direction. Whatever future changes are made, the public assistance system will remain an important part of our social welfare system.

School Social Welfare

Although perhaps not commonly thought of as a social welfare structure, there are several ways in which the public school system may be seen as performing social welfare functions. The first is a human enrichment function, in which young people are taught to use their capacities to think and grow as distinctive human beings. Second, the societal preparation function teaches the child the cognitive processes and behavior patterns that will enable him to function successfully in society (i.e., a socialization function). Third is the social control function, in which socialization and child-care services combine to help the child avoid deviant behavior contexts and permit other family members greater mobility. Given the societal mandate to perform these social welfare functions, there are several problems in their achievement that create the need for a variety of social welfare professionals in the school system.

Although society encourages education for all, not everyone has equal access to it or equal probability of succeeding in the system. In a highly mobile society, children often need help in adjusting to moving, utilizing resources in new environments, making new friends, and adjusting to new school curricula. Standardized curricula can create problems for the unusual child, whether he is unusually gifted, slow, or artistic. Initial school entry problems pose a potential trouble area, as the child has to adjust to separation from the home, a new peer group, and the discipline of the school. Finally, children sometimes have one or more barriers to learning, including personal or family problems, deficient learning backgrounds, or deviant subcultural values and behaviors.

There are many social welfare professionals involved in the school system in addition to teachers and administrators, including the pupil personnel worker, the school social worker, the school guidance counselor, special education teachers, the school nurse, and a variety of recreation personnel. Many of these professionals do not work in the classroom, but instead work with teachers, parents, other social welfare personnel, and students in nonclassroom settings. They provide an excellent example of a team of relatively specialized professionals performing related but separate tasks.

The school nurse, school guidance counselor, special education teachers, and recreation personnel work within the school itself, and can spot physical and behavioral problems that are then referred to pupil personnel workers and school social workers; teachers are also a valuable referral source. The pupil personnel worker usually focuses on school attendance and working with other community resources such as the courts and departments of social service to try to insure a child's attendance at school. The school social worker attempts to follow through on problems identified by the other personnel, and may consult with teachers, provide counseling and referral service for children and their families, and utilize other community social welfare services as needed and appropriate. In all cases, the social welfare personnel attempt to enable the child to express himself, learn and develop as a person, and obtain needed physical and emotional resources. They also help the school system operate more effectively and with minimal disruption.

In looking at some of the issues in social welfare work in the public school system, several problems and prospects become clear. Among the problems is the obvious one of coordinating the various specialties involved, so that, for example, school guidance counselors are not giving children unrealistic expectations, which the school social worker cannot realistically help them attain. There is the related need to insure that all personnel are aware of what the others are doing, so that a teacher, for example, doesn't unwittingly extinguish behavior that a pupil personnel worker is trying to reward. Another problem can be one of professional jealousy, whereby each specialty guards its prerogatives regardless of logic and the best interests of the clients. For example, pupil personnel work commonly requires an education background, while school social work normally requires a social work background, despite the fact that the actual tasks are quite closely related. Finally, there is the problem of social welfare in a host setting. Since a school may see its basic function as classroom education, it may be unwilling to adapt its program to facilitate the tasks of the other social welfare personnel working within the larger educational system. This can minimize referrals, create problems in the areas of professional autonomy and responsibility, and generate crises in professional identification among some of the social welfare personnel.

Much like public assistance, the school system is a uniquely important social welfare context despite the problems that may exist. The school system, because of its powerful societal mandate and the pervasiveness of the service structure, offers an unparalleled opportunity to create an institutional social welfare structure affecting virtually the total population. The services are also provided early enough in the child's life to have strong preventative value. Linking social welfare services with a strongly mandated resource such as education provides a pleasant environment for the social welfare worker, and gives him legitimacy to enter problem areas otherwise resistant to intervention. In summary, then, social welfare work in the public school system can be a significant resource in the early identification and treatment of problems, despite the organizational difficulties that may exist.

Medical Social Welfare

The medical institution is basic to social welfare because of its focus on physical well-being as an essential part of human functioning and happiness. The fact that most medical personnel are primarily concerned with the physical functioning of the patient, rather than his total biopsychosocial totality, generates the need for a variety of other social welfare professionals to supplement the care given by the medical staff. The need

---

EXHIBIT 10–2
The Future of Public Assistance: NASW's Proposed Draft Bill

Among the several legislative proposals to revamp public assistance and the public social services is a model bill by the National Association of Social Workers (NASW) called "Social Services Amendments of 1972." A summary of this proposed social services draft bill, which appeared in the February 1972 issue of NASW News, is presented here. Although this proposed legislation was due for further revision, it is an excellent example of the significance that public assistance agencies are likely to have in the social welfare system of the future.

Reason for the bill. This is a time of great change in public assistance programs. An essentially federal system is likely to replace the existing federal-state system of public assistance, and it seems clear that—for the first time—income maintenance programs and programs providing social services will be administered separately. These major shifts will inevitably lead to changes in the social services mechanism. In the main, the states have been providing public social services as *incidental* to providing an adequate level of income for needy persons.

Public social services and public assistance in the form of cash payments now have a common statutory base. The authority for both is interwoven in the Social Security Act and related legislation. Separation of the income maintenance authority means that at least minimum changes must be made in the social services aspect of the law. It is conceivable that a workable social services system could be devised by making only minimum changes. To a certain extent, that is what HR 1 does. However, the historic creation of a federal income maintenance system for the needy offers a unique opportunity to reexamine the statutory base for social services, to make changes that reflect current needs and current techniques for meeting these needs, and to develop a comprehensive, effective program of social services.

The proposed bill, called the "Social Services Amendments of 1972," offers such a program. It retains and builds on the existing federal-state system, and is based on the assumption that—once HR 1 is enacted—the states will be only slightly involved, if at all, in

From *NASW News* 17 (February 1972): 9. Used with permission.

for social welfare personnel in medical settings includes the following:

1. Physical and emotional functioning are related, with emotional problems often accompanying illness and the need for medical treatment.

2. Illness usually interferes with normal role functioning, and has ramifications throughout the individual's social setting. This includes helping others to accept and adapt to an individual's illness.

3. Since much medical care is voluntary and private, it is necessary to reach out into the community to identify need and find ways for those in need to obtain resources.

4. Given the complexity of contemporary medical practice and services, there is need for a referral and coordination service.

---

administering public assistance. All state welfare agencies are currently performing some social service functions, although the extent and quality vary sharply with locale and area of work; the total impact is inadequate.

This bill provides ways to capture the good in the present system, make up for some present omissions, and alleviate shortcomings. Its enactment would put fresh momentum behind existing social services efforts and immediately move the states' public welfare resources in a social services direction.

There was never a more urgent need for a broad program of social services. Indeed, the enactment of the new federal system of income maintenance will emphasize that need. Even now, effectiveness of the cash-benefit social security program is handicapped by social services inadequate for dealing with human problems related to but separate from income maintenance. Protective services for children and the aged are obvious examples, but there are many others. Medical programs have created an urgency for planning—with individuals and families—forms of care alternative to institutional care. And all the insurance programs are so complicated that people must have some place in the community where they can find out what resources are available and how to obtain them. This new social services program, when placed beside the existing programs of cash benefits and medical insurance under social security, will serve as one vast case-finding device.

The emphasis HR 1 gives to employment programs for the needy further points up the urgency of a broad services program. HR 1 already recognizes the need for "supportive services." These include personal counseling, day care for children of women who are to work outside the home, and a variety of other essential services that enable the potential wage earner to concentrate on job training and work. The report accompanying HR 1 admonishes the Department of Labor to use existing resources rather than set up its own supportive services. The "Social Services Amendments of 1972" supports the development of available services to go along with the employment programs and maximize their effectiveness.

Structure of the bill. The social services program would be a state program with federal financial assistance and standard-setting. The bill requires that a single state agency be designated or established either to administer the program or supervise the administration. That agency is to be the one, if an appropriate agency exists, generally recognized in the state as already having a broad range of services—sometimes called an "umbrella" agency. The

There is a variety of social welfare practitioner positions in medical settings. To some extent there is variation among settings—a community health center will have different personnel from a birth control clinic. Nevertheless, there are certain major social welfare professional groups that have general importance in medical settings, especially occupational and physical therapists, medical social workers, psychiatric nurses, visiting nurses, and a variety of medical technicians. Of these groups, medical social workers and visiting nurses provide the broadest range of social services, with the others being more concerned with the services of their particular specialty.

The range of functions the social welfare practitioner may perform is also varied. An important function is helping the patient to adapt to his illness, including necessary treatment and implications for the future

---

reason for this proviso is that the bill aims to consolidate and coordinate services—an urgent need because services at both state and community levels are usually fragmented and uneven, and there are often gaps in types and locale of coverage.

In addition to the required umbrella agency, other means encourage a coordinated continuum of services. A second means is the granting of federal funds to finance the planning of coordinated services, research, experiments, and evaluations. A third means is a proviso giving the Secretary (Department of Health, Education, and Welfare) authority to modify plans or requirements for any health, education, welfare, or manpower programs under his direction—including the requirements in this title—if necessary to achieve a coordination.

Each state is to select local agencies to administer the program in its political subdivisions. Local officials are to have an opportunity to appeal directly to the state if they are not satisfied with any aspect of state supervision or administration, including state directives, priorities, and interpretations.

Services to be provided. The bill specifically defines all services the program covers. It indicates those the states must provide at the outset and those optional for a time but eventually mandatory. Rather than using general terms like "strengthening family life" or "help to realize the individual's potentials," the bill breaks such general services down into hard, visible components. Definitions have been carefully drafted so that the services are broad and comprehensive, though specific; there should be no gaps in services because authorization is lacking. Services are to be offered in the following areas:

adoption	housing	self-care
caretaker services	information and referral	services to meet special
child welfare	marriage counseling	health needs
day care for adults	nutrition	special services for the
family planning	protective services for adults	blind
foster care	protective services for	temporary emergency
homemaker service	children	services

Services are to be provided, in part, through community multiservice centers accessible to the population. Such centers are to provide—as a minimum—information and referral services, temporary emergency services, services to meet special health needs, family plan-

(physical limitations, discomfort, occupational training, etc.). A second task is to help others to accept the patient's illness, including participating in the treatment if appropriate, restructuring role relationships to take account of the patient's limitations, and avoiding stigmatizing the patient. Third, there has to be planning for aftercare and rehabilitation, so that the transition from the medical setting to the home is as easy as possible. This includes the exploration of resources to help in aftercare, the re-establishment of social contacts, and the follow-up to insure that the total treatment plan is carried through. Finally, there is the need for the informed social welfare practitioner to participate in institutional and community planning so that needed services may be provided in an attractive and accessible manner.

The problems of social welfare work in medical settings are similar

---

ning services, and housing services. The centers may offer additional services. Also the states are to provide certain "core services," which may be offered either through the centers or other governmental agencies or by grant, contract, purchase, or other arrangements with voluntary agencies. These core services initially are to include information and referral services, adoption services, foster care services, protective services for adults and children, homemaker services, and special services for the blind.

From among the other services the bill covers, the Secretary from time to time is to select additions to this list, with the objective that by July 1, 1976, all the services will be provided throughout each state. States may initiate, on a less-than-statewide basis, services they select among the nonrequired services.

Staff for carrying out the services will have a wide range of skills and education. They should include neighborhood workers, new-career personnel (low-income neighborhood people trained and employed to provide social services), professional social workers, and members of other professional groups. The social services program is to be coordinated, not only with public welfare agencies, but also with vocational rehabilitation, health, and education agencies, as well as all types of voluntary agencies. In addition plans are to be coordinated with area and community economic development agencies, such as regional authorities interested in broad planning.

Who is eligible? Public social services are to be made available as rapidly as possible throughout each state to all persons requesting them. Certain levels and types of local financing are provided for. In moving beyond minimum core services, states may set up a system of priorities for the services they will provide, but they must emphasize the needs of low-income people. In addition, states must put into effect methods prescribed by the Secretary to make sure that they bring to the attention of the needy the services presumably available to all in the community. Charges for services rendered will take into consideration the financial ability to pay of users of certain services.

Relationship to income maintenance programs. The program this bill proposes would be administered apart from income maintenance programs. The bill provides, however, that the states are to arrange for referrals of service from federal and state income maintenance programs. Essential social services needs having an impact on income maintenance are to receive the attention of social services agencies. The temporary emergency services, which

to those in school settings, including the same problems of professional coordination, identification, and autonomy. These problems tend to be accentuated by the fact that medical personnel have responsibility for life-and-death decisions, and tend to emphasize strongly the physical aspects of human functioning. However, the utility of combining social with physical treatment is increasingly recognized, and the perceived need to break down the isolation of "total institutions" has also helped to unite a range of medical and other social welfare personnel. The advantages of a medical setting include the legitimacy of the medical mandate (as with the school system), and the superb resources which are frequently available in medical settings (rehabilitation equipment, funds, and space). In addition, the medical setting is, for the most part, a clean, attractive, prestigious one in which a social welfare practitioner

---

the centers are required to provide, are not intended to be another income maintenance program, but rather a personal service program having strictly limited funds available for aid in cash or kind during a specifically limited period.

Episodes causing severe social dislocation. At present the federal government can take few actions promptly at the onset of an episode severely dislocating a community. For example, tensions within a city, often interracial, have sparked many episodes destroying and dislocating services. This bill would open another channel of action to the federal government. It authorizes the Secretary to make grants of up to 100 percent federal funds to state or local agencies administering services under the bill or to other community agencies whenever such an episode occurs or is threatened. Funds are to be used to finance services directed toward disastrous effects of these episodes or, in some instances, toward preventing a threatened outbreak. The grants would be time-limited but should prove useful in dealing with urgent crises—for example, in urban affairs.

Financing the program. The states pay the costs for providing services, administration, and training; the basic percentage of federal funds paid to the states toward these costs is 80 percent. There is special funding, with the percentage of federal funds going up to 100 percent, to finance projects having specific objectives. The Secretary will have some money to finance training, research, and experiments. He can use a variety of means, including grants to states and contracts with public and private nonprofit organizations. The Secretary will have another fund from which he can make grants to states to help bring about coordinated, comprehensive services. Grants can also be made for new-career programs.

In addition, the bill includes an amendment to Title II of the Social Security Act, authorizing the transfer of up to $50-million a year from the Social Security Trust Fund to finance the cost of protective services for aged, blind, and disabled adult beneficiaries and child beneficiaries of social security when such services are essential to individuals for the effective use of their social security benefits. This money is to be transferred by the Secretary to the state and local agencies providing the needed protective services. Currently, such urgently needed services are either not provided or are provided irregularly and undependably by public or voluntary agencies.

Democratic involvement. The bill includes several provisos assuring community involvement in administering and evaluating the program. It establishes a National Advisory

can work. The tremendous strides which medicine has made have stimulated related social welfare professions to develop new ways to create a total treatment environment. In the process, many dynamic and interesting work contexts have been created.

Settlement Houses

Settlement houses (also called neighborhood houses or community centers) occupy a niche in the social welfare system very different from those contexts already discussed. The name derives from their original purpose of helping immigrants to settle in new communities, and this educational-recreational-community focus persists today. They are social welfare facilities in their objectives of providing recreational facilities to

---

Council on Individual and Family Services to be composed of members representing various geographic sections of the country and including beneficiaries of the services. This council is to have authority to advise and make recommendations to the Secretary on major policies, scope, objectives, and operation of the program. There are to be parallel state councils with similar authority.

There is ample provision for program analysis and evaluation, both by the federal agency and by the states, independently of the federal government and in conjunction with it. Results of evaluations are to be made available to the national council, and the Secretary's annual report on this program is to include the national council's comments on program evaluation studies.

Relationship to existing programs. As already mentioned, this bill aims to achieve a coordinated, comprehensive program of social services to respond to human problems throughout the states. To achieve this goal, some consolidation of services is desirable, and coordination of all related services is essential. This bill does not attempt to direct the manner in which this is to be accomplished or the programs to be involved. If a state makes a convincing case to the Secretary that it is organized to achieve a coordinated, nonduplicating continuum of services to those who need them, this fulfills the requirements of the new title. It seems likely that most states will wish and need to consolidate services somewhat.

It is not the bill's intent to bring different programs under the same roof just because they have purposes crossing over into the bill's area. Education or health agencies, for example, can no doubt continue to operate most effectively apart from the agencies administering individual and family social services, although certain common purposes and certain aspects of their programs should be coordinated by various arrangements. New agencies envisioned under this bill may well help to support, through purchase agreements, some services provided by other agencies.

This bill allows room for child care programs to grow separately. Although it authorizes child welfare services, the initiation of a major program is not intended if existing agencies are providing the services. The same applies to agencies providing legal services, housing agencies, certain health agencies, and the like. In planning a national program, possibilities of varied arrangements or lack of arrangements for services in different communities must be taken into account. Some programs authorized under this bill may not be needed in some communities because the service is already provided.

improve the quality of life in a community. They also encourage individual growth and development by providing instructional facilities to increase knowledge and improve living skills, and by promoting community identification and involvement. The worker in a settlement house context performs four major functions, the first of which is to provide professional leadership in recreational, instructional, and community programs. In this task, the professional utilizes his interventive skills as appropriate, but much of his importance is as a knowledgeable person and role model in a wide range of activities. A second task is to provide professional leadership in the community's attempts to identify and express its needs, and organize to meet them. This is much more likely to call upon the worker's interventive skills. Third, the settlement house worker is a local person to whom neighborhood residents can go in times of need. Being locally situated in an agency structure that is relatively informal and nonbureaucratic, the worker becomes an accessible social welfare resource. Carrying the previous function a step further, the fourth task of the worker is to serve as a referral source and mediate between the community and the rest of the social welfare system, including referrals, outreach, follow-up, and so on.

EXHIBIT 10–3
The Social Welfare Career Packet

As a guide for those wishing to explore a career in social welfare, some materials compiled in 1970 and distributed by the Health and Welfare Council of Central Maryland, Inc. are included in Appendix B. These materials were prepared under the auspices of the Social Welfare Careers Service of the Health and Welfare Council and Social Welfare Manpower Project of the Social Services Administration of the Maryland Department of Employment and Social Services. Copies of these and other related materials may be obtained from the council, 200 East Lexington Street, Baltimore, Maryland 21202.

The materials included in Appendix B are the following:

1. Social Welfare Workers
   a. What does the social welfare worker do?
   b. What qualities should the social welfare worker have?
   c. What jobs are included in social welfare?

2. Exploring a Career in Social Welfare
   a. Is social welfare the career for you?
   b. Sources of career information
   c. Sources of paid and volunteer jobs

3. Social Welfare Jobs
   a. Jobs and salaries as related to educational level

In addition to the wealth of information in Appendix B, the following points are worthy of your consideration if you are seriously thinking about a social welfare career:

A major issue in settlement house work is the blending of the professional and nonprofessional roles. This enables the worker to identify with the community and achieve a level of trust and communication often difficult in more formal, bureaucratized settings. However, the worker can also experience role ambiguity and role conflict when trying to help the community obtain needed services from more distant, bureaucratic, and unresponsive agencies. Indeed, many settlement house personnel have limited professional training, an indication of the dual focus of this type of agency and the problems that such a focus implies. A second consideration is the resource base of such agencies. Since they are usually privately funded and dependent on community support, they often operate with very limited resources. Mobilizing the community to obtain needed resources can be an important part of a worker's strategy to involve it in the agency's program. It can also be a chronic problem.

Concluding this discussion of the settlement house as a context of practice, it is important to reemphasize its significance as a locally based social welfare service. Its potential for helping to decentralize other services and achieve a more effective relationship between them and the community is very important. As bureaucracies proliferate and certain

---

1. You should have a solid foundation in the social sciences, and actively try to relate such theory to practice contexts.

2. You should like people in a meaningful way. That is, it must matter enough to you what happens to people that you are willing to give up some of your own comforts if necessary to help others.

3. You must have persistence and tenacity. Social and personal problems are notoriously long lasting, so you can't give up half way through. After a while problems get repetitious, so you must be able to remember that as old hat as they are to you, they are new and meaningful to the person experiencing them.

4. You must be honest with yourself. People in need can often be easily manipulated and deceived. You must care enough about them and yourself to help others because you believe in man's commitment to man, not because you enjoy feeling superior to others.

5. You must be able to accept discouragement and try again. As with Freddy's family, some clients are hard to reach and seem to enjoy deceiving or disappointing you. This is sometimes also true of professionals. You must be able to accept some set-backs and a snail's pace forward and still keep trying.

Social welfare work isn't easy. The emotional drain and personal frustrations can't be appreciated until they are experienced. The rewards are often remarkably few for the work involved. As idealistic as it seems, you have to *have* to do it to be a good social welfare worker. Of course there are many mediocre and incompetent social welfare workers for whom the job is immeasurably less trying . . . but do you really want to become one of them?

population groups come to feel increasingly alienated, the mediating function of agencies such as settlement houses becomes increasingly important—a type of ombudsman, in a sense. For the social welfare professional seeking a relatively flexible work structure, whose interests lean towards the recreational, arts and crafts, and community involvement in a total way, and who isn't threatened by a weak professional identification and limited resources, settlement house work can be exciting and rewarding.

Conclusion

Hopefully, this brief review of four major contexts of practice gives some idea of the incredible diversity of social welfare practice, and helps the reader sort out the type of context of particular interest. However, a book can only give a second-hand, limited view of the social welfare field. There is no substitute for actually going out to visit agencies, talking to welfare professionals, writing the national organization appropriate to your interests, and doing volunteer work to test out your interests. Social welfare is an occupational area full of frustrations and rewards, inconsistencies and sound programs, impossible bureaucracies and life-maintaining services. It is best served by people who have a mixture of idealism, practicality, dedication, strength, sensitivity, intelligence, and hardheadedness. Ultimately, the only way to know if you can thrive on its peculiar diet of rewards and frustrations is to try it, although it is hoped that this chapter will help you make an intelligent first step.

SELECTED READINGS

The best source of information about specific practice contexts is to actually visit the kind of agency in which you are interested. Observe the activity there and make an appointment to speak to a worker. Written information can also be obtained from the sources in Appendix B. However, the following may be of interest for the information about social welfare work they provide, and the issues they raise.

Addams, Jane. *Twenty Years at Hull House*. New York: Macmillan, 1910.
Collins, Alice. *The Lonely and Afraid*. New York: Odyssey, 1969.
Green, Hannah. *I Never Promised You a Rose Garden*. New York: Holt, Rinehart and Winston, 1964.

IV
CONCLUSION

THINKING AHEAD

11

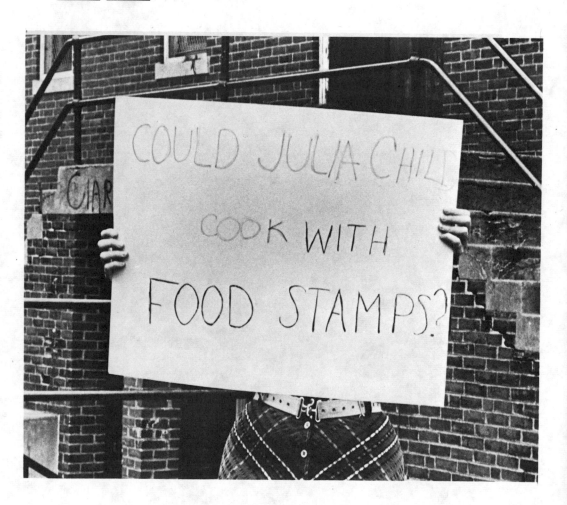

Perhaps an effective way to end an introductory social welfare text is to cite a recent newspaper article entitled "States Move to Reverse Wide Welfare Expansion."[1] In this article, it is stated that

A decade of liberalization and expansion of the nation's welfare program has come to a halt this year, with state after state focusing on public assistance programs to cut costs.[2]

Some of the techniques used to cut costs are attempts to reintroduce residence requirements, programs of fraud investigation, lack of welfare appropriations by some state legislatures, threats of dropping welfare programs completely, and forcing employable public welfare recipients to work in return for their grants. Clearly the states are finding it difficult to meet welfare costs, and competition among public services for scarce funds is developing as a result.

Education, health and transportation programs in every state have long-established and powerful lobbies that fight for public dollars. Only recently, with the formation of the National Welfare Rights Organization, has welfare had a comparable lobby, and it is only just beginning to function. In the scramble for public money, welfare usually—but not always—loses.[3]

Another way to grasp the dimensions of the crisis is to look at the figures on recent costs and recipients of public welfare (see Exhibit 11–1, p. 176).

No matter how committed one may be to the need for adequate welfare services, the problems are apparent, and the future of welfare for some time to come is going to lie in attempts to solve such problems. Several threads emerge to help us predict where solutions may ultimately materialize. Probably most important is the fact that welfare recipients and professionals are only now beginning to become politically active. This, juxtaposed with the fact that our welfare system is primarily a public one in which the major policy decisions are made in political contexts, suggests that the development of a welfare lobby can be a powerful mechanism to insure that welfare needs are recognized and adequately met.

The social welfare professional of the future will of necessity be a political being, as will many more welfare recipients. This must happen if welfare is to maintain itself in competition with other public services. It isn't so much a question of welfare being any less deserving as it is a question of the squeaky wheel getting the grease. It also is not cause for welfare paranoia; politicians are not out to destroy welfare as much as they are out to get reelected. Most Americans take pride in a political system that is responsive to the will of the majority. The welfare professional of the future will have to be much more aggressive in bringing the needs of those he serves to the attention of those who have the political strength to affect the nation's social policy and legislation.

A second step is necessary if welfare is to find a secure, effective future, and that is the development of economically, politically, and socially feasible social welfare programs. One of the facts that should be obvious from this book is that the present welfare structure is a massive, sprawling, poorly coordinated, often ineffective network of services. There are too many instances of duplicated effort, inefficient administrative and service structures, and glaring gaps in the services offered. The costs of operating this structure are skyrocketing, while users of the services continue to have their needs inadequately met. Providers of the services are similarly disadvantaged by having to cope with inadequate resources, and consequent personal and professional frustration. The present patchwork of services cannot continue, as critics of it are all too fond of saying—and people believe them. The question is, what can replace the present sys-

---

EXHIBIT 11–1
Costs and Recipients of Public Welfare, 1955–1971

Year	Recipients	Costs
1955	5.8 million	$ 2.7 billion
1960	6.8	3.7
1965	7.7	5.3
1970	13.4	12.8
1971	14.4 (estimated)	13.0 (estimated)

© 1971 by The New York Times Company. Reprinted by permission.

---

tem? Ruthlessly dropping services is one solution, and one which some would accept. Obviously the welfare professional is committed to a restructuring of the system to make it more efficient, effective, and comprehensive—but how?

It appears that the states are indeed feeling a financial pinch, and that their ability to provide uniform, adequate welfare services with only their own resources is limited. The federal government's resource base is much greater, and organizational structures already exist at the national level that efficiently administer certain kinds of welfare programs—Social Security, for example. It seems logical, then, that a reasonable strategy would be to utilize the federal government's resources and organization to bring about a federal welfare system that provides basic services and meets economic needs. This would be supplemented by state, local, and private social service programs planned and organized in cooperation with the various consumer groups to be served. The fact that funding would then be distributed among all the states would avoid much of the present local political resistance to welfare programs in some localities, and would help equalize the financial burden.

The best kind of federal system is currently being hotly debated. The general point that financially based concrete needs may be different from social service needs has been accepted in principle, and most major proposals separate economic services from social services. This is recognition of the fact that economic need does not necessarily imply personal or social inadequacy, and should greatly facilitate the simplification of the provision of economic services. At the same time, social welfare personnel trained in the provision of social services will be relieved of the administrative and emotional burdens resulting when economic and social services are joined in the same service delivery structure. Many of the current proposals to revamp the welfare system focus on income transfer as the major federal goal, with changes in the social service system less clearly defined and relegated primarily to state and local levels. Most welfare proposals are very complex, and are not easily summarized. However, some of the major proposals will be briefly discussed below for comparative purposes. This material is based on Romanyshyn, and his discussion of these programs should be consulted for more details and an excellent analysis of problems and prospects.[4]

Family Assistance Plan (FAP). Proposed by the Nixon administration, FAP is a plan to provide basic economic support to families with children, even if parents are unemployed or, if employed, do not earn an adequate subsistence income. Childless couples and single persons are not covered (although they would fall under the new adult program similar to the present public assistance programs for the aged, blind, and disabled). Recipients of FAP would be required to work (except under limited circumstances), and the program clearly attempts to support the work ethic. The level of economic support would be very limited ($1600–$2400 has been proposed for a family of four), and the program would be federally financed and operated. Although FAP would establish a guaranteed, uniform, federal income-support program for families with children, there are several negative features: income levels are minimal; childless persons are not covered; and the obligatory work provisions are both morally questionable and of dubious effectiveness in a society with an unemployment problem.

Children's Allowance. This plan, used in numerous other countries, automatically pays parents a cash allowance for each child. Since the allowance is automatic, it reduces the stigma attached to the receipt of welfare payments. On the other hand, it provides money to those not in economic need, and as such is a poor utilization of resources (although changes in the tax structure could mitigate such effects). Some question whether this type of plan would lead to an increase in the number of children per family. Even assuming this to be undesirable, experience in other countries does not support such an apprehension. This plan does, however, discriminate against those without children.

Negative Income Tax. The Internal Revenue Service (IRS) would pay those whose income falls below a certain level, just as it in turn is paid by those whose income is above set levels. This plan gets somewhat complicated by a work incentive, whereby low-income persons would have only a portion of their work income used in the computation of the payment they receive from IRS. There is some debate over whether the negative income tax still perpetrates the stigma of relief, and there is some societal resistance to payments without a work stipulation.

Social Dividend. This plan would provide a universal payment to all regardless of income or status. It is the most costly of all plans, but insures equality of treatment to all and has no work provisions. It would be funded out of federal income tax revenues.

NASW's Draft Proposal (see Exhibit 10–2, pp. 164–169). Romanyshyn, in summarizing the various proposals, notes that "there seem to be no adequate ways to reconcile the conflicting aims of social adequacy, economy, equity, and work incentive."[5] As is always the case in social welfare, any action requires consideration of many basic societal values. In revamping the welfare system, once again the core questions emerge: For whom is society responsible? To what standard of life is society committed, and do all groups in society have a right to the same standard? What groups in society have a responsibility to contribute to the needs of others? Who decides on the allocation of societal resources, and through what decision-making structures? Each of the alternative plans to revamp the welfare system is possible economically. Enactment of specific legislation will depend on the society making choices of priorities—who will be served, how will they be served, and who will pay? Such choices inevitably involve the use of power by those groups interested in the outcome. A major task for the social welfare professions is to band together and agree on the type of revision most suitable to social welfare goals. Then the development of political sophistication, influence, and strength must be achieved to make their choice the nation's choice.

Once a restructuring of the basic welfare system occurs, what remains? Although basic economic security is a necessity, there are many other areas in which the future of welfare will be shaped. Two of the most important are practice techniques and societal values. There are several forces promising to make practice techniques an area of future interest. The rapid growth of the social science bases of intervention is expanding the theory base that practitioners have to work with. Demands for practical relevance being made on social scientists are encouraging them to help practitioners find stronger bridges between theory and practice. A link between theorists and practitioners has already been formed in the area of methodology. Social welfare practitioners must find methods of proving the effectiveness of their services if they are to successfully compete for scarce societal resources. Social scientists can help to develop research methods to test the effectiveness of practice, and are being encouraged to do so as a way of validating their own theoretical constructs. These complementary needs may form a sounder basis for co-operation between social scientists and social welfare practitioners than has existed in the past.

Additional practice developments can be seen in new types of delivery systems. As social welfare becomes increasingly institutionalized, it must serve an ever-increasing population. Traditional service delivery systems are simply inadequate to cope with substantially greater numbers of users. The way in which new systems will develop is not clear, although multiservice, decentralized service centers seem quite promising. A notable increase in intermediary professions whose function is to provide only referral and follow-up services is another possibility. Service delivery systems are also changing in the direction of crisis-oriented, short-term services. This is partly in response to the increased number of users, but is also an outgrowth of new theories suggesting that short-term crisis-focused services are more effective than long-term supportive services for the average user of welfare services. The adequate conceptualization of crisis is a task that still remains, the achievement of which must precede the design of adequate crisis-focused structures. The most effective way of providing short-term services is also an issue for the future, with new ideas already beginning to emerge.

Achieving changes in social values sometimes seems a hopeless task. Although there is no question that the social welfare structure is solidly institutionalized in the United States, this book points out that adequate services are still needed in many areas. Certain basic social values must be changed if these needed services are ever to be feasible. The prognosis for such change appears to be slim, and yet the perspective of history is encouraging. When one thinks of the centuries it took to achieve the breakthrough of the Social Security Act, the lesson is clear—social change is slow and tedious. This country has made progress in social welfare. We do care for others in ways and at levels unthinkable not too many years ago. Yet we as a society still value individualism, discrimination, and laissez-faire capitalism, and these values often conflict with social welfare goals. Any projection that attempts to predict the resolution of this conflict would require a prediction about the future of the society. This is an impossible and perhaps sterile task. What the issue of value change in the future does suggest in a practical way is that all of us as citizens will affect the values of the future. Values are made and can be changed. If we as human beings, citizens, and social welfare practitioners believe in certain values, we must fight for their adoption. It is a worthwhile project for the future of each of us.

It always comes down to us. We are society. We are the social welfare system. We are human beings. We make our own decisions. The study of social welfare is so wonderful because it calls to us to assume the responsibility of our human heritage by using ourselves to make the life of everyone better. It involves us totally: our feelings, our values, our ability to think, learn, and reason. It can be a life-encompassing task, or a part of other tasks. But it is there. The future? I hope that here, at the end of this book, the future presents itself to you in a different way from before. I hope that you see it as rich with many opportunities, theoretical and practical. Most of all, I hope you see it as an active challenge to assume the responsibility for making everyone's social welfare a part of your life.

REFERENCES

1. Bill Kovach, "States Move to Reverse Wide Welfare Expansion," *New York Times*, August 16, 1971, pp. 1ff.
2. Ibid., p. 1.
3. Ibid., p. 36.
4. John Romanyshyn, *Social Welfare: Charity to Justice* (New York: Random House, 1971), pp. 258–290. See also the President's Commission on Income Maintenance Programs, *Working Papers* (Washington, D.C.: Government Printing Office, 1969), Part III, pp. 407–455.
5. Romanyshyn, op. cit., p. 268.

APPENDIX A

THE STRUCTURE OF SOCIAL WELFARE SERVICES: SOME ILLUSTRATIVE EXAMPLES

Social welfare programs change rapidly: old programs are modified or dropped, while new ones are created. Any static picture of the social welfare system will soon be out of date in its details, but the following illustrations of existing programs should help the student of social welfare as a social institution in contemporary United States society get a better sense of the whole and some of its major parts. The analytical framework used is explained and discussed in Chapter 3.

I. Public Programs: Some Illustrations

A. *Transfer Payment Programs*

    1. *Social Insurances*—In social insurance, the recipient pays into a fund and then essentially receives his own money back when he is eligible to collect. His payments may be supplemented by contributions from other sources (employer, for example).

        a. *Objectives*—Insurance (income replacement) and income redistribution.

        b. *Programs*

            (1) *Old Age, Survivors' and Disability Insurance (Social Security)*[1]

                (a) Objective—To provide a basic income for retired people and their families, and for those disabled or widowed.

                (b) Legislation—Social Security Act of 1935 and subsequent amendments.

                (c) Funding—Payroll tax on specified amount of earnings ($10,800 effective July 1, 1973), shared equally by employer and employee.

                (d) Administration—Social Security Administration (federal government); tax paid to the federal government and benefits paid by it.

                (e) Eligibility—"Insured status" required, obtained by having worked for a specified period of time in employment in which tax withholdings are taken; benefits paid at age 65 (or age 62 at lower benefit rates) to insured retired persons, their surviving minor or disabled children and spouse, and insured disabled workers and their dependents.

(f) Coverage in 1968—Retired workers and dependents—15,345,-493; survivors—5,815,987; disabled workers and dependents—2,257,793.

(g) Adequacy—Benefit rates tend to be higher than public assistance, but even so, in 1967 the average monthly payment to a retired worker with an eligible wife was $165. Irregularly employed farm and domestic workers, and employees of certain religious and nonprofit organizations are not covered (plus railroad workers and federal, state, and local government employees, who have their own retirement plans).

(h) Equity—All workers are not covered; the tax is regressive in that taxes are withheld only up to a certain amount; in order to qualify for coverage, the work history must have more stability and continuity than is usually possible for low-income workers.

(2) *Unemployment Insurance*[2]

(a) Objective—To provide cash for normally employed persons during periods of involuntary unemployment.

(b) Legislation—Federal Unemployment Tax Act of 1933 and subsequent amendments.

(c) Funding—payroll tax paid by employers on a specified amount of earnings per employee.

(d) Administration—Federal government collects part of the tax (through the Internal Revenue Service) for administrative expenses and to support the Employment Service, and also holds state-collected benefit funds in trust for each state. The individual states establish methods of computation of benefits, maximum benefit amounts, and maximum benefit duration. Benefits are paid through state unemployment offices. Railroad workers, federal government employees, and unemployed ex-servicemen have separate programs.

(e) Eligibility—Benefits based on earnings or employment experience during a recent, specified base period (varies by state). Must register at the state employment office, seek work, and be available for work.

(f) Coverage in 1968—Insured unemployed were 1,110,600, while uninsured unemployed were 1,997,400.

(g) Adequacy—Several categories of workers are not covered by unemployment insurance: state and local government employees; domestic workers; employees of nonprofit organizations; farm workers; employees of very small firms (less than four employees); the self-employed; unpaid family workers; young workers seeking their first job; and reentrants into the labor force. In 1968, the average weekly benefit was $43.43, and the average duration of benefits was 11.6 weeks; benefit computation and distribution differ widely among states.

(h) Equity—All workers are not covered; there are variations in requirements and benefits by state; in order to qualify for coverage, the work history must have more stability and continuity than is usually possible for low-income workers.

(3) *Workmen's Compensation*[3]

  (a) Objective—Compensation of a worker for work-connected injury regardless of assessment of fault.

  (b) Legislation—Each state has its own; the earliest was in 1911. The federal government also has such legislation covering its employees; the first federal legislation was passed in 1908.

  (c) Funding—Employers contract with a private company for insurance, or in some states there are state-run insurance programs. An employer may also choose to be self-insured.

  (d) Administration—Benefits are paid by the insurance agent. In most states, employees make no contribution, the cost being borne by the employer as a cost of business operation. Scope of coverage, benefit provisions, and administrative procedures vary by state.

  (e) Eligibility—See (g).

  (f) Coverage in 1967—approximately 2.2 million workers.

  (g) Adequacy—Casual labor, agricultural, and domestic work is *not* covered, nor is some work in religious and charitable institutions. There are three categories of coverage with varying benefit procedures: permanent total disability; permanent partial disability; and temporary total disability.

  (h) Equity—All workers are not covered; there are variations in benefits and procedures by state.

2. *Tax Transfers*[4]

a. *Objectives*—Special deductions, credits, exclusions, exemptions, and preferential rates designed to achieve various social and economic objectives. They represent income lost or deferred for the federal government, and therefore may be seen as payment transfers.

b. *Programs*—There are numerous, complex tax transfers. Some of the ones particularly relevant for social welfare will be briefly noted below.

  (1) *In Commerce:* Individuals may exclude $100 of dividends from taxable income, and deduct interest paid on consumer credit; corporations may get tax benefits from expenses for research and development.

  (2) *In Community Development and Housing:* Mortgage interest and property taxes may be deducted from taxable income by homeowners.

  (3) *In Health and Welfare:* The aged and disabled get special tax deductions, and need not declare Social Security benefits; Unemployment Insurance and Workmen's Compensation benefits need not be declared, nor need Public Assistance payments; both employer and employee get exemptions relating to pension plans; interest on life insurance savings is not taxable; most philanthropic contributions are deductible; certain medical, child and dependent care, and casualty loss costs are deductible.

(4) *In Education and Manpower:* Deductions for students and contributions to educational institutions; scholarship and fellowship deductions can sometimes be taken.

(5) *In Veterans' Benefits and Services:* Veterans Administration benefits and payments are nontaxable.

(6) *In Aid to State and Local Government Financing:* There is a variety of tax benefits extended to state and local governments.

c. *Summary and evaluation*—Tax deductions represent substantial income transfer programs. However, many of them serve to benefit the non-poor (property tax and mortgage deductions, for example), and reduce the federal funds that could otherwise be used to provide more adequate social welfare services. To the extent that tax programs are not specifically seen as income transfer programs, there may be an inaccurate assessment of social welfare services being provided or needed. In some cases, it would be very legitimate to question whether the tax system is the best way to achieve various social welfare goals.

3. *Public Assistance*—Direct cash grants from local, state, and federal tax monies to individuals or families in financial need.

a. *Objectives*—To provide adequate financial aid to insure that everyone has basic physical needs.

b. *Programs*[5]

(1) *Old Age Assistance* (OAA)

(a) Objectives—To provide for basic, unmet needs of persons 65 and older.

(b) Legislation—Social Security Act of 1935 and subsequent amendments.

(c) Funding—Combination of state, federal, and local funds. In 1968, on the average, 66.1 percent of the total cost (payments and administrative costs) was federal money, 28.8 percent was state, and 5.1 percent was local. The amount of the federal contribution (which comes from general revenue funds) varies according to the characteristics of the state's program, the state's ability to meet the costs, and the general economic condition of the state.

(d) Administration—The federal government established general requirements which states must meet to qualify for federal funds (to insure some uniformity and equity in programs), but the individual states administer or supervise the program and set major eligibility requirements. At the federal level, financial participation and supervision is through the Department of Health, Education, and Welfare, Social Rehabilitation Service, Assistance Payments Administration. At the state level, there is usually a state department of social services (or similar structure) which sets standards and administers the state program, while actual services are provided through county or city social service departments (there is some variation by state).

(e) Eligibility—Eligibility varies by state. The *federal guidelines* that state programs must observe include administrative standards, state-wide operation with opportunity for all to apply and be considered, grievance procedures, standards of confidentiality, use of income and other resources as one standard of eligibility, limitations on unreasonable state eligibility requirements and payments, and certain legal requirements. *State requirements* usually include proof of age (65 or over), limitations on property and income, application to and agreement with the requirements set by the appropriate state facility (including a social study and home visits). Residence requirements have twice been declared unconstitutional, but are still being contested in some states.

(f) Coverage as of January 1, 1969—Of the total estimated population age 65 and over of 19,485,000, 2,024,000 received OAA.

(g) Adequacy—In June 1969, the average monthly assistance payment per recipient (excluding medical payments) was $71. OAA payments may be supplemented by Social Security benefits as long as the recipient still falls within the need category established by the state.

(h) Equity—OAA is equitable in that all states have such programs, and any citizen may apply. However, while in theory the principle of "unmet need" is used to determine payments (amounts needed to live less resources available), in only twenty-four of the fifty states is this amount actually paid. In the others, there are maximum payments permitted which leave many recipients with less than their unmet need.

(2) *Aid to the Permanently and Totally Disabled* (APTD)[6]

(a) Objectives—To provide for basic, unmet needs of persons defined as permanently or totally disabled. It is not a program to cover medical expenses.

(b) Legislation—Created in the 1950 amendments to the Social Security Act of 1935.

(c) Funding—Same as Old Age Assistance; in 1969, the average federal share of costs was 58.6 percent, with state and local costs representing about 41.4 percent of the total.

(d) Administration—Same as Old Age Assistance.

(e) Eligibility—The federal guidelines are the same as Old Age Assistance. The state guidelines are also the same, except the age requirement is usually 18 to 65, and medical proof of disability is required.

(f) Coverage in January 1969—711,000 individuals received APTD in 1969.

(g) Adequacy—In June 1969, the average grant was $86 per recipient (excluding medical payments). As with OAA, payments may be supplemented by Social Security benefits.

(h) Equity—All states except Nevada have APTD disabled. As with OAA, the recipient's unmet need is not always covered by his grant. In addition, state variations in defining disability create inequality in eligibility, and, while payments are similar in size to OAA, the disabled are likely to have greater needs. APTD would more logically be a health service rather than an income-maintenance program.

(3) *Aid to the Blind* (AB)[7]
- (a) Objectives—To provide for basic, unmet needs of blind persons.
- (b) Legislation—Social Security Act of 1935 and subsequent amendments.
- (c) Funding—Same as OAA and APTD; in 1969, the average percentage of federal, state, and local funds were 56.8, 35.5, and 7.6 respectively.
- (d) Administration—Same as OAA and APTD.
- (e) Eligibility—Same as OAA, except that in the state requirements the minimum age is usually 18, and medical proof of blindness is necessary (according to the state definition of blindness).
- (f) Coverage in January 1969—80,500 recipients.
- (g) Adequacy—In June 1969, the average grant was $95 per recipient (excluding medical payments). Social Security benefits may supplement these grants.
- (h) Equity—All states have Aid to the Blind programs. AB grants tend to be the most adequate of any public assistance program, but even so, they are minimal.

(4) *Aid to the Aged, Blind, and Disabled*—A 1962 amendment to the Social Security Act of 1935 permitted states to combine Aid to the Blind, Aid to the Permanently and Totally Disabled, and Old Age Assistance. In 1963 only 17 states had made these changes; the change has made little difference in actual operation of the programs.

(5) *Aid to Families with Dependent Children* (AFDC)[8]
- (a) Objectives—To provide for basic, unmet needs of children who are "dependent" (deprived of the care and support of at least one parent).
- (b) Legislation—Social Security Act of 1935 in the form of Aid to Dependent Children. Subsequent amendments include the ones in 1950 that included the children's caretaker, thus making it Aid to Families with Dependent Children.
- (c) Funding—Same as previous public assistance programs discussed. In 1969, the average federal, state, and local percentage contributions were 56.1, 30.6, and 13.2, respectively.
- (d) Administration—Same as other public assistance programs.
- (e) Eligibility—Federal guidelines same as OAA. The state guidelines are the same with the following exceptions: age limit for the child of eighteen (twenty-one if still in school); caretaker must prove child deprived of the care and support of one parent by death, desertion, or incapacity (in twenty-one states, unemployment is also considered grounds for eligibility); in desertion cases, the father must be reported and a warrant for nonsupport sworn out; cooperation in making a plan leading to self-support in the future.
- (f) Coverage as of December 1968—There were 6,086,000 recipients, including 1,522,000 families and 4,555,000 individuals.
- (g) Adequacy—In 1969, the average grant (excluding medical payments) was $173 per family and $44 per recipient. From its original passage, AFDC benefits have been lower than benefits

in the other public assistance programs. This can be understood considering the societal values surrounding such issues as work, sexual mores, and dependency, which are integral parts of AFDC. In addition, those who benefit most—women and children—are likely to have the least political power.

(h) Equity—All states have AFDC programs, although not all have unemployment as an eligibility criterion. Unmet need is usually substantial, given the size of permissible AFDC grants. Furthermore, eligibility requirements are such that family breakup is encouraged by making it more economically feasible in many cases for the father to disappear if he cannot support the family, and to have illegitimate children rather than burdening a man only marginally able to support the family by getting married. The fact that women are required to report husbands who have

---

EXHIBIT A–1
Public Assistance in the United States: Some Illustrative Data

The following data show the diversity in public assistance payments created by the federal-state system of funding. These differences theoretically reflect regional differences in the cost of living, but in fact are more nearly indicative of political realities (the low level of payments in the southern states, for example, where many recipients are black and legislators are whites).

Aid to Families with Dependent Children: Recipients and Grants (February 1971)

State	Number Recipients	Average Grant	Number Families	Average Grant
Alabama	171,000	$15.20	43,600	$59.55
Arizona	63,200	31.95	16,300	123.80
Arkansas	63,300	25.05	17,000	93.45
Florida	267,000	24.10	71,200	90.15
Illinois	535,000	56.55	128,000	235.95
Louisiana	233,000	19.70	57,300	80.05
Maine	56,100	40.35	15,300	147.80
Maryland	167,000	43.50	44,900	162.10
Mississippi	131,000	12.05	33,900	46.60
Montana	18,600	45.85	5,500	156.05
New York	1,262,000	70.95	337,000	265.90
Oregon	106,000	46.50	29,400	167.55
Pennsylvania	596,000	61.45	152,000	241.45
Puerto Rico	299,000	9.00	58,700	45.85
Texas	352,000	29.20	87,400	117.80
Utah	40,000	42.15	11,000	154.05

Source: Public Assistance Statistics February 1971 (NCSS Report A-2 [2/71]), U. S. Department of Health, Education, and Welfare, Social and Rehabilitation Service, Program Statistics and Data Systems, National Center for Social Statistics, p. 15.

deserted them creates ill will between the man and woman, and between the recipients and welfare and law enforcement personnel. Although the 1967 amendments allow a working mother to deduct her work expenses from the income considered in computing unmet need, and keep $30 plus one-third of the remainder of her income, persons with low-paying jobs are still not likely to make enough to noticeably improve their financial position over what it would be receiving assistance and not working. Recent legislation now requires that employable recipients accept work if available as a condition of receiving assistance.

(6) *General Assistance* (GA)[9]

    (a) Objectives—To provide for basic, unmet needs of those ineligible for federally aided programs: single persons; childless couples under age sixty-five who are not disabled or blind; families with children having employed male heads (the underemployed); and families with children having unemployed male heads in states not having unemployment as an acceptable AFDC eligibility criterion.

    (b) Legislation—None at the federal level; a state and local program.

    (c) Funding—Exclusively from state, state-local, or local funds.

    (d) Administration—Varies greatly; some combination of state and local administration, or just local administration.

    (e) Eligibility—At the discretion of the funding body; often dire need is necessary, either of an emergency nature or one that cannot be met in any other way.

    (f) Coverage in June 1969 (rough estimate)—769,000 recipients.

    (g) Adequacy—In 1969, the average recipient grant was $47.65 (rough estimate).

    (h) Equity—Virtually impossible to discuss because of enormous variation. In general, General Assistance is a residual category poorly funded and erratically administered. It provides a last resort to those in extreme need.

4. *Health—Transfer Programs*

    a. *Objectives*—To provide basic health services for the sick, and to insure adequate prenatal and infant care.

    b. *Programs*

      (1) *Medical Assistance for the Aged (Medicare)*[10]

        (a) Objectives—To cover the hospital and medical needs of the aged.

        (b) Legislation—Medical Assistance for the Aged (Kerr-Mills bill), passed in July 1965.

        (c) Funding—A combination insurance–payment-for-service program, paid for by the federal government and the recipient. Hospital costs are covered by part of the individual's Social Security payment (shared by employer and employee). Medical costs are met by: a small monthly fee paid by the recipient; half of the total cost paid by the federal government out of general funds; and a $50 deductible paid by the recipient. The medical program part of Medicare is optional.

(d) Administration—The Social Security Administration.

(e) Eligibility—Coverage under Social Security for hospital care, and payment of required costs (optional) for medical care.

(f) Coverage as of June 1968—Persons covered in hospitals—19,697,000; medical coverage—18,798,000.

(g) Adequacy—Adequate coverage for those enrolled.

(h) Equity—There is the built-in limitation that only those covered under Social Security (or similar programs) are covered for hospital care. In addition, for medical care, the individual must have adequate resources to pay the monthly fee and deductible amount.

(2) *Medical Assistance for the Aged (Medicaid)*[11]

(a) Objectives—To cover the hospital and medical needs of the aged.

(b) Legislation—Same as Medicare.

(c) Funding—Same as Medicare, plus the following extension: to cover the medical costs of Medicare for all persons receiving public assistance and aged people not qualifying for OAA but whose medical costs would make them legally indigent, a local-state-federal sharing plan was established to insure such persons.

(d) Administration—Through the public assistance structure set up in each state. Benefits are paid directly to the providers (vendors) of the needed medical service. At the federal level, Medicaid is administered through the Department of Health, Education, and Welfare through the Social and Rehabilitation Services Division.

(e) Eligibility—All public assistance recipients must be covered for a state to receive federal shares for medical payments. Each state may set its own benefit levels, and may elect to cover the medically indigent aged.

(f) Coverage in November 1967—Approximately 4.6 million people had payments for medical care made for them, including payments to the medically indigent aged.

(g) Adequacy—Adequate coverage for those involved.

(h) Equity—Only those receiving public assistance are covered under age 65. Over age 65, only those who would otherwise be medically indigent are covered (in addition to those receiving public assistance).

5. *Housing—Transfer Programs*

a. *Objectives*—To improve the quality and supply of housing, and to minimize housing as a barrier to economic and social well-being.

b. *Programs*

(1) *Public Housing*[12]

(a) Objectives—To improve the quality of low-income housing, and housing available to large families.

(b) Legislation—Wagner-Steagall Act of 1937 and Housing and Urban Development Act of 1968.

(c) Funding—Rents cover operating costs and an operating reserve; federal contributions cover capital costs; local communities usually exempt the land from taxes and provide public services.

(d) Administration—Local public housing authorities incorporated under state law to develop and maintain public housing units. Federal supervision is done by the Housing Assistance Administration.

(e) Eligibility—Determined by local public housing authorities, and vary widely. Eligibility requirements usually include substandard housing, low income, and disadvantaged status. The median annual income eligibility for an average family of four is about $3,700. Large families with very low incomes have their rents subsidized by the Housing and Urban Development Act of 1968.

(f) Coverage in 1969—There were approximately 650,000 habitable units of public housing, with a waiting list of over 500,000 families.

(g) Adequacy—The physical space and conditions provided in public housing are adequate. The social environment is often unattractive to residents, and can encourage rapid physical deterioration of public housing units.

(h) Equity—With such long waiting lists, large numbers of eligible families are obviously being excluded. Although subsidized public housing helps get better housing for the money, the very poorest families do not qualify due to requirements of minimum rental payments. Housing management also tends to be very selective among cultural, racial, and ethnic groups, while public housing often destroys pre-existing neighborhood patterns and creates new ghettos.

(2) *Rent Supplement*[13]

(a) Objectives—to improve the quality of low-income housing.

(b) Legislation—Housing and Urban Development Act of 1965, and 1968 amendments.

(c) Funding—Federal Housing Administration supplements rents for amounts needed for maintenance and amortization. Rent payments are tied to income level. Subsidies cannot exceed 70 percent of the housing unit's cost.

(d) Administration—Department of Housing and Urban Development authorizes program allocations to private developers in local communities through the administering agency of the Federal Housing Administration.

(e) Eligibility—Locally determined and therefore variable. Usually includes substandard housing, low income, and disadvantaged status.

(f) Coverage in 1968 (first year of operation)—Only 11,000 units were to be constructed, although 3–4 million families qualified.

(g) Adequacy—Minimal effect so far.

(h) Equity—As in public housing, the poorest families don't qualify. Accommodations for large families are minimal.

(3) *Housing Loan Program*[14]

(a) Objectives—To stimulate home building and purchasing.

(b) Legislation—National Housing Acts of 1934 and 1954.

(c) Funding—Federal Housing Administration guarantees home loans at set interest rates; also insures construction of homes and rental housing in urban renewal areas.

(d) Administration—See (c).

(e) Eligibility—Families displaced by urban renewal and other government action; families who can meet the credit standards of lenders.

(f) Coverage up to 1965—Approximately 6,664,250 homes and 48,000 rental units were insured.

(g) Adequacy—Has stimulated home building and enabled many to own their homes with manageable mortgage payments.

(h) Equity—Limited to moderate-income families that can meet the credit requirements of lenders.

(4) *Urban Renewal*[15]

(a) Objectives—To relieve blighted areas and reclaim land for more productive uses through clearance and rehabilitation.

(b) Legislation—Housing Act of 1949 and subsequent amendments.

(c) Funding—Renewal Assistance Administration (of the Department of Housing and Urban Development) obtains and clears the land to be developed. Urban renewal projects qualify for housing loans (above).

(d) Administration—Local or state agency requests the Renewal Assistance Administration to obtain and clear land, after which it is turned over to private or public developers.

(e) Eligibility—Approval of plan presented to the Renewal Assistance Administration by state or local agencies.

(f) Coverage up to 1969—About $7 billion given in grants for renewal, redevelopment, and rehabilitation.

(g) Adequacy—Has had a major impact on the low-income housing market. Since 1956, relocation allowances are granted to affected residents.

(h) Equity—Low-income neighborhoods are often destroyed, with inadequate provision made for the relocation of the residents.

(5) *Rural Housing*[16]

(a) Objectives—To provide decent housing and essential farm buildings for rural residents.

(b) Legislation—Housing Act of 1949 and its amendments; Housing and Urban Development Act of 1968.

(c) Funding—Farmers Home Administration (USDA) makes small grants and loans to rural residents not able to qualify for regular market loans; grants are also made to local governments for construction and improvement projects. Department of Housing and Urban Development provides assistance for land purchase and building.

(d) Administration—See (c).

(e) Eligibility—Financial need; lack of qualification in the regular loan market; need for community development.

(f) Coverage in 1968—400,000 low-income rural residents.

(g) Adequacy—Has stimulated rural community development.

(h) Equity—Primarily to benefit those excluded from the regular loan market, and residents of depressed areas.

(6) *Leased Housing*[17]

(a) Objectives—To provide more adequate low-income housing while scattering low-income persons throughout the housing areas in established neighborhoods.

(b) Legislation—Sections 23 and 106 of the National Housing Acts.

(c) Funding—Federal government subsidizes rents paid by tenants.

(d) Administration—The Housing Assistance Administration administers the federal shares, cooperating with local housing authorities, which negotiate with landlords for acceptance of tenants. The selection of tenants varies by agreement between the local authority and the landlord, but the authority can obtain significant control.

(e) Eligibility—Determined by the local authorities and varies widely, although low income is usually one criterion.

(f) Coverage as of August 31, 1968—22,704 leases had been executed.

(g) Adequacy—Gives the renter a much wider selection of rental choices than would otherwise be the case, but there has been limited success in achieving sociocultural integration.

(h) Equity—As with other housing programs discussed, there is a maximum subsidy specified so the lowest income persons are effectively excluded. Local control permits considerable inequities in operation.

6. *Food-Transfer Programs*

a. *Objectives*—To improve the nutrition of low-income families, recognizing the relationship of nutrition to normal growth and development.

b. *Programs*

(1) *Commodity Distribution Program*

(a) Objectives—To use surplus agricultural commodities for the benefit of low-income families.

(b) Legislation—Agricultural Adjustment Act of 1935.

(c) Funding—Department of Agriculture provides food acquired through price-support and surplus-removal purchases free to states requesting such food. Costs of distribution borne by states.

(d) Administration—A voluntary program; request by the governor of a state required, as well as obeying rules of the program. Commodities delivered to specially designated agency of the state for distribution. The food is usually distributed through the public welfare structure in the state. In some cases where demonstrated need exists, the Department of Agriculture may pay the costs of distribution for a county or operate its own program in a county.

(e) Eligibility—The standards used to determine eligibility for public assistance are used.

    (f) Coverage in 1969—3.8 million participants.

    (g) Adequacy—It is estimated that less than half of those with sub-standard diets take advantage of either the Commodity Distribution or Food Stamp programs.

    (h) Equity—Working through the welfare structure builds in the inequities of variable eligibility and limited outreach. In addition, limited distribution points, bulk form of the commodities distributed, and lack of choice in commodities obtained all serve to limit the utility of the program. No cooking instruction is provided to maximize the utility of the commodities obtained.

(2) *Food Stamp Program*[18]

    (a) Objectives—Increasing the food purchasing power of low-income consumers using the normal market system.

    (b) Legislation—Food Stamp Act of 1964.

    (c) Funding—Department of Agriculture subsidizes the recipient's food budget by allowing him to purchase more food than the market value of the amount he spends; determination of eligibility and operational costs are borne by the state.

    (d) Administration—States submit plans for Department of Agriculture approval. The program is operationalized through the existing public assistance structure.

    (e) Eligibility—Generally public assistance income eligibility requirements prevail; application for food stamps on the part of the recipient is voluntary. The recipient must pay a "purchase requirement," an amount determined by the Department of Agriculture on a sliding scale according to income, which is then supplemented by stamps of greater value than the amount paid.

    (f) Coverage in 1969—2.9 million participants.

    (g) Adequacy—See 1(g).

    (h) Equity—The limitations imposed by the public assistance structure exist. Households with no income cannot participate since they cannot meet the purchase requirement. No budgeting counseling is provided to maximize the program's effectiveness.

(3) *Child Feeding Programs*[19]

    (a) Objectives—To improve the nutrition of children and increase food consumption.

    (b) Legislation[20]—National School Lunch Act of 1946 (School Lunch Program), Agricultural Act of 1954 (Special Milk Program for Children), Child Nutrition Act of 1966 (School Breakfast Program and Equipment Program).

    (c) Funding—School Lunch Program: Department of Agriculture funds matched by the state (usually obtained from what school children pay for their lunches); Special Milk Program: Department of Agriculture funds supplemented by the institution using the milk; Equipment Program: 75 percent/25 percent matching federal/state-local.

    (d) Administration—School Lunch and Special Milk Programs: federal money and commodities distributed through the state educational agency on the basis of school requests (the Special

Milk Program also covers other types of child care institutions).
(e) Eligibility—Children at the covered schools or institutions. The Equipment Program exists so that schools needing the other programs but lacking the facilities may obtain what is needed.
(f) Coverage—School Lunch Program: about 20 million children participate out of 36 million eligible; 137,462 (in 1966) of these received reduced price or free lunches under a Special Assistance provision. Equipment Program: in 1967, about 586 schools received grants. Special Milk Program: in 1967, about 95,000 institutions participated. School Breakfast Program: in 1968, about 1,000 schools participated.
(g) Adequacy—The School Lunch Program is the most extensively developed, and yet the coverage noted above is well under what it could be.
(h) Equity—These programs generally require that the child pays something to participate (Special Assistance reduced and free provisions are sometimes available), which excludes many.

B. *Social Service Programs*[21] "Organized activity that aims at helping toward a mutual adjustment of individuals and their social environment."[22] Social Service programs are composed of: (1) concrete, identifiable activities (meals on wheels, homemaker services, etc.); (2) relationship activities, usually in clinical settings (counseling of various kinds); and (3) educative activities (birth-control clinics, legal aid, etc.).

1. *Relationship to income maintenance programs:* Social service programs supplement income maintenance programs by providing the concrete skills, counseling, or information that are often essential to an individual's understanding of his situation as well as the steps needed to become economically independent. Social services are rarely completely paid for by the recipient of the service; tax-supported or charitable subsidies are usually involved.
   a. *Objectives*—"Social Services appear to be designed to assist people who are not capable of normal participation in the usual areas of life. The failure to perform may be permanent, temporary, individually determined, or imposed by society and circumstance. There is always a presumption of need for help."[23]
   b. *Programs*
      (1) *Social Services in Public Assistance*[24]
         (a) Objectives—To improve the level of functioning of recipients of public assistance grants.
         (b) Legislation—See IA3.
         (c) Funding—See 6A(3) (b).
         (d) Administration—See 6A(3) (b).
         (e) Eligibility—Anyone receiving a public assistance grant.
         (f) Coverage—The actual percent of public assistance recipients who also receive social services varies by assistance category, problem area, and manpower resources.
         (g) Adequacy—Social services in public assistance are generally inadequate for many reasons. Inadequate funding is a major

one, reflected in the fact that in 1967 the median caseload of AFDC was 64 cases each, and in adult programs the median was 160 cases each. (The recent separation of income support payments and the provision of social services should help solve this problem.) In addition, there is societal value ambiguity which leads to low grants and the provision of few social services.

(h) Equity—Social services provided through public assistance are inherently inequitable for two major reasons: (1) they are tied to the receipt of public assistance, and are not available to those who do not qualify; and (2) they become part of the social control mechanism in public assistance, whereby receipt of a grant and social services is tied to obeying set rules.

(2) *Child Welfare*[25]

(a) Objectives—To supplement or substitute for parental care and supervision.

(b) Legislation—Social Security Act of 1935 and subsequent amendments.

(c) Funding—Department of Health, Education, and Welfare, through the Children's Bureau, makes grants to state welfare departments on a variable matching formula.

(d) Administration—The Children's Bureau on the federal level, and the state public assistance network on the local level.

(e) Eligibility—There is usually a test of prospective clients' ability to pay, but most services are not by intent tied to income. Eligibility is usually determined by need for the service and application for it.

(f) Coverage in 1967—607,900 children were receiving services (48 percent in their own or relatives' homes, 34 percent in foster homes, 10 percent in institutions, and 7 percent in adoptive homes).

(g) Adequacy—There are five major child welfare services: foster home care; adoptions; protective services; day care; and services to unmarried mothers. These services seem to include most circumstances of possible need. AFDC might also be considered a related program, along with school food programs.

(h) Equity—The provision of child welfare services through the public assistance network has tended to restrict usage of the services to low-income persons who are familiar with public assistance, or who will (or must) accept the social stigma of receiving services through that network.

(3) *Neighborhood Service Centers*[26]

(a) Objectives—To provide decentralized, coordinated, and improved services within easy access to users.

(b) Legislation—Economic Opportunity Act of 1964, and the Public Works and Economic Development Act of 1965.

(c) Funding—See (d).

(d) Administration—A cooperative program between four federal agencies and selected cities, through which grants are made to the cities.

(e) Eligibility—At the present time, pilot studies are being undertaken.

(f) Coverage—Too early for adequate data.

(g) Adequacy Too early for adequate data.

(h) Equity—Too early for adequate data. However, by intent the Neighborhood Service Center attempts to maximize equity by reducing transportation and information barriers in the provision and receipt of services.

(4) *Vocational Rehabilitation*[27]

(a) Objectives—To prepare the disabled for jobs.

(b) Legislation—Smith-Fess Act of 1920, Social Security Act of 1935, and subsequent amendments, and Vocational Rehabilitation Act of 1965, Medicare amendment of 1965.

(c) Funding—Federal-State cooperative program.

(d) Administration—Federal grants are administered through the Department of Health, Education, and Welfare, the Social and Rehabilitation Service division, and specifically the Rehabilitation Services Administration. State programs are administrated through State Vocational Rehabilitation agencies, which present a plan to the federal administration for funding. There are federal guidelines that state plans must follow, but beyond that, there is considerable flexibility at the state and local levels.

(e) Eligibility—Federal guidelines require that a state have a non-discriminatory program without a means test or age requirement, and with certain administrative characteristics. Determination of existence of disability and rehabilitation potential are state-determined within broad federal guidelines.

(f) Coverage in 1966—There were over 900,000 persons being helped by state rehabilitation agencies.

(g) Adequacy—It is estimated that 3.7 million people could benefit from vocational rehabilitation services. However, for those rehabilitated, it is a much more efficient service economically and psychologically than only providing income support.

(h) Equity—The variability of state eligibility requirements and ambiguity in definitions of disabled status lead to inequities. These problems are accentuated by large worker caseloads.

(5) *Health—Social Services*[28] (*Maternal and Child Health; Neighborhood Health Centers*)

(a) Objectives—To provide for the health needs of mothers, children, and crippled children; to provide accessible neighborhood health services and train resident, unskilled workers for positions in the health field.

(b) Legislation—Social Security Act of 1935 and subsequent amendments; Economic Opportunity Act of 1964.

(c) Funding—Neighborhood Health Centers; costs charged back to other public or private sources; other costs met through cooperation with other health services. Maternal and Child Health: variable federal-state sharing formula, federal HEW grants being paid to state Health Departments and/or Crippled Children's agencies.

(d) Administration—Federal grants used by state to develop and operate services through Health and Crippled Children's agencies in the state. Neighborhood Health Centers are operated by the Office of Economic Opportunity in conjunction with other federal, state, and local programs.

(e) Eligibility—Based on need for services.

(f) Coverage—In 1968, Neighborhood Health Centers treated about 500,000 persons. Maternal and Child Health service coverage in 1967 was well over 20 million persons.

(g) Adequacy—Neighborhood Health Centers have great, but as yet unrealized, potential. Maternal and Child Health services are more extensive, including maternity clinics, family planning, public health nurse visits to the home, well-child clinics, pediatric clinics, school health programs, dental care programs, immunization programs, and mental retardation and illness programs.

(h) Equity—Primarily serve low-income persons because of their lack of access to other service resources.

(6) *Employment Service*[29]

(a) Objectives—To provide employment information and counseling, and to administer unemployment insurance claims.

(b) Legislation—Wagner-Peyser Act of 1933 reestablished the United States Employment Service; there have been subsequent revisions.

(c) Funding—Federal Unemployment Tax, plus funds from the tax surcharge enacted in 1969.

(d) Administration—Federal administration and federal guidelines operated through the Department of Labor, Bureau of Employment Security. Employment offices are state operated although federally funded.

(e) Eligibility—All workers legally qualified to work. Disabled persons and veterans are given preference.

(f) Coverage in 1966—5.72 million people were placed by the Employment Service during 1966.

(g) Adequacy—In 1966, 47.8 percent of the total unemployed were placed by the Employment Service. The service also operates or administers numerous programs oriented toward the disadvantaged (Youth Opportunity Centers, Job Corps, Neighborhood Youth Corps, New Careers Program, Operation Mainstream, and the Work Incentive Program are among the best-known).

(h) Equity—Equitable in that any legally qualified worker must be served. However, there is a great deal of attention given to unemployment rather than employment counseling created by the relationship with the Unemployment Insurance program. Questions are also raised as to whether the Employment Service ought to give greater emphasis or priority to certain particularly disadvantaged groups in the job market.

(7) *Area Redevelopment*[30]

(a) Objectives—To provide new industry and permanent jobs in areas of chronically high unemployment and low income.

(b) Legislation—Public Works and Economic Development Act of 1965, creating the Economic Development Administration.[31]

(c) Funding—Federal loans, training programs, contract priorities, technical assistance, and public works programs.

(d) Administration—administered by the Department of Commerce with the Department of Labor handling training programs. Regional commissions are established to work with local government and groups in designing and implementing programs.

(e) Eligibility—Areas of chronic high unemployment and low income.

(f) Coverage—Appalachia, upper Great Lakes, Ozarks, the Four Corners, and Indian reservations.

(g) Adequacy—Has been relatively unsuccessful, with spotty coverage and success, high loan-default rates, and high out-migration.

(h) Equity—Does not cover small pockets of need, tends to help those already employed, firms benefit rather than the area and its people in many cases.

(8) *Neighborhood Youth Corps*[32]

(a) Objectives—To encourage completion of high school by providing part-time and summer work opportunities, and working with high school dropouts.

(b) Legislation—Economic Opportunity Act of 1964.

(c) Funding—Federal funds supplemented by work-sponsor contributions (sometimes on an in-kind basis).

(d) Administration—Office of Economic Opportunity, through the Department of Labor's Bureau of Work and Training Programs, distributes federal funds and approves locally sponsored projects. Sponsors include community action agencies, public schools, social agencies, and employers.

(e) Eligibility—Ninth to twelfth grade in school, local standards of low income, or school dropout status.

(f) Coverage—In 1968, 133,000 part-time school jobs were provided, 251,000 summer jobs, and 68,000 jobs for dropouts.

(g) Adequacy—It is unclear whether, even for the population covered, there are long-term effects. It has been successful in prolonging school attendance, but the dropout program is dubious as anything other than a temporary income-maintenance program.

(h) Equity—The programs require local initiative and hence are not equally available to the total target population. These programs can have a potentially adverse effect on the regular employment market, which could otherwise fill many of these jobs.

(9) *Manpower Development and Training*[33]

(a) Objectives—To reduce unemployment through job training and retraining.

(b) Legislation—Manpower Development and Training Act of 1962.

(c) Funding—Federal funds with state contributions.

(d) Administration—The Manpower Administration of the Department of Labor has overall federal administrative control. In the Institutional Training Program, the Office of Education

(Department of Health, Education, and Welfare) provides curriculum, instruction, and facilities, while the state employment
offices handle testing, screening, and job placement. In the
On-the-Job Training Program, contracts are made with employers at the local level, and the employers (often with the
state employment office) recruit and select candidates.

(e) Eligibility—Institutional Training Programs: unemployed status,
or desire to upgrade job skills, with a focus on the hard-core
unemployed or marginally employed. On-the-Job Training program: the employer sets hiring standards for the unemployed
applicants or selection procedures for employees who want to
upgrade their skills.

(f) Coverage in 1967—176,500 received training in Institutional
Training Programs, and 109,900 in On-the-Job Training Programs.

(g) Adequacy—These programs cover a small percentage of the
unemployed, the marginally employed, and those who will
probably be displaced by technology in the near future.

(h) Equity—There is some tendency toward "creaming" (taking
those with the best probability of success), especially in On-
the-Job Training Programs where employers make the final
hiring decisions. Coverage is limited, and the size and focus of
the programs tend to be responsive to employment market
conditions rather than individual needs.

(10) *Job Corps*[34]

(a) Objectives—To help disadvantaged young people prepare for
responsibilities of citizenship and increase their employability
through training in residential settings.

(b) Legislation—Economic Opportunity Act of 1964.

(c) Funding—Federal.

(d) Administration—Office of Economic Opportunity contracts with
large corporations to operate urban centers, and with universities, nonprofit organizations, and state agencies (in cooperation
with the departments of Agriculture and Interior) to operate
rural centers (called Civilian Conservation Centers).

(e) Eligibility—Disadvantaged status, ages fourteen through twenty-
one; focuses on the most poorly educated youth (data published in 1967 showed average years of school to be 8.8 with
an average reading level of 4.8 and math level of 5.0).

(f) Coverage in 1968—100,500 enrollees received training.

(g) Adequacy—One of the few training programs that seems to
reach the really hard-core disadvantaged. However, many leave
the program before it can have an impact—in 1967, 22 percent
left after one month.

(h) Equity—Seems to be equally available to all in the target group,
and to offer usable training to all enrollees. The residential
nature of the program is sometimes seen as undesirable by
participants, especially the rural settings.

C. *Programs for Special Groups*

1. *Veterans*[35]

   a. *Objectives*—To provide income support, health services, and readjustment aids to people serving in the Armed Forces during wartime, during a recognized period of armed conflict, or during the Cold War period between January 31, 1955 and August 5, 1964.

   b. *Programs*—There are numerous programs, some of which will be summarized below. All require veteran status as defined above, plus, in some cases, evidence of need. All services are funded and administered by the Veterans Administration.

   (1) *Veterans Compensation*—Provides monthly compensation checks to veterans with service-connected disability, as well as payments for dependents. Also provides monthly support payments to surviving dependents of deceased veterans who died of service connected causes (in addition to Social Security death benefits).

   (2) *Pensions*—Pensions are paid to war veterans who were not injured in service, but who are needy and unable to work, as well as to needy survivors of veterans who died of causes not related to their military service. Economic need is an eligibility requirement. Social Security benefits are counted as income determining need.

   (3) *Life Insurance*—Low-cost government-sponsored life insurance is available to veterans under a variety of plans.

   (4) *Health Services*—Free hospital and medical service is provided to veterans and their dependents at military medical facilities and Veterans Hospitals. Free drugs are also included. Long-term domiciliary care is provided for eligible veterans in Veterans Hospital facilities.

   (5) *Vocational Rehabilitation*—Vocational rehabilitation services are provided when needed (as determined by the Veterans Administration) for veterans with service-connected disabilities. Generally, training is available for up to four years, and vocational counseling is also provided. Eligible veterans may enroll in schools and colleges, institutional training, on-the-job training, or combination programs. During training, subsistence payments are made in addition to disability payments.

   (6) *Dependent's Educational Assistance*—A monthly grant is available to wives and children of deceased or permanently and totally disabled veterans (service-connected) for a maximum of thirty-six months. This payment is in addition to death or compensation payments.

   (7) *GI Bill Education and Training*—Veterans and servicemen are eligible for payments for approved study toward a specified career objective. Thirty-six months is the maximum study period for which payments are made, and grants are larger for veterans with dependents. Disadvantaged veterans can complete their high school education or take deficiency courses required to continue their training without any loss of time from the thirty-six months permitted.

2. *Farmers*[36]

    a. *Objectives*—To cushion the downward trend in the price of farm prod-
    ucts (due to technological advances), smoothing out income fluctua-
    tions, and supporting farm incomes.

    b. *Programs*

        (1) *Farm Price Supports*—Prices for farm products are supported by
        the federal government at levels above regular market levels through
        loans, purchases, and payments. In some cases, eligibility for this
        program is contingent upon willingness to adjust production levels,
        techniques, and items. Since amount of support is tied to amount
        produced, the larger and wealthier farmers get the most benefit. For
        example, in 1965, farms with $40,000 and over in commercial sales
        received an average government payment of $3,196, while those
        with $2,500 to $4,999 in sales received $441, on the average. This
        program also amounts to subsidizing an inefficient industry. How-
        ever, surplus items obtained by the federal government are used in
        other welfare programs, such as the Commodity Distribution and
        School Lunch Programs.

        (2) *Credit*—There are numerous programs to enable farmers who would
        not commercially qualify for loans to obtain them at favorable
        rates for the purposes of purchasing land or equipment, or improv-
        ing their property, equipment, and farming practices.

        (3) *Insurance*—Since hail insurance is the only commercial crop insur-
        ance available, the government offers (in limited areas) an all-risk
        insurance to protect income in cases of unavoidable losses.

        (4) *Hired Farm Labor*—The Office of Farm Labor Service (Department
        of Labor) establishes interstate standards for the recruitment, pay-
        ment, and treatment of farm labor. It also attempts to match the
        available labor supply with area of labor need. The tighter regulation
        of the influx of foreign farm labor has also helped the labor picture
        for domestic hired farm labor.

3. *Indians*[37]

    a. Objectives—Programs to improve the level of Indian education, health,
    housing, and employment are provided separately to native Indians,
    Eskimos, and Aleuts.

    b. *Programs*—In all programs, eligibility includes living on a reservation
    or being listed on a tribal register.

        (1) *Education*—Operated by the Bureau of Indian Affairs (Department
        of the Interior). Indian students may receive tuition, school hous-
        ing, or school operation payments from the government. Indian
        children and adults are eligible, and payments include school con-
        struction as well as operation.

        (2) *Employment*—Also operated by the Bureau of Indian Affairs, voca-
        tional training is provided for Indians who will agree to relocate
        in urban environments. Counseling, transportation, subsistence, and
        eventually home ownership assistance is provided to help in ad-
        justment away from the reservation.

(3) *Health*—Operated by the Public Health Service, hospital, health, and sanitation programs are operated specifically for Indians, or, where feasible, other existing programs are utilized on a contract basis. Training of auxiliary personnel, and family planning services are also provided. Indian illness and mortality rates are still well above those of non-Indians, but the discrepancy is decreasing.

4. *Military*

a. *Objectives*—To minimize the potentially disruptive effects of military life, and provide for the basic needs of military personnel in active duty or retired from military careers.

b. *Programs*

(1) *Housing*—On-base housing is sometimes provided for servicemen and/or their dependents; in other cases, housing allowances are paid which enable military families to purchase housing in the civilian housing market. Provision of housing can be especially important in other societies where servicemen and their families may be unfamiliar with the housing market and general social customs.

(2) *Consumer Goods*—Post Exchanges (PXs) are provided on military installations to provide common food and other household, clothing, and recreational products to servicemen and their dependents tax-free and at substantial discounts from prevailing market prices.

(3) *Health*—Servicemen and their dependents are provided free hospital, medical, and drug facilities at the medical centers on military installations. When appropriate, medical services are also provided in the home, and long-term medical and rehabilitative care can also be furnished at no cost to the recipients.

(4) *Insurance and Pensions*—Free life insurance and supplementary low-cost insurances are available. Upon retirement from a military career, a pension calculated on rank and number of years' service is paid in addition to regular social security benefits.

(5) *General Social Services*—Many social services are available to military personnel and their families, including the services of a lawyer, personal counseling related to home/interpersonal problems, work problems, and career planning, planning assistance to dependents in case of death or injury, appropriate community service referrals, and vocational training.

II. *Private Programs: Some Illustrations*

A. *Introduction.* It should be clear by now that the network of public social services is a wide-ranging, complex one, with a variety of services being provided by diverse organizational structures. Yet in spite of the size of the public social service system, it is far from comprehensive, and suffers from inadequate resources in many areas. The private social welfare system has tended to shape itself around the public system, servicing special groups (religious groups, for example), extending the range of services available (particularly noticeable in recreation), and duplicating public services when their supply is inadequate for the demand. Obviously, then, private social services are a valuable supplement to public services, and although the historical progression of welfare services has very much accented the dominance of the public sphere, private services continue to play an important part in the total social welfare system. Unfortunately, private services are themselves often inadequately funded, and sometimes have very variable service standards, both of which restrict their effectiveness. But even given their problems, they are of considerable value.

B. *Transfer Payment Programs*

   1. *Social Insurance*
      a. *Objectives*—Insurance (income replacement) and savings.
      b. *Programs*
        (1) *Life insurance (individual or group)*[38]—Protects survivors in the event of loss of life (or total disability, in some cases). *Term insurance* decreases in value each year but has low premiums; savings occur yearly in minimal payments for maximum protection. *Whole life insurance* maintains a stable value (usually plus interest), but has relatively high premiums; savings occur when the policy matures (usually at age 65) at which time the insured may get his money to use as a retirement income.
        (2) *Supplemental Unemployment Benefit Plans*[39]—Supplements unemployment insurance.
        (3) *Guaranteed Annual Wage*[40]—Guaranteed salary for a specified number of weeks each year.
        (4) *Employee Pension Plans*[41]—Objectives: to supplement Social Security benefits in retirement, and to improve employee morale and productivity. *Programs:* approximately one-third of the civilian labor force is covered in private pension plans. Such plans are financed entirely by the employer (noncontributory), by both employer and employee (contributory), or occasionally entirely by the employees; contributions are tax-deductible. The employer may administer the fund, or may use an insurance company program. Workers receive benefits only when they meet either age or time eligibility requirements established by the employer, which may serve to limit job mobility. Workers with high turnover typically do not qualify for later payments. Workers who withdraw from pension programs may always receive their own contributions back, but programs vary whether they get back the employer's contribution. In general, eligibility requirements and the fact that many programs do not pay the employee the employer's contributions, if he leaves the plan before eligibility requirements are met, tends to discriminate against low-paid, unskilled workers whose work careers tend to be erratic.
        (5) *Health Insurance*
          (a) *Objectives*—To protect insured persons in the event of costs arising from illness or hospitalization.
          (b) *Coverage*—In 1963, 65.8 percent of families had complete private hospital insurance coverage, and 11.7 percent had incomplete coverage.

2. *Charity*

    a. *Objectives*—The transfer of income as a unilateral gift.

    b. *Programs*—Voluntary giving to social welfare is often centralized in one community drive called the United Fund. The monies collected through this drive are then apportioned along criteria developed in the community to the private social welfare agencies in the community.

        (1) *Philanthropy*[42]—Voluntary gifts by individuals, groups, and corporations to charitable organizations. In 1967, they totaled $14,569,000. Includes religious contributions, contributions for civic and cultural activities, for health and education, and "human resources" (youth activities, recreation, welfare, etc.). Only 6 percent went for the last named category or approximately $1.6 million in 1967. Philanthropy is encouraged through tax laws allowing tax deduction of such gifts.

        (2) *Alimony and Child Support*[43]—Legal obligations for the support of adults and children in the case of divorce. Partially voluntary in that such agreements are often difficult to enforce. In 1965, there were about 479,000 divorces, with over 4 million children from families broken by divorce.

C. *Private Social Services*

    1. *Objectives*—There is a wide variety of privately funded and administered programs providing various types of social services to members of a given community. These services may be entirely independent (a community settlement house, for example), or may be part of a national organization (Family Service Association of America, Big Brothers, etc.). These private programs attempt to meet social needs they have identified in their community, and usually work closely with public programs in the community.

    2. *Programs*—Out of the enormous variety of programs that exist in one community or another, a few major categories of private programs will be discussed. Since the funding base of private programs is much more limited than for public programs, they usually do not attempt to provide income maintenance assistance, and frequently have a scaled fee adjusted to client's income. As a mechanism of community involvement as well as a way to stretch very limited resources, many private programs utilize volunteer help (as do some public programs). Some private programs, such as the American Red Cross, Camp Fire Girls, Big Brothers, etc., have most services performed by a volunteer staff, with the small core of paid professionals performing advisory, planning, and supervisory functions.

    a. *Counseling Services*

        (1) *Objectives*—To advise persons in areas of interpersonal difficulty, and serve as a referral source to the range of community social welfare resources.

        (2) *Programs*—There are several major private counseling programs. Among the most prominent are: *Family Service Association and Child Welfare League of America* programs, which provide personal and family counseling to applicants, and which charge a fee based on ability to pay for such counseling. *Social Service branches of religious denominations*, operating much like Family Service except

for having the built-in referral source of ministers, priests, and rabbis; *Traveler's Aid Association,* providing counseling help, appropriate referral assistance, and limited financial resources to persons encountering difficulty while traveling.

b. *Recreation Services*

   (1) *Objectives*—To provide constructive recreational outlets for children and adults. Participants can derive pleasure from developing their physical capabilities and learning how to interact more successfully with others.

   (2) *Programs*—Out of the wide variety of recreational programs, three will be discussed briefly: the *Boy Scouts, Girl Scouts,* and *Camp Fire Girls,* while separately administered, are similar in that they provide structured recreational services, utilizing volunteers extensively, to provide youngsters with recreational, cultural, and educational opportunities facilitating the child's physical and social maturation. There are some costs involved in belonging to any one of these organizations. *Settlement houses* are neighborhood facilities providing physical and social recreational resources as well as limited educational programs. Neighborhood cultural elements are used extensively, and costs are minimal. *The Young Men and Young Women's Christian Association (YMCA, YWCA)* provide facilities similar to settlement houses, except with a more national than neighborhood perspective. Eating and sleeping facilities are often available at moderate cost. The cost of recreational programs is minimal.

c. *Training and Rehabilitation*

   (1) *Objectives*—To provide training and counseling needed to assist those with personal or physical handicaps to reestablish themselves as autonomous, satisfied societal members.

   (2) *Programs*—Three significant training and rehabilitation services that are privately operated include: *The Salvation Army* provides food, housing, and occupational training for needy individuals, maintaining retail outlets for the sale of products made by program participants. Costs are minimal, and men, women, and children are served. *Missions* are church-related social welfare organizations dealing primarily with homeless and alcoholic males. Food, housing, and minimal occupational training are provided, usually at no cost. Both the Salvation Army and the Missions usually attempt to develop a religious foundation in clients as part of their rehabilitation program. *Halfway houses,* such as Synanon in California, exist to enable drug addicts to rehabilitate themselves. Others exist to help ex-mental patients and ex-criminals to become reintegrated into the community. Along with counseling and group therapy, vocational training or employment is provided or encouraged. The halfway house concept is also utilized in some public programs.

d. *Health Care*

   (1) *Objectives*—To provide for the daily physical and mental health of the community.

   (2) *Programs*—Since widespread public health programs are relatively recent, the private health network has traditionally been well developed and operated on a pay-as-you-go basis; while hospitals and

clinics have traditionally been operated on a non-profit basis, private physician and psychiatric services have usually been operated for profit. Many of the current public health programs utilize private facilities, making vendor payments for covered services. These same services, when provided for persons not covered under public health programs, must be paid for by the individual or his insurance. A relatively recent addition to the private health care network are private nursing homes, providing long-term physical care, and in many instances, surrogate family care.

e. *Surrogate Services*

  (1) *Objectives*—Surrogate services are those that attempt to provide services that the client does not perform himself.

  (2) *Programs*—A few of the better-known surrogate services include: *Big Brothers* and *Big Sisters,* organizations to provide same-sex adult companionship for a child lacking such a meaningful figure in his or her life. This helps the child enjoy companionship, and provides an appropriate role model. The *Red Cross* provides a wide range of services. These include life saving instruction, blood banks, disaster relief, and transportation resources for those lacking access to other transportation facilities. *Meals-on-Wheels* brings hot meals to the homes of those both unable to prepare such meals for themselves, and those who are unable to leave their homes to obtain meals.

f. *Community Coordination and Planning*

  (1) *Objectives*—To organize existing social welfare services into an integrated network, and plan for new or reorganized services as community need and community desire develops.

  (2) *Programs*—Four major programs of interest are: *Health and Welfare Councils,* that seek to provide information about community resources to interested citizens' groups and agencies, in order to facilitate coordination, planning, and usage. Health and Welfare Councils are frequently involved in United Fund drives and the allocation of their resources. *Block Clubs* are organizations of persons on one or contiguous blocks for purposes of social interaction and community action to obtain needed resources or express member feelings on important issues. *Civic Organizations* are similar to block clubs, except that they typically include larger geographic areas and may encompass several block clubs. The larger size enables members to become involved in more issues and sometimes to have greater effectiveness. *Research* activities, such as the March of Dimes, are important for the generation of data needed for planning, and the basic treatment research that will ultimately improve practice methods.

REFERENCES

1. President's Commission on Income Maintenance Programs, *Background Papers* (Washington, D.C.: Government Printing Office, 1970), pp. 167–184.
2. Ibid., pp. 191–199.

3. Wayne Vasey, *Government and Social Welfare* (New York: Henry Holt, 1958), p. 111.
4. President's Commission, op. cit., pp. 223–232.
5. Ibid., pp. 260–264.
6. Ibid., pp. 264–268.
7. Ibid., pp. 268–272.
8. Ibid., pp. 273–279.
9. Ibid., pp. 279–283.
10. Ibid., pp. 321–322.
11. Ibid., pp. 323–329.
12. Ibid., pp. 339–342.
13. Ibid., pp. 342–344.
14. Ibid., pp. 344–345.
15. Ibid., pp. 345–346.
16. Ibid., pp. 346–347.
17. Ibid., pp. 347–349.
18. Ibid., pp. 356–361.
19. Ibid., pp. 361–364.
20. Office of the Federal Register, *United States Government Organization Manual 1970–71* (Washington, D. C.: Government Printing Office, 1970), p. 262.
21. President's Commission, op. cit., pp. 299–318.
22. Ibid., p. 299.
23. Ibid., p. 301.
24. Ibid., pp. 303–309.
25. Ibid., pp. 309–311.
26. Ibid., pp. 311–312.
27. Ibid., pp. 312–318.
28. Ibid., pp. 333–336.
29. Ibid., pp. 367–378.
30. Ibid., pp. 383–385.
31. *U. S. Government Organization Manual*, op. cit., p. 286.
32. President's Commission, op. cit., pp. 389–391.
33. Ibid., pp. 391–395.
34. Ibid., pp. 395–397.
35. Ibid., pp. 201–211.
36. Ibid., pp. 285–295.
37. Ibid., pp. 295–297.
38. Ibid., pp. 217–220.
39. Ibid, p. 184.
40. Ibid., p. 185.
41. Ibid., pp. 213–217.
42. Ibid., pp. 220–221.
43. Ibid., pp. 221–222.

APPENDIX B

THE SOCIAL WELFARE CAREER PACKET

Social Welfare Workers and Their Work

What Does the Social Welfare Worker Do? The social welfare worker is concerned with society and its social problems. He deals with the causes, the prevention, and the treatment of such problems. The social welfare worker may work with individuals, with groups, and/or the community. He may also work with adults, with teen-agers, with children, or with all three.

At the present time our society is seeking new approaches to the increasingly serious questions of poverty, sickness, inferior education, urban ills, and racial injustices. Such new approaches are affecting, and will affect, the role of the social welfare worker. The student considering social welfare as a career, therefore, needs to know that if he enters the field he will become part of a dynamic but rapidly changing scene: new services are being offered and new methods are being developed to meet today's problems.

What Qualities Should the Social Welfare Worker Have? Social welfare needs those who are willing to accept the challenge of working in a field that is searching for ways to become more effective in solving the problems of an increasingly complex society. Social welfare requires individuals who have drive, imagination, intelligence, understanding, patience, and a genuine commitment to do the job. For those who are able to accept the challenge, for those who are willing to invest in further educational preparation, this can be a most satisfying and rewarding career.

What Jobs are Included in Social Welfare? As stated above, social welfare encompasses a wide variety of jobs and job titles. Each category may or may not include workers on all educational levels from below high school through the Master's degree. The examples of job titles listed are representative samples only and by no means include all titles possible. Although there is considerable overlap with other fields and some lack of clarity in the structure of the jobs, most social welfare jobs fall into the categories listed below:

1. *Social Workers*—Includes social work and social work assistant positions. (Examples: Social Worker, Social Work Assistant, Psychiatric Social Worker, Medical Social Worker, and School Social Worker.) Community workers and

Materials presented in this appendix are parts of mimeographed handouts provided by the Health and Welfare Council of Central Maryland, Social Work Careers Service, Baltimore, Maryland. Used with permission.

group workers can be included in this category or in the appropriate category below.

2. *Financial Assistance and Benefit Workers*—Includes positions of those workers primarily responsible for determining eligibility for benefits including welfare, medical assistance, social insurance, veterans' benefits, etc. (Examples: Public Welfare Interviewer, Eligibility Technician, and Claims Representative.)

3. *Community Workers*—Includes positions of those working in social welfare planning and research (Examples: Community Organizer, Planning Assistant, and Researcher); those working at the neighborhood level to improve or stabilize conditions (Examples: Neighborhood Development Assistant, and Community Organizer); and race relations workers (Example: Assistant Inter-group Relations Representative).

4. *Employment Workers*—Includes positions related to job development, job counseling, vocational rehabilitation, and staff development. (Examples: Vocational Rehabilitation Counselor, Staff Development Assistant, Employment Counselor, and Job Developer.) Excludes personnel officers and school guidance counselors.

5. *Youth and Recreation Workers*—Includes positions of those whose duties primarily consist of working with groups for purposes of recreation or youth development. (Examples: Group Worker, Youth Worker, and Recreation Leader.)

6. *Correction Workers*—Includes positions both in the field of adult correction (Examples: Correction Officer and Correctional Classification Counselor), and juvenile correction (Examples: Youth Supervisor and Juvenile Probation Worker). Excludes those who are primarily law enforcement workers such as policemen.

7. *Specialized Health Counselors*—Includes positions of counselors working with specialized health problems (Examples: Alcoholism Counselor, Family Planning Counselor, and Drug Abuse Counselor).

8. *Supportive Aides*—Includes positions which are usually, though not exclusively, entry level positions open to those with a high school education or less and which support or augment the services of the Associate, Master's, or Bachelor's degree worker. (Examples: Homemaker, Day Care Aide, Social Service Aide, Relocation Aide, and Psychiatric Aide.)

9. *College Teachers* of graduate and undergraduate courses in social work and social welfare. (Examples: Professor, Assistant Professor, and Instructor.)

10. *Administrators*—Includes all social welfare administrative positions above the rank of supervisor. (Examples: Executive Director, Assistant or Associate Director, Division or Bureau Chief, Program Director, Project Director, and Coordinator.)

Exploring a Career in Social Welfare

Is social welfare the career for you? Do you think it might be, but want to know more about it? Will you like the work? Do you really have an aptitude for it?

It's well to ask these questions now and there are a number of steps you can take to help find the answers for yourself.

First, review all of the information you can about a social welfare career. Your college or public *library* contains pamphlets and books about social work, recreation, corrections, job counseling, community organization, and other related helping occupations within the broad field of social welfare. *Your college vocational or placement office* also has such materials. The counselor in the placement office, or your college adviser, can help you plan which courses you should take to prepare for this career. He can also tell you whom to contact for additional information.

Sources of additional written career information include:

1. Social Work—National Commission for Social Work Careers, 600 Southern Building, 15th and H Sts., N.W., Washington, D.C. 20005.

2. Recreation—National Recreation and Park Association, 1700 Pennsylvania Avenue, N.W., Washington, D.C. 20006

3. Rehabilitation Counseling—American Rehabilitation Counseling Association, 1605 New Hampshire Avenue, N.W., Washington, D.C. 20009

4. Vocational Counseling—National Vocational Guidance Association, Inc., 1605 New Hampshire Avenue, N.W., Washington, D.C. 20009

5. Public Welfare—American Public Welfare Association, 1313 East 60th Street, Chicago, Illinois 60637

6. Child Welfare—Child Welfare League of America, 44 East 23rd Street, New York, New York 10016

7. Mental Health Careers—Mental Health Materials Center, 419 Park Avenue, South, New York, New York 10016

8. Group and Neighborhood Work—National Federation of Settlements and Neighborhood Centers, 232 Madison Avenue, New York, New York 10016

Books, pamphlets, and information can help, but how do you really know if this is the career for you? How do you find out if you'll like the work; how will you know if you're suited for it? Career testing opportunities are needed to help you begin to answer these questions. *Volunteer work* is an excellent starting point—not just any volunteer job, however, but one where you can be involved with people; where you have a chance to see what a social service organization is doing; where you have an opportunity to talk with the workers in the agency; where you can have a small piece of the action yourself.

Volunteer work is available both for a few hours per week during the college year and for any time from a few hours to the entire week during the summer. Students can call any social agency in which they are interested to offer their services and inquire about the opportunities and requirements. Among those local organizations throughout the state that use volunteers are: community action agencies; groups working with retarded children; state mental hospitals; county or city departments of social services; youth serving organizations such as YWCA, Girl Scouts, Catholic Youth Organization, and Jewish community centers; bureaus of recreation; and the American Red Cross.

Another means of career testing while still in college is through *paid part-time jobs in the field of social welfare.* The number of such opportunities available during the school year is limited and students who volunteer in or live near an agency often have a better opportunity of securing those part-time jobs which are available. In addition your college placement office may have some listings of such jobs.

If you have a particular *skill which you can teach* you may be able to find a part-time job during the week or on Saturday working in a *recreation or youth serving agency.* In the process of teaching the skill, you will learn about the work of the agency, and very importantly, about your own ability to relate to and work with people, perhaps including those of backgrounds other than your own. Some of the skills for which there is a demand are: arts and crafts, ballet, sports, music, and swimming. To inquire about such opportunities call youth serving agencies near your home or college.

Paid summer work experience in a helping profession is one of the best ways of preparing for a social welfare career, although such work opportunities are limited in most areas. Some possibilities are the following:

1. *Summer Camps* provide an ideal opportunity for students to gain experience working with children. A number of camps, including both day and overnight camps, hire college students. The salary varies considerably from camp to camp. Students interested in camp jobs should seek further information from their placement office or the American Camping Association, Bradford Woods, Martinsville, Indiana 46151. Public libraries also have listings of camps approved by the American Camping Association.

2. *Recreation Departments* often hire high school and college students to work in their summer programs. For example, Baltimore City Bureau of Recreation hires students seventeen years old and up as day-camp aides, playground aides, portable-pool guards, leaders for the handicapped, and traveling play leaders. Apply between January and mid-March at your local recreation department.

3. The *VISTA* program provides another means of testing an aptitude for a social welfare career. VISTA, Volunteers in Service to America, recruits, trains and assigns volunteers to work for one year fighting poverty in urban slums, on Indian reservations, in Appalachia, in mental retardation programs, etc. Applicants must be at least eighteen years of age and have no dependents under eighteen. The volunteers are sponsored by state and local agencies—public and private—and are paid only a minimum subsistence allowance and a $50 monthly stipend. For further information, write VISTA, Box 700, Washington, D.C. 20506.

4. Some large cities have *Summer Jobs in Social Work Programs,* in which young people are hired by agencies specifically so they can experience social welfare work first hand. To see if there is one in your city, contact the local chapter of the National Association of Social Workers, the local health and welfare council, or the local department of social services.

In summary, both information and career testing are essential in making a career choice. After such exploration you may or may not decide that social welfare is the career for you, but you will have a sound basis for your choice.

Social Welfare Jobs: Matching Training with Tasks

The field of social welfare can be entered at all educational levels from less than high school graduation through the Master's or Doctor's degree. Below is information about jobs and salary ranges at each educational level. Jobs may be in governmental service at the local, state or federal level, or they may be in private agencies such as those supported by the United Fund or other voluntary sources.

High School Graduation. A person with a high school diploma (and sometimes less) may obtain a beginning job in a social welfare organization such as a community action agency, a bureau of recreation, a department of housing and community development, a day care center, a department of social services, a child-caring institution, or a health service agency of a hospital. The student should be aware, however, that many of such jobs are available only to residents of certain neighborhoods or to members of the client group which the employing agency serves. Beginning social welfare positions are quite varied, but the worker usually does some of the following:

1. Goes out in the neighborhood to explain the services of the agency and to encourage the people to use the services.

2. Follows up clients who have been receiving the services of the agency.

3. When necessary, refers clients to other workers in the same agency or to other agencies for further service.

4. Helps the professional working with a recreation, community or therapy group, or with an individual or family.

5. Keeps simple records and reports.

6. Cares for and supervises children and/or adults in an institution, recreation center, or their own home.

   Most workers with a high school diploma or less start at a salary of $4500–$6000 and receive increases with experience and training. Some of the positions provide for career advancement following additional experience, training, and/or formal education.

   Some examples of the titles or jobs one may hold with a high school diploma are: Neighborhood Development Assistant I, Recreation Assistant, Health Aide I, Homemaker, Community Worker, and Youth Supervisor I.

Associate of Arts Degree (two years of college). A person who has an Associate of Arts degree (AA) may be employed in interviewing and beginning counseling positions with employment and manpower agencies, county and city departments of social services, hospitals and clinics, mental hospitals, and other organizations. He can work as a recreation leader, housing relocation aide, administrative secretary in a social agency, or serve as an assistant in urban planning.

   The worker with an Associate of Arts degree often does some of the following:

1. Interviews clients and/or examines written information in order to determine eligibility for service including financial, medical, or other benefits.

2. Provides some of the services of the agency including elementary counseling.

3. The following duties are similar to those performed by workers with a high school diploma. The AA worker, however, usually would be assigned to situations of a more complex nature than those assigned to the high school graduate.

   a. Goes out into the neighborhood to explain the services of the agency, and to encourage people to use the services.

   b. Follows up clients who have been receiving the services of the agency.

   c. When necessary refers clients, whose problems indicate the need for such referral, to other workers in the same agency or to other agencies for further service.

   d. Helps the professional in working with a recreation, community, or therapy group, or with an individual or family.

   e. Keeps simple records and reports.

The salaries are varied, but most workers with an AA degree start at a salary of $6000–$7000. Most of the AA degree positions provide for salary increases and career advancement following additional experience, training, and/or formal education.

Examples of the titles of jobs one may hold with two years of college are: Public Welfare Interviewer, Health Aide III, Relocation Aide, Beginning Casework Assistant, Mental Health Associate, and Intake Interviewer. Some of the above jobs require additional experience beyond the AA degree.

Bachelor's Degree (four years of college). The largest number of employees in the social welfare field are those holding a Bachelor of Arts or Bachelor of Science degree. Although one may obtain a job in the social welfare field with a college major in any subject, many employers prefer someone who has majored or taken courses in the social sciences (sociology, psychology, social welfare, economics, etc.). Most of the provision of direct services to individuals, groups, and organizations is carried out by persons with a four-year college degree.

The worker with a Bachelor's degree and no experience usually does some of the following:

1. Provides specific services for clients, such as placement of a foster child; preparation for parole; preparation for hospital release; location of jobs, etc.

2. Assists clients and families, both individually and in groups, in discussing their problems and in developing and making the most of their abilities.

3. Assists clients in using agency, hospital, or community resources to help them solve their problems.

4. Works with a community, recreation, or therapy group.

5. Determines financial or service eligibility.

6. Gathers information, analyzes material, makes recommendations, keeps records, and submits reports.

7. Keeps in close contact with other agencies and organizations; makes referrals when necessary; works with other agencies concerning community problems.

The Bachelor's degree worker with no prior experience usually starts at a salary between $7000 and $8000. Some examples of the titles of jobs one may hold with a Bachelor's degree are: Casework Assistant I, Street Club Worker, Employment Counselor I, Assistant Intergroup Relations Representative, and Juvenile Probation Worker. Some of the above jobs require additional experience beyond the Bachelor's degree.

As the Bachelor's level worker gains experience, his duties become more complex. With considerable experience and increased responsibility, some Bachelor's degree workers earn as much as $11,000 to $14,000.

Master's Degree. The Master's degree in social work (variously titled MSW, MSSA, MA, etc.) is often specified for positions in the social welfare field, although for certain jobs other Master's degrees are acceptable and sometimes preferred. The Master's degree in social work currently requires two years of college beyond the Bachelor's degree. Only a small percentage of employees in the field of social welfare possess a Master's degree. (In social work alone, only approximately 20 percent of all employees hold a Master's degree.)

The duties of the Master's degree worker may include the following:

1. Works with clients on more complex situations.

2. Develops and works with groups established for the purpose of therapy, personal development, and/or recreation.

3. Works with neighborhood or community groups to analyze their needs and develop plans to meet the needs.

4. Develops, coordinates, and evaluates programs and policies.

5. Supervises and trains staff.

6. Interprets the work of the agency through writing and speaking.

With experience, the Master's degree worker may advance rapidly either to the provision of direct service on a deeper level, to supervision, and/or to administration. In actual practice, outside of private agencies, very few persons with a Master's degree and experience are engaged primarily in the direct provision of services to clients. Advancement for Master's degree workers is almost always in the direction of supervision, staff development, planning, and/or administration.

Some examples of the titles of jobs one may hold with a Master's degree are: Social Worker I, Senior Community Organization Advisor, Counselor II, Juvenile Services Regional Supervisor I, Deputy Commissioner, and Assistant Administrator II. Some of the above jobs require additional experience beyond the Master's degree.

The Master's degree holder with no previous experience usually starts at a salary between $8,000 and $10,500. With increased experience and job responsibility a Master's degree worker may earn $12,000 to $25,000, and sometimes more.

INDEX

INDEX